Peter Munk

The Making of a Modern Tycoon

Donald Rumball

Published in 1996 by
Stoddart Publishing Co. Limited
34 Lesmill Road
Toronto, Canada
M3B 2T6
Tel. (416) 445-3333
Fax (416) 445-5967

Stoddart Books are available for bulk purchase for sales promotions, premiums, fundraising, and seminars. For details, contact the Special Sales Department at the above address.

Canadian Cataloguing in Publication Data

Rumball, Donald
Peter Munk: the making of a modern tycoon

Includes index
ISBN 0-7737-2943-7

1. Munk, Peter, 1927–   . 2. Barrick Gold Corp. 3.Horsham Corporation.
4. Businessmen – Canada – Biography. 5. Executives – Canada – Biography.
I. Title.

HD9506.C32R84 1996   338.7'622'092   C95-933297-9

Cover Design: Pekoe Jones/multiphrenia
Computer Graphics: Mary Bowness
Cover photograph: Joy von Tiedemann

Printed and bound in Canada

Stoddart Publishing gratefully acknowledges the support of the Canada Council, and the Ontario Arts Council in the development of writing and publishing in Canada.

For my mother and Nathalie

CONTENTS

Acknowledgments   vii

1   The Dilemma of Success   1

2   Early Dreams, Early Disaster   30

3   Strong Foundations Built on Shifting Sands   67

4   Takeover Two-Step   96

5   The Arab Connection   142

6   Breakthrough   166

7   Black Gold, Yellow Gold   204

8   Goldstrike   240

9   The Lac Takeover   272

10 Strategies for the Encores   301

11 The Man and His Machine   332

    Index   353

ACKNOWLEDGMENTS

This book would not have been possible without the enthusiasm and support of Peter Munk, who not only gave me freely of his time, but encouraged his colleagues and associates to do the same and opened his archives to me. His frankness on sensitive topics was extraordinary. His openness about his own highs and lows is rare indeed among successful people. His business career is so absorbing that it wrenched the book in directions I had never intended, but do not regret! I thank him most sincerely.

The 40-plus people who spoke to me for this book all gave me as much time as I asked of them. They are too numerous to mention individually, but I would like to single out a few who made unusually important contributions to my research. Bill

Birchall's remarkable memory and meticulous commentary have helped keep errors to a minimum; he also gave me the context and the reasons for many decisions and actions I would not otherwise have understood. Bob Smith's shrewd observations were a touchstone on some of the more fundamental issues. David Gilmour, Pat Samuel, and Roger Kirby not only shared their unique perspectives of Peter Munk, but extended their gracious hospitality to me in the South Seas. David Wynne-Morgan eased the birth of the book and offered unflagging support through some of the anxious moments; his sense of humor and subtlety were always a pleasure. Vince Borg organized an instructive and enjoyable trip to the gold mine in Nevada. Lurlene, the head librarian at *The Australian*, allowed me full access to her invaluable microfiche records. I owe Kerr McGovern and Sheila Fennessy a particularly heartfelt thank-you. They were unfailing in their helpfulness, they organized my access to roomfuls of documents, they smoothed my path in many, many ways — and they made me laugh.

Jack Stoddart immediately saw the potential of this book, and gave it the support it needed. Don Bastian was always encouraging and knew how to nurture my sense of urgency without ever pushing. Lynne Missen's editing was meticulous and sensitive. My agent, Bruce Westwood, was an enthusiastic supporter.

Tarra Dunphy read the manuscript and provided both encouragement and insightful comments. Last, but never least, I would like to thank my daughter Nathalie for understanding when I couldn't be as good a father as I would have liked to have been.

1

THE DILEMMA OF SUCCESS

It was the summer of 1995, and as Peter Munk looked back over the previous 18 months, he was exasperated. His company, Barrick Gold Corp., had not had a good year on the stock market in 1994. Despite a banner year when the company's earnings and production broke all records, its stock price drifted erratically downward from a peak 18 months earlier. Admittedly, the market was sliding for everyone, but Barrick's stellar performance should have insulated it from the limp parade of less dynamic companies. It was tough to understand. After several years of exponential growth, Barrick had just swallowed one of its larger competitors, Lac Minerals, in a $1.7 billion[1] takeover

---

[1] All dollar figures are in U.S. dollars unless otherwise specified.

that vaulted it into the top spot among North American gold mining companies. Barrick had become the third largest gold mining company in the world and the most profitable. To have done this was noteworthy. To have done it from scratch, less than 12 years after entering the gold mining business, was exceptional. Yet its stock could not break out of its dreary pattern, ending up the year 22% below its high in January 1994.

Even when stock prices recovered a bit in the first half of 1995, Barrick's insipid recovery had trailed the market. It would have been enough to upset anyone coming off two fabulously successful years, but what infuriated Munk, the company's chairman, founder, and driving force, was that his company had suffered more at the hands of this dog market than had the other three first-tier gold companies — Placer Dome Inc., Newmont Mining Co., and Homestake Mining Co. — which had all performed worse than Barrick over those two years according to every available yardstick of performance.

When Munk is infuriated about something, he doesn't stew on it. He gets the issues on the table by talking about them with his trusted colleagues and associates. He listens intently, drawing out fresh perspectives to lay a foundation for action. Munk prefers one-on-one sessions where he can explore issues with complete openness. He knows that big meetings lead to posturing as executives compete for the high ground among their peers. Still, Barrick's senior managers do sit around their Arthurian round table once a week and Munk joins them whenever he's in town. To call these get-togethers "meetings," however, would be misleading. They are more like brainstorming sessions where Munk and his people discuss current issues and bounce around their ramifications. Barrick's culture is not one of formal position papers and layered decision making. Executives figure out the implications of the issues and then leave it to the competent managers to do something about them.

It was inevitable that the sluggish performance of Barrick's stock would surface in the weekly sessions that summer.

"Find out why people have bought Placer Dome shares and Newmont shares, but not our shares in the last 18 months," Munk rapped out to his senior managers. "Just find out."

The price of his shares is at the very heart of Munk's business philosophy, although not in a conventional way. He believes passionately that the goal of a company's managers must be to maximize the benefits flowing to the shareholder — and maximizing shareholder benefits does not mean increasing earnings per share by 10¢ a year. It means doubling the stock price every three or four years. In his 40 years as an entrepreneur (and latterly tycoon), he has drummed that message into every single person with whom he has worked, making it a mantra that defines and drives his companies. Every employee in Barrick receives, *every day*, a one-page sheet with a "market update." On the first few lines of that sheet, in boldface, is Barrick Gold's closing price and volume on the Toronto and New York stock exchanges over the previous week. Then comes the same information for the holding company, Horsham Corp., followed by the key statistics for Barrick's major competitors — the Newmonts and Placer Domes whose stock prices had provoked Munk's irritation.

When Peter Munk focuses on something, it defines his entire existence until he has resolved it to his satisfaction. He's happiest when he's focused, at home and at work. His wife, Melanie, says he is a terrible driver in normal conditions, but superb when he's behind the wheel on a treacherous road covered in black ice.

When something really bothers him, everyone knows about

it. He is a tornado, his energy pulsating, creating waves you can feel from the room next door. At five feet ten, he's not tall, but he dominates people's attention as he glides between offices in Barrick's plush new surroundings on the 27th floor of the Royal Bank Plaza in downtown Toronto. Even inside his own office, he is constantly on the move, pacing restlessly as his words flow out in torrents. Not for him the sedentary authority of a conventional chief executive officer, reflecting on portentous corporate reports in the isolated dignity of a corner office. Munk believes that executives are not paid to read in the office, so he uses all his "working hours" to meet with people, usually individually. And every evening, his secretary, Sheila Fennessy, gives him his pile of reading, which he invariably returns the next morning, each item meticulously read or discarded.

At 67, he is in superb shape, radiating the enthusiasm of a 35-year-old. On a bad day, he can get tired toward five o'clock, but that rarely happens. He works out regularly and paces himself carefully, maintaining his taut build without an ounce of fat. (If someone else in the office gets a bit overweight, he is not shy in suggesting ways to remedy the situation.) He dresses impeccably, his conservative dark blue suits styled with an elegant flair that hasn't changed in 40 years — unbusiness in a most businesslike way, especially when he adds to the ensemble the old-fashioned fedora that gives him an air of European mystery. Most of all, however, you notice his face. The dominant forehead, framed by receding white hair with a suggestion of the deep red that once caused him so much distress, is balanced by his lower jaw, jutting out after a lifetime of leading with his chin. And the eyes — intense green, sharp, penetrating, their prominence amplified by his blond eyelashes.

The Hungarian accent is still strong more than 50 years after he left the country where he was born, but you never notice it because he speaks with his whole body. He touches the people he likes and respects, constantly gripping their arm or their knee or patting them on the back. If he doesn't feel comfortable with his visitors, he doesn't touch them — and if he still can't touch them after several meetings, he starts avoiding them, even if he needs something from them.

When he's talking with someone, he gives them his total, undivided attention, looking intently into their eyes, searching for signs of understanding that will allow him to leave his current sentence unfinished and move on to his next thought. Munk has that extraordinary knack of encouraging people in their belief (not always mistaken) that their opinions and advice will weigh heavily in his considerations. His associates, including some who are powerhouses in their own right, proudly recount the occasions when they changed his mind.

That summer, as Munk mounted his impeccably logical assault on the market's frivolous treatment of his company, his intensity was greater than usual. As he warmed to his theme in that weekly get-together with his senior managers, he ticked off the key facts in the argument he had so meticulously researched.

"It's not earnings — we've got much better earnings," he told them. "It's not cash flow, because we've got much better cash flow. It's not track record — we've got a much better track record."

Indeed, Barrick's earnings per share had risen 5% over the year and a half from the end of 1993, while Placer Dome's earnings per share fell 47%. Yet Barrick's share price fell 11% during the same period compared to an *increase* of 5% in the market valuation of Placer Dome.

Earnings per share is not, of course, the only thing that affects the price of shares — not in the short run, at any rate. In the long run, the profit earned for each share is the only thing that matters, since it determines a company's ability to grow and make even more money. But in the short run, expectations of an uncertain future play a vital role, and the forum for assembling those expectations is the collected opinions of the financial analysts in the investment banking firms that run the machinery of the stock market. If the financial analysts expect a company's earnings to improve dramatically, they will encourage investors to bid up the market price far beyond the justification afforded by their actual performance up to that point. And vice versa.

So why, then, were these analysts and their investors excited over Placer Dome, at the expense of Barrick Gold? Peter Munk's executives spent more than $100,000 on surveys and consultants to find the answer to that question, which is perhaps as old as stock markets themselves. The analysts liked Placer Dome, they discovered, because it was in a lot of "plays," while Barrick had focused on its handful of mines, investing its time, energy, and money developing them into the most profitable gold mining company in the world. The analysts knew exactly what was in store for Barrick and decided they preferred the uncertain potential of huge gain from Placer Dome's risky exploration program to Barrick's guaranteed flow of solid profits.

Munk is no stranger to analysts, whom he has sweet-talked for most of his working life, but he could barely contain himself when he heard the information his $100,000 had bought.

"In banking, in retailing, in construction, any other sector of the stock market, the analysts look for performance, track record, reliability of earnings," he snapped. "Here, they like Placer Dome and Newmont."

Munk was infuriated that the mining analysts seemed to be far more interested in the geological plays than in their financial implications. "They get turned on by a guy saying, 'I'm in Uzbekistan and I'm in the lower slope of the so-and-so trend in Indonesia . . .' The fact that three years later they write off $30 million is goddamn irrelevant. In any other business, the analysts would not tolerate that. Here, the analysts look at them in their dreams. They say, 'God, Newmont has five projects. Poor Barrick, how can they get a chance to catch up?'"

It's a sensitive issue, because the foundation of Munk's success with Barrick was his decision to avoid a risky exploration program as the route to growth, choosing instead to grow by acquiring producing properties. Back in 1983, when he took his first faltering steps into the gold business, his vision was crystal clear. The big pension funds and mutual funds in Europe and North America were major investors in gold stocks, but they were getting nervous because most of their holdings were in South Africa, which was heading deeper and deeper into political trouble. But there were no other suitable gold stocks to take their place outside of North America — and the pickings were very slim on that continent. All but a half dozen of the gold companies were "juniors" — small companies with limited resources, owned by promoters or prospectors looking for an "elephant," a huge discovery that would catapult them into the major leagues overnight. Pension funds, however, don't invest in prayers. They want solid, producing companies with a strong cash flow that have some prospect of performing well in their portfolios for many years to come.

To meet that need, Munk decided in 1983 he would start buying small mines that were in production 'but were not performing to their maximum capability. He would buy them cheaply and wring the last ounce of potential out of them through superior management. Exploration was out. The only drilling he wanted to do was development drilling on properties where he already knew there was gold in commercial quantities.

As it happened, this was an inspired plan. Four years later, he had bought several producing mines that he was able to improve beyond his wildest dreams. This success, of course, only confirmed the wisdom of staying away from "grassroots" exploration on properties where there was no guarantee of success, so his exploration budget languished accordingly. From 1987 to 1993, he averaged a little more than $5 million a year on exploration, a pittance next to his cash flow, which soared from $37 million to $317 million over the same seven years. This did not escape the attention of the analysts, who couldn't help noting that, between 1992 and 1994, Placer Dome committed itself to spending about $70 million every year on grassroots exploration — more than a quarter of its cash flow.

This didn't mean that Barrick wasn't spending heavily on development. Once the Barrick executives had realized in 1987 that they were sitting on a genuine elephant in their Goldstrike property in Nevada, they poured all their energies into developing that mine. During the next eight years, Barrick sank more than $1.6 billion into its six mines, with Goldstrike accounting for more than $1 billion. Placer Dome was no slouch either, spending $2.2 billion over the same period. But Placer didn't come close to matching Barrick's results. Despite its late start, the company mined 7.7 million ounces of gold in the eight years to 1994, by which time it had accumulated proven and probable reserves of 37.6 million ounces of gold. Placer Dome, with a proud corporate lineage stretching back to 1910 and already a substantial gold company long before Barrick drew on its first line of credit, mined 11.4 million ounces in the same period and could count on proven and probable reserves of 19.8 million ounces.

During the heady years when Goldstrike was emerging from obscurity to become the biggest gold deposit on the continent, there was real excitement in the stock market over the gradual unveiling of its treasure house, and investors showed their appreciation by awarding Barrick a premium on its stock price to reflect its status as a growth company. Now they had taken that premium away. The company's very success had raised the ante in the analysts' demand for an encore.

The stock market's bias toward Placer Dome was especially galling because Munk already knew that the prospects down the road for Barrick were even more promising than the analysts dreamed. He knew that the Chilean properties of Lac Minerals, which Barrick had bought a year earlier, in the summer of 1994, were much better than anyone at Lac had ever dreamed. Unfortunately, the laborious process of delineating the orebody was a long way from finished and he would have to wait another year before he could *prove* just how big it was. And, until he could prove it, he couldn't tell the market about the fabulous wealth of his new-found assets. He had to bite his tongue.

All his life Munk had painted alluring pictures of the enormous potential of his assets, showing them off in their most advantageous light. He can take an improbable idea that defies the imagination and develop a flawlessly constructed argument that can convince even the most hard-bitten, skeptical audience of the inevitability of its success. Give him some moose pasture in the middle of nowhere and he'll find ways to make it the most attractive place on earth. Not only that, he'll persuade investors to give him millions of dollars to prove it. This is not idle speculation — he has actually done it. Now, he was not allowed to talk up his Chilean ace-in-the-hole to its real potential when he tried to answer the analysts' simple question: "How are you going to find enough new deposits to replace those 3 million ounces you are pulling out of your reserves every year?"

Munk, in fact, was way ahead of the analysts. The purchase of Lac Minerals was a direct result of his own realization of the validity of their question. And the scope of his thinking was broader than anything that most of them could imagine.

More than two years previously, in the first half of 1993, Munk had started wrestling with the dilemma of his success. He worried about his company turning into an institutional bureaucracy. With the $1 billion development of its Goldstrike mine behind it, the company was beginning to feel large and profitable; the first signs of flabbiness were starting to show. The staff was still small enough and the culture was still strong enough that there was no danger of the operation becoming blah, but the spigots were opening and the cash was flowing. Munk knew that, without a jolt from him, the sense of urgency that kept the company taut and entrepreneurial would begin to fade.

In the winter of 1993, he took off four months to ski at his chalet in Klosters, Switzerland. He is a fanatical skier who throws himself into the sport with the intensity he brings to everything he does. He's not a natural skier, but he has mastered it enough to ski at the same level as good skiers many years his junior, including his wife, Melanie. (In fact, the two first met in Switzerland, where their relationship bloomed after their first day on the slopes together, when Melanie broke her leg.) But, as in most things he does, the fun is edged with his relentless competitiveness. If he is skiing with younger people (which is all the time, because there aren't too many 67-year-olds who can ski with him), he won't leave the *piste* until every younger man, woman, and child has called it a day. When his skiing partners stretch out their day, he'll return to his chalet gray with exhaustion — but victoriously the last to come in.

He has spent a good part of every winter since the mid-1970s at his chalet, *Viti Levu,* named after Fiji's main island. That was where he made his first fortune, part of which paid for the chalet. However, he always interspersed the skiing with chunks of time in Toronto to take care of business; 1993 was the first year he made only short, infrequent visits to Canada between Christmas and April. He was in touch with the office every day, faxes and phone calls flying between his chalet and points around the world, but Toronto saw very little of him during those four months. His colleagues thought that he was slowing down: that he had started the process of passing the baton to the next generation of managers after his string of successes.

Little did they know that he was staying up late into the night, pacing up and down, worrying how he could re-inject his entrepreneurial spirit into his business, now in danger of being spoiled by its success. He experimented with various ideas, bouncing them off his long-standing partners — men like Bill Birchall who had fought with him in the trenches, who had stuck with him as they pulled themselves out of one quagmire after another to make his first real fortune in the 1970s. What he came up with was his own unique two-track strategy — a blend of entrepreneurial verve and financial caution.

On the one hand, he knew that Barrick had to switch its attention to exploration now that the development phase had been completed at Goldstrike. Having great reserves is one thing. It's quite another to find enough new mines to replenish those reserves as they deplete at 2 million ounces a year (as it was at that time, before they bought Lac with its annual production of 1 million ounces). For a company the size of Barrick, moreover, those new mines had to be substantial. Barrick couldn't afford to toy with deposits of 100,000 ounces here and 250,000 ounces there, and annual production of a few thousand ounces. For an orebody to have any impact on its reserves, there had to be a million ounces or more — and mines like that are hard to come by.

On the other hand, he reluctantly faced the prospect of a regretful retreat from the industry that had made him a multi-millionaire: perhaps Barrick had become a "commodity play" — its price no longer determined by its own performance, but by the vagaries of the gold index on the stock market.

Munk has never been a fan of the stock market. He considers it a casino with the dice loaded against the players. So why does he live and die by the stock price of his own companies? Because owning stock in a company you manage yourself is not the same as investing in companies run by strangers. Munk feels he can control the performance of his company and, with good management, that performance will be reflected in the stock price. He holds virtually no stock market investments outside his own companies. So when he felt he was less and less able to influence Barrick's stock price by managing it better than anyone else, the logical conclusion was that it was time to start selling his holding of Barrick and diversify into new fields.

"I'm European," he says. "If your grandfather told you [to diversify] when you were nine years old, whether it's currencies or properties or countries, you have to diversify." His grandfather probably really did tell him that, because he was a wealthy investment banker in Hungary between the two world wars. That wealth provided Peter Munk with a superior early education and a sense of familiarity with the trappings of wealth, but it never gave him a privileged start in business because the family lost its money in the Second World War. Ever since, Munk has doubted the sustainability of whatever business he was in, always searching for ways to build on his base by branching out into bigger and better things. Up to that winter of 1993, that instinct for the vulnerability of success had been right in four out of the five businesses he had started — five out of six if you count the business he started as a student at the University of Toronto. Each one soared initially with unlimited promise, only to hit a wall plunked down in his path by a flippant fate. And each time, when the bottom fell out, he was saved by an alternative interest he had nurtured.

One of the few characteristics shared by almost all successful entrepreneurs is a high tolerance for ambiguity. They can pursue conflicting strategies simultaneously, delaying any choice between the two until they can see which one works best. Munk's ambiguous, two-track strategy — strengthening his investment in gold by beefing up the effort to find new gold reserves and diversifying out of gold — was the basis of his moves in the second half of 1993.

First, in October, he created a senior corporate development group at Barrick, which he chaired, and charged it with the mandate to find new gold deposits in South America and Asia by whatever means were appropriate. In the space of a few months, he wanted the company to shed its image of a strictly North American company in pursuit of producing properties that it could manage better than anyone else. He wanted instead an internationally minded, aggressive explorer.

Earlier in the year, he had brought onto his board the recently retired prime minister of Canada, Brian Mulroney, the unhappy lightning rod for the angst of a whole nation, in office and out.

13

Munk was well aware of these feelings toward his new recruit, of course, although he clearly felt differently, but he also knew that Mulroney enjoyed immense prestige outside Canada. After nine years trotting around the world to meet world leaders, he had incomparable access to presidents and prime ministers in all the key spots where Munk wanted to take Barrick. Through Mulroney, Munk knew he could get to meet the presidents of Chile or Argentina or the premier of China. With that access and Munk's irresistible ability to pitch an idea, he knew — he just knew — he could launch Barrick into new mining fields at a speed that would turn heads around the world.

He was most excited about China. He visited the country himself and Mulroney arranged the necessary access to the key decision makers. Munk was starting to salivate at the prospect of an inside track into the huge Chinese territory that was known to have significant gold deposits. He teamed up with Paul Desmarais of Power Corp. in Montreal, another great Canadian entrepreneur who has built a global business empire. Desmarais has impeccable Chinese contacts, having served for many years on the Canada–China Business Council. With Mulroney and Desmarais in tow, the Barrick Power Gold Corp. of China (75% owned by Barrick and 25% by Power) looked like a winner.

Munk's colleagues weren't as enthusiastic. They were the ones who had to sit down to interminable, confusing, obfuscating meetings with lower-level Chinese bureaucrats in the provinces, and they knew that the chances of ever reaching an agreement that they could live with were minimal. The whole world knew that China was dicey, its negotiators notoriously devious. Toward the end of 1993, David Wynne-Morgan, head of communications in Horsham and Barrick and a director of Horsham, gently told his boss how he felt about it.

"Peter, the market is beginning to ask, 'Is there life after Goldstrike?,'" he said. "We have expounded the philosophy that we are a North American gold company and one of the things they like about us is our total focus on gold and the fact that we operate only in North America because of the economic and political stability it provides. If we come in now and say, 'Yes, there is life after Goldstrike — and it's China,' I fear your shares will fall another $5."

Munk turned on him, snapping out his perspective on the eye-popping potential of China, impatient at Wynne-Morgan's reticence. He soon found, however, that his colleague's views were supported by other senior people, including Barrick's president, Bob Smith, whose steady hand had guided the company safely through its explosive growth. Smith had no illusions about where the Chinese were coming from. He fully expected them to pursue a relationship until they had sucked all the technology they needed from Barrick and then wave goodbye. Munk eventually accepted the consensus and backed off China, but it was a tactical retreat, not a strategic withdrawal.

When Peter Munk sets his mind on something, he is in a league of his own. He will scavenge for every scrap of relevant information, phoning people all over the world for leads. He summons streams of people into his office for urgent discussions. He grabs the corporate jet to meet people who may be able to help him, even for a lunch. He builds his case with disciplined logic and relentless energy until he has put together an argument that defies disagreement.

And woe betide any executives who disagree with him without

being able to back up their point of view with cogent logic. Munk devastates unprepared opponents with the intellectual equivalent of slash and burn. They seldom make the same mistake again. Yet he appreciates — and understands that he needs — a valid contrary point of view. When people show signs of being able to meet that bill, he encourages them to keep on trying, even if he doesn't accept their advice. He admits that he doesn't feel right about a big decision until he has talked it through in arguments with his colleagues. Remarkably, he has trained his colleagues to accept his approach.

Their view is best articulated by Greg Wilkins, the young accountant who came to Barrick from Coopers & Lybrand and worked his way up to president of Trizec Corp., the real estate giant controlled by Munk's holding company, Horsham Corp. Wilkins had spent time in Barrick where he ended up as executive vice president, then in Horsham where he is also president — all before he had reached 40.

"You've got to have one guy who is ultimately the decision maker," Wilkins says. "If you have a couple of major guys who want to be the boss, there's just not enough room for that. We work very effectively as a team. A lot of the people around Peter today certainly show a lot of respect and loyalty to him, but they recognize that ultimately, [if you don't agree with] his judgment, we have every opportunity to convince him otherwise. If you fail to convince him, it's not Peter's fault, it's your own fault. Peter won't always make the right decision — we're going to have to live with that — but we all put our egos in the drawer and think about what's best for the company. Peter is part of the team — team leader, perhaps — but he's prepared to put his ego in the drawer and let the prevailing wisdom go forward, even on very important strategic decisions."

Munk conceded defeat on his dream of putting China at the center of the company's diversification program. (Barrick is still in China, although with greatly reduced expectations and exploration budget.) But he still had to move out of North America, where government regulations were becoming onerous and omnipresent prospectors had worked over most of the potential orebodies. By the spring of 1994, he had shifted his gaze to South America, where Mulroney was already making friendly calls on the presidents of Chile, Argentina, and Peru, among others. On the back of Mulroney's introductions, Munk became more familiar with the key countries of Latin America and his excitement grew rapidly. He was among the first to see that there was a historic shift under way. The dictatorships that had, for centuries, blighted the prospects of an entire subcontinent were giving way to democracies that were opening up their economies to the power and dynamism of foreign capital. At last, companies like Barrick could contemplate, with some degree of comfort, investing in the immense mineral deposits of such countries as Chile, Peru, Argentina, and Brazil. These governments now recognized the benefits that would accrue to their own people if they allowed foreigners to take their profits home after they invested in their countries.

The following year, in the fall of 1995, the Society of the Americas invited him to speak to one of their meetings in New York's elegant Pierre Hotel. For most of this century, the U.S. administration's interest in the region had been mainly political. Its interest in the region's economies and business had been driven by the exigencies of rescue missions and the drug trade rather than economic self-interest. Now here was Peter Munk getting excited about the business prospects in Latin America for North American companies. He had his august audience on their feet, cheering, as he told them:

"An enormous shift has taken place over the past ten years in the affairs of our hemisphere . . . the fundamental change from the rhetoric of poverty-driven socialism, from the bankrupt ideas of Marxism, to the fabulous emergence of free enterprise, democracy, and all the things which we stand for, we believe in, in Latin America . . . In years to come, when professional historians will look back at this generation and analyze the significant events to find answers to the major inexplicable events, there will be two fundamental issues that will preoccupy their thinking. One will be the enormous shift in Latin America . . . The second is the most fundamental development of our generation — the voluntary abandonment of the most powerful tyranny mankind has known in Soviet Russia."

Delivered with his usual force and conviction, without a single note, filling the room with his passion, he took his audience's breath away. One man stood up in the question period and said the speech had changed his life.

By the time he delivered this speech, he had already taken a giant step toward implementing his new-found focus on Latin America. After he returned from Switzerland in the spring of 1994, his hankering for China in cold storage, Munk set in motion a comprehensive review of Barrick's options in generating its next growth phase. He let everyone know that this was still "his" company and it was still entrepreneurial. He asked Bob Smith to put together an aggressive plan to acquire new mines and called a board meeting in the dog days of summer to approve it. His message was simple. We can no longer afford to amble along our growth path. We've got to sprint. That means an acquisition.

Within weeks, he bought Lac Minerals, largely on the strength of its Chilean properties. He had not identified the company as a target, but its annual production of 1 million ounces fitted his strategy perfectly and he grabbed it enthusiastically when it unexpectedly came up for sale.

While he was initiating the first part of his two-track strategy — strengthening his investment in gold by beefing up the effort to find new reserves — he was equally engaged in the second part: diversifying out of gold. In the spring of 1993, he started to breathe vitality into his holding company, Horsham Corp. He had founded Horsham, named after the English town where Melanie's parents lived, in 1987 intending to use it as a vehicle to invest Barrick's profits in other industries. He put all his and his partners' holdings of Barrick shares into the company, which then controlled about 30% of Barrick (those shares now represent $16\frac{1}{2}$% of Barrick after several issues of new shares, including those for the purchase of Lac).

Horsham languished as a "shelf" company for a year until one of Munk's acquaintances, Tony Novelly, dropped one of his companies into Munk's lap. Novelly's business strategy was not compatible with Munk's, but they were good friends at the time because they had helped each other out. A flamboyant businessman with a penchant for gambling, Novelly needed some fast cash to pay for the serious losses he suffered from a disastrous fling on the market for oil derivatives. So it seemed only natural for Novelly to turn to Munk and ask him to take a 60% stake in his company, Clark Refining and Marketing, to pay for his debts. Munk obliged. This was no rinky-dink company, however. It was in the Fortune 500 list of biggest companies in the United States, the fourth largest independent refinery in the country. It owned three refineries and 820 gas and convenience stations in the mid-West. Munk acquired his 60%

for $454 million, all but $28 million of it either borrowed or financed from cash in Clark.

Horsham subsequently diversified further, investing in real estate in Berlin, but even then, in early 1993, it was still an ad hoc appendage designed to keep the accounting systems tidy and having no clear role.

That spring of 1993, Munk was ready to start molding Horsham into a more substantial vehicle for organized diversification. His new program started slowly. He first issued $8\frac{1}{2}$ million common shares in May, raising close to $100 million. Then he went ahead at the end of the year with an issue of $600 million of 25-year debentures, which gave him the muscle to make a really significant acquisition.

It was a unique financing, as much of Munk's fund-raising is. He had many options in setting a strategy for diversifying. He could have relied on dividends paid to Horsham by Barrick, but that would have been a very slow process — $5 million or so a year does not buy a lot of mega corporations. He could have sold the Barrick shares, but that would have meant ditching the goose that laid the golden egg. Or he could have borrowed money using the Barrick shares as collateral. The only problem with this idea was that Horsham did not actually have a candidate for a takeover bid, and Munk didn't want to pay the banks their usual high interest rate for money that would be sitting in short-term securities for an indefinite period.

None of these options suited Munk. With classic entrepreneurial ambiguity, he wanted to have his cake and eat it, too. A year and a half before the debenture was floated, he had assembled his key finance men in Horsham (Greg Wilkins and Paul Melnuk, who was then president of Horsham but later became president of Clark) and told them he wanted to cash in

Horsham's Barrick shares without selling them. That was a tall order in and of itself, but he wanted even more. The riskiest strategy for a diversification program is to pay for it with borrowed money, because, if the diversification goes awry, the creditors are likely to force the sale of all the company's other assets to get their money back. Usually, this is not in the company's best interests. So Munk told his whiz kids that he wanted the cash to be as far away from a straight loan as possible. Wilkins and Melnuk were soon joined by Bill Biggar, who had come to Horsham from Bunting Warburg Inc., and the three of them, led by Biggar, spent many, many hours jawboning investment dealers as they tried to find a formula to fit Munk's criteria. "We were searching," says Munk, "for the one formula that allowed me to keep control, allowed me to get the cash today and allowed me to defer my taxation."

They tried dozens of different ideas with the underwriters. "Every top investment banker came in," he says. "We were offered a hundred deals — conventional lines of credit, conventional convertibles — you name it." The strategy that emerged was to borrow cash and repay it with something other than cash. "We didn't want to deliver money [when the debentures are redeemed]. If the shares [of the diversification vehicle] go down, and I don't have the money, then they take away my company. So that's out." Instead, he wanted the debenture holders to accept Barrick shares as repayment for their loan. "We wanted to deliver a fixed number of shares. So I say, 'We will give you shares and I won't give away one share more.' I know today how many shares I have to deliver to satisfy the $600 million indebtedness 25 years from now."

No one had ever done a deal like it before — borrowing money in return for shares to be delivered a quarter of a century later at whatever their value might be at that time.[2] To top up the ambiguity, Horsham retains the option to repay its debentures with the pledged Barrick stock or the cash equivalent, so it doesn't have to decide until 2018 whether to keep its money in Barrick or sell. If Barrick's prospects are better than its other investments, it will pay off the debentures in cash, selling other investments if necessary; if Barrick's prospects are worse in 2018, it will pay in Barrick stock.

The debentures carried a coupon of $3\frac{1}{4}$%, so the investors were, in effect, buying Barrick shares and getting an additional yield of $3\frac{1}{4}$% on their investment in return for giving Munk the option to redeem the debentures at any time after 1998, in cash or in shares. Munk, in turn, was getting very cheap money — $3\frac{1}{4}$% at a time when he would have paid $8\frac{1}{2}$% for a straight loan — and the flexibility to keep or dispose of his Barrick shares once he knew whether or not Barrick shares were working out better than the diversification program. Whatever happened, it was a pretty good deal for Horsham. The Barrick shares, then trading at about $30, would have to rise to $150 by 2018 to raise the overall yield on the debentures to $8\frac{1}{2}$%. This may sound ambitious, but at the time the debenture issue was floated, Barrick was coming off a year when its price

---

[2] Horsham backed each $1,000 debenture with between 32.4675 and 35.7143 Barrick shares. When the debentures are redeemed in 2018, the holders of each $1,000 debenture will get back exactly $1,000 if the Barrick shares are trading between $28 and $30.80. But if the Barrick shares are trading higher than $30.80, each debenture will be worth 32.4675 Barrick shares and the debenture holders will pocket the full appreciation of the stock over $30.80. If the shares are trading at $35 at redemption, for example, each $1,000 debenture will be paid $1,136. If they are trading at $50, the debenture will fetch $1,623. By the same token, if the Barrick shares are trading at less than $28, the debenture will be worth 35.7143 Barrick shares. If the shares are trading at $25 at redemption time, each $1,000 debenture will fetch only $893.

almost doubled in 12 months. So going up five times in 25 years did not (and still does not) seem out of reach.

Munk's first golden rule:
Never raise money when you need it.
Raise it when financial markets are buoyant;
invest it when markets are depressed.

It was a classic Munk financing — exchanging short-term, guaranteed cash benefits to his company in return for long-term possible capital gains for his investors.

"The worst that could have happened was instead of having 57 million shares of Barrick 25 years from now, I would only have 36 million shares," says Munk. "That I can live with. That's 25 years down the line. If I am going to diversify out of gold, I want to do it without risks. Any ass can roll the dice. I'm too old to do that. When we bought Clark, it was not because I strategically love refining and employing 4,000 workers in Texas, believe me. I bought it because I could buy it for an amount of money that if everything blew up, I knew I could afford to lose and I could still go and do things again."

By the time Munk purchased Clark, Horsham was big enough that it could easily survive the loss of a paltry $28 million if everything went wrong. The major attraction, however, was that the upside was huge. Tony Novelly was in trouble with Clark because profit margins in the refinery business had collapsed and Munk knew that when the refinery margins recovered, Clark would begin to throw off huge profits. "If I was right with the refining margins, it is a large enough company that I could have done something spectacular with it." A mere six years later, the value of that $28 million had grown to $180 million[3] — and that was before refining margins had really recovered.

"These are things I like doing. That is the difference between business and gambling. A gambler rolls the dice. If it doesn't come up, he's lost everything. With business, you roll the dice, but if you lose out, you're not hurt. That's my job. That slows you down. But what's wrong with that? That's a fair price to pay not to be wiped out. That's my strategy."

Munk's second golden rule:
Always give away some of the upside
to protect the downside.

(Slightly more than two years later, in January 1996, Munk repeated the debenture exercise, raising $250 million for Horsham, this time with an interest rate of 3% with no right to cash in the debentures for the shares for at least ten years.)

When Munk departed Toronto for Switzerland in December 1993, his diversification program was ready to roll. The $750 million he had stuffed into Horsham's stocking was enough to make a dramatic acquisition — and he didn't have long to wait. Before the ink was dry on the $600 million debenture, Munk got a call from Tony Fell, the chairman of RBC Dominion Securities, the biggest investment broker in Canada, and the lead underwriter for the debenture issue.

"Would you like to buy one of the largest real estate companies in North America?" he asked. "If you can write a check for between half a billion and a billion, it's got the cash flow

---

[3] Clark subsequently bought out the balance of Novelly's shares to own 100%. Then it raised $120 million by giving a 40% share to an institutional money manager. This valued the company at $300 million, putting a value of $180 million on Horsham's 60% share.

and you can ride this into something really significant."

Munk agreed to take a look at it and a few months later, he teamed up with New York real estate financier Jerry O'Connor and investment bankers J. P. Morgan to buy a controlling interest in a faltering Canadian real estate giant called Trizec, which owned almost $5 billion of assets. It cost Horsham $477 million to buy 48% of Trizec, after revaluing the assets to about 3\frac{1}{4}$ billion to reflect the rock-bottom prices at the end of a drastic slump in real estate prices. In 1994, when the Trizec deal was finalized, commercial real estate properties were worth about the same as they had been in the late 1970s, having soared 75% during the early 1980s, then tumbled right back down.

It was the ideal diversification. "If I was right on Trizec," says Munk, "then I have got the best pool of real estate in North America that I got at bargain prices at a cyclical low. That can give us potential." And if he was wrong, his downside was covered by the terms of the debenture.

By the end of 1994, Munk felt confident that he had set Barrick and Horsham on their new paths. That summer, he had spent $2.3 million buying Lác Minerals and Trizec, putting a completely new face on his companies. The financial analysts, surely, would sit up and take notice.

But they didn't. Horsham shares languished and Barrick's continued to lag.

It was too much for Munk. His exploits had been the most spectacular business story in Canada that year and the stock market was yawning at him. The analysts had torched one of Canada's most explosive business competitors. It had become personal, because his story was just too good, he felt, to be treated with such indifference. After ruminating during his next sojourn in Klosters, in the winter of 1995, Munk decided to end the malign neglect by feeding the analysts' expectations. He would give them what they craved — exploration plays for Barrick and a whole new concept for Horsham.

On Munk's return to Toronto in the spring of 1995, he launched another series of bold initiatives. First of all, he more than doubled the budget for exploration. The budget for 1995 had been $30 million, which represented a healthy increase from the previous year's $20 million, which in turn was a big increase from 1993's $7 million. He changed the 1995 budget to $80 million. About half this money was earmarked for joint ventures with individual prospectors or very small gold companies looking for a partner to do the development drilling to assess the extent of a promising find. The rest was for drilling on existing mines to gauge the extent of their reserves. At that stage, Barrick still did very little real grassroots exploration — sending geologists out into the field to take rock samples in virgin territory. This kind of exploration is extremely labor intensive and high risk.

Even without the pure grassroots exploration plays, Barrick's exploration budget still represents a fearsome challenge for its top executives. Alan Hill, Barrick's executive vice president of corporate development, the man in charge of developing new orebodies, knows only too well that his neck's on the line. "You know, we're better than anybody else, but there's 150 companies out there looking for the same thing. You've got to kiss a lot of frogs before you find a prince."

The army of prospectors who roam the world looking for geological anomalies are the best source of prospects for new mines. Big mining companies seldom attract geologists who will stick their necks out for the wild hunches that lead, in a fraction of the cases, to elephant orebodies. The trick for a large company like Barrick is to get the prospectors to come to Barrick rather than its competitors when they are seeking a partner. Munk's geologists around the world now have strict instructions to treat every lead from a prospector as a serious possibility and to give them a prompt reply when they come calling.

The company still won't develop anything under a million ounces of gold, but it will look seriously at anything that any prospector brings to it. To drive the point home on how *not* to implement this strategy, Barrick suffered a huge disappointment in the fall of 1995 when a small company it had narrowly missed signing up as a partner announced it had made the biggest gold discovery in the world that year. The owners of Calgary-based Bre-X had come to Barrick looking for a partner in late 1993. Barrick's geologists liked the look of its property in Indonesia and the company made an offer: it would buy a million Bre-X shares at C$1.25 to C$1.50 a share in return for the right to an 80% share of any future Bre-X developments. It was an aggressive proposal, which didn't leave a lot on the table for Bre-X and the negotiations fizzled. A year and a half later, Bre-X revealed that reserves on its Indonesian property were at least 15 million and maybe as much as 30 million ounces of gold. Its shares, which had by then risen to C$4, shot up to C$59. A few months later, as more details emerged of the enormity of the find, the shares continued their climb, passing C$270[4] in May 1996. At this price, the market was guessing that Bre-X's orebody contained more than 50 million ounces of gold. In the spring of 1996, Bre-X's president, David Walsh, felt he could tell *The Financial Post* that he wanted C$2 billion for 25% of Bre-X. That priced the shares at C$360 each, when it was trading at C$220.

---

[4] C$27 after a 10-for-1 stock split.

It was exactly the kind of opportunity that Munk wanted to nail down for Barrick and he was thoroughly disappointed. To make sure that nothing more falls between the cracks, he has embarked on a strategy to systematize the whole process of making deals with junior companies and multiply the projects that Barrick gets involved in.

"The analysts want us to have more projects," he says. "Well, if that's what the public wants, that's what the public will get — and we'll do it better than everybody else."

At the end of 1995, Barrick announced it had arranged a revolving credit facility for $1 billion from the Royal Bank of Canada for a term of up to eight years. This, plus Barrick's annual cash flow of half a billion dollars, will buy a lot of deals, even after the heavy development spending planned for ore-bodies in mines they already own.

"Five years from now," he says, "this is what will give us the windfalls for the next three Goldstrikes." He paces round his office, punching his left palm with his right fist. "We are sending a message to the market that there's more to it than just reserves. We are going to send a message out to them that this management is not lying down. We are going to send them a message that we are able to carry on a component in this mining company that is totally independent from mining — that's sheer business. . . We are not going to become an institutional mining company.

"I hate excuses and if I can't change my own company, then you may as well believe in the karma of your chorus book. I will never be able to put gold in the ground — but to bring an entrepreneurial component into my company when I've got cash flow of half a billion dollars a year — if I can't do that, then I should be shot through the head or be fired."

Of course, having a cash flow of half a billion dollars makes it harder, not easier, to bring an entrepreneurial component into a company, no matter how intense the leader's passion.

The success in this endeavor, however, will lie in whether Munk owes his success so far to luck or good management. In a career of dramatic ups and downs, he has had some astounding luck, both good and bad, but he also forged the competitive edge of someone who has consistently tested the furthest limits of his own capacity. Over the past four decades, he has built six businesses, any one of which could have made him a multimillionaire. In each case, he shot for the stars, reaching for goals that few would dare to dream, let alone attempt. Inevitably, they didn't all work. The first two were initially highly successful, but fell off the rails; the third was a spectacular success; the next two were abandoned before ever making a profit; and the sixth was fabulously successful. His three businesses in Horsham are all on track to succeed, but the jury is still out on them.

He has himself said on a number of occasions that he's been lucky. That begs the question of whether people create their own luck. Every successful person admits that luck plays a part in their success. Was it inevitable that Munk would hit the jackpot sooner or later? Or did lightning strike twice?

Peter Munk has set himself the goal of proving that luck is only a part, and a small part at that, of the enormous business empire he has built. The only way he can prove he's right is to do it again. And so, in the spring of 1996, he announced at Barrick's Annual General Meeting that he had set his company a new goal — to become the leading gold company in the world.

2

EARLY DREAMS, EARLY DISASTER

Almost 100 people came to the reunion. The Park Plaza Hotel in Toronto, October 21, 1989. They flew in from cities right across Canada and countries around the world — Fiji, Hungary, Israel, Britain, South America, and the United States — to remember and to be remembered, with laughter and tears of happiness. In that same hotel 31 years before, Clairtone Sound Corporation had burst onto the scene, embarking on a spectacular adventure that entranced an entire nation for almost a decade, before it collapsed into distressing oblivion.

Clairtone was Peter Munk's first really big challenge. In those tumultuous years, which spanned his 30s, he formulated his first mega-dream and discovered he had the capacity to make it come true. After its exuberant, if short-lived, success in markets all around the world, the tiny company became one of the most spectacular business failures of the 1960s, still remembered by many even in the 1990s. But Munk credits Clairtone for teaching him lessons that have guided him for the rest of his life. Much later, he would tell anyone who would listen that Clairtone was the classic impossible dream. "Everything I've been able to achieve afterwards is because of Clairtone. The biggest thing I got from the whole experience is self-confidence. I can achieve anything I set my mind to. We learned that the impossible is attainable."

Indeed, the Clairtone alumni were not at the Park Plaza to sing dirges and gnash their teeth. They were there to celebrate the glory years — the nine short years when they had all experienced the joy of believing in the impossible and of stretching their capacities to the outer limits of their potential. After dinner, they lined up to bear witness.

"After Clairtone, there was nothing I couldn't do," said one, an accountant. Another couldn't attend but passed on a message: "Those were the happiest working days of my life." Oscar Peterson sent a warm greeting.

The feeling was summed up best by Ziggy Hahn, the vice president of finance who had kept score in the wildest financial ride in business that Canada had seen since the Second World War: "Clairtone was a learning experience. We learned something about the meaning of courage. We certainly learned something about leadership. We learned what vision and strength meant in times of great success and difficulty. If you work hard enough, if you're convinced enough, then everything is possible . . . We weren't better. In some mysterious way, there was a human synergy that made very ordinary people do quite extraordinary things."

Later, in his keynote speech, Munk let it all hang out. "If we had told people, when we first started our operation, that within two years, Clairtone would be the youngest industrial company, and the first since the war, to be accepted for listing [on the Toronto Stock Exchange], if we had told them that for the following three years, it would be the top performing stock, that we would move from a bucket shop to a prestigious Canadian company dealing with E. F. Hutton, which at that time was the crème de la crème of New York, those people would have laughed us out of court . . . And you know, these impossible achievements, these impossible obstacles have created a unique phenomenon. It created among the people in Clairtone a commitment to common goals, an acceptance of a mutual ideal that transcends individual interests . . . It became a symbol for a new Canada."

It was vintage Munk, his whole body radiating the intensity of the message, no trace of a smile, his eyes burning, his passion rising: "Clairtone created the spirit of Clairtone. Clairtone created a commitment to a common bond that bound us together, that gave us courage, that gave us the belief, that gave us the confidence to achieve our objectives. The Clairtone people were magic."

Later, in his quiet dénouement, spoken softly: "To me that bond is priceless. Nobody can buy it, no school or university can teach it, and no parent can hand it down to their children. For that I would like to thank you today, because what you have given me is one of the most precious assets I possess."

A standing ovation. It wasn't a reunion, it was a spiritual revival. They called it "reliving the magic."

Just before Munk's speech, his first and still-active partner, David Gilmour, told an apocryphal story about his partner. The two of them, Gilmour said, had visited two of the company's financial advisers, and after the meeting, they had all gone down in the elevator together. One of the advisers, a woman, stood next to Munk and told him that she thought his product was wonderful, his vision was inspiring, and his leadership was admirable (or words to that effect). Then, in dulcet tones, according to Gilmour, she said: "I want to make love with you." The other two, staring intently at the numbers flashing above the elevator door, waited with baited breath for Munk's response, which came soon enough. "That's OK for you, but what's in it for the company?"

The Munk-and-Gilmour partnership was the essential component of the Clairtone magic and it has survived, with unswerving loyalty, almost 40 years of amazing vicissitudes, of dizzy highs and crushing lows, of incredible might-have-beens and of extraordinary luck, both good and bad.

David Gilmour had never experienced privation when he first met Munk. He had private tutors as a child, then went to the elite Trinity College School. His parents moved confidently through the inner circles of high society in an emergent Toronto. His mother, Doris, the daughter of a British colonel, was an operatic soprano whose artistic flair fused with her husband's monied sportiness to create an ideal social couple. Major Harrison Gilmour, decorated in the First World War, loved to hunt foxes and ski when he wasn't fueling the destiny of Canadian industry as managing director of one of Canada's leading investment houses, Nesbitt Thomson. He had hoped his fourth child and only son would follow in his footsteps at Nesbitt and proselytized the free enterprise gospel, never missing an opportunity to drum it into his son that he could achieve whatever he set out to do. His message fell on fertile ground but had unintended results, because the goals that David chose to set for himself did not mesh with his father's dreams for him. When the Major offered his son some money and suggested he could build it into a nest egg, David demurred, preferring to blow it all in a glorious travel binge in Europe.

He had always known exactly how he wanted to live — the fox hunting, the travel, the beautiful people with their villas in southern Spain and the south of France. He grabbed the opportunity his father's small gift gave him. He had it all, navigating the byways in the convertible Volkswagen his father had provided, never pausing to wonder what would happen when the money ran out.

On one occasion in his European travels, when the Gilmour family was in Monte Carlo, Harrison thought he would inject some financial responsibility into his errant son, so he took him to the casino. Hoping that an evening at the tables would suitably demonstrate the inevitable consequences of gambling and maybe even plant the seeds of financial husbandry, he gave his son 50 French francs. David bought two Fr25 chips and put them both on the number 7. When *la balle* landed on 7, Harrison gave up, despairing of ever imparting the sober demeanor appropriate to a scion of the arbiters of Toronto society. The two went off and got drunk on the winnings.

But the money did run out, of course. "There is nothing so diligent," Gilmour says, "as a remittance man without a remittance." In a classic rich-kid ploy, he wired his father for money: "Four tires worn out — very dangerous to drive. Please send $300." In an equally classic response, Harrison replied: "Son, love you very much. Park car beside road and abandon. Return home immediately."

Gilmour cut a dashing figure. Tall, slim, elegant, he exudes his background. His crisp, well-modulated voice carries a hint of aristocratic languidness, with an accent somehow un-North American, but not European either. His hazel eyes flick around the people and the place, detached somehow, even when his attention is focused. Always ready with a diplomatic *bon mot*, he can, when he wants to, make people feel comfortably at ease in the most trying circumstances. Later, when he and Munk laid the foundations of their business empire, that facility became important. "They would all prefer to deal with Gilmour," Munk said 20 years after they first met. "He's much nicer to deal with. But I don't want to be the guy everybody likes. I want to get things done. And, to get things done, you've got to argue, poke, prod, wrestle, push."

On David's return to Canada, Harrison urged him to join Nesbitt, but the thought of life in an investment house was abhorrent to the putative playboy, so he chose something about as far away from finance as he could get. He moved to Montreal where he sold pots and pans door to door, mainly to Polish immigrants. He held demonstrations in his own kitchen where he would cook sample meals. He says he chose this job because he wanted to learn how to make cold calls in a business setting. He knew he could function effectively in the social setting of mutual friends and supportive referrals, but could he apply his social skills to situations where he did not have the advantage of automatic acceptance? He managed to make a half-decent living with his pots and pans, but his family soon worked out a plan to lure him back to Toronto a year after he left.

Gilmour's sister, Shelagh Vansittart, was his Rock of Gibraltar. She herded him through his indulgent 20s like a substitute father, straddling two roles in his life — his friend who moved in the same exuberant social circle in Toronto and his mentor as he eased into the world of business. Shelagh had built a solid business in Yorkville, *the* trendy quarter in Toronto, with a furnishing store called "Shelagh's of Toronto." She and her father hatched a scheme to expand the business by importing Scandinavian furniture, which was just then beginning to gain a following in North America. They asked David to look after the new business, which he quickly agreed to, because it suited his designer tastes. "Scantrade" was born and David Gilmour was finally in an occupation that didn't embarrass his father, who unfortunately died before he could savor the success of Clairtone only a few years later.

Gilmour still wasn't giving any time to thinking about how to please his father, however. He had quietly made a decision about the lifestyle he wanted and was trying to figure out how to pay for it when he met Peter Munk. "I couldn't have done it if I hadn't had someone to bond to of such strength and excitement," he says.

David Gilmour was the perfect foil for Peter Munk. Munk also came from a privileged background, his grandfather having been a prominent financier in Budapest, but his family lost all their wealth long before Munk set foot in Canada. The early years of servants and the grand family complex in a block of apartments left their mark, however. When he recently revisited his childhood home for the first time since he left it, a 92-year-old neighbor who still lives in the same block reminded him of the time when he threw his grandfather's gold watch into the garden below. Munk didn't remember the incident, although he did acknowledge he had been a naughty child and had hated school. What he *did* remember, however, was the wall safe, from which his grandfather used to take gold coins and give them to the only child of his son.

That world came crashing down on the Munk family when the Nazis occupied Hungary in 1944. A small group of wealthy Jews — Munk, his grandfather, and father included — were able to buy their way out of the developing persecution, exchanging all the gold they possessed for a train ticket to Switzerland. Munk's mother, divorced since Peter was an infant, wasn't as lucky — she was interned in a concentration camp, which she survived. Her son escaped all that and spent the rest of the war in Zurich, where he finished his high school. An average student, he worked hard to get good marks, but no amount of work could raise his marks high enough to pass the grade for Zurich's prestigious Polytechnic University. His parents decided instead to send him to the New World, and he left for Canada in 1948, armed only with $350 to pay for his tuition fees at university.

Between Zurich and Toronto, he managed to blow that $350 on a beautiful woman he met on the boat, lavishing meals, drinks, and gifts on her with his customary single-mindedness. He was counting on his rich uncle, Nick, who lived in Toronto, to lend him the money for the tuition until he could pay him back. The uncle decided to teach him a lesson instead and refused. Desperate, Munk found out that he could earn good money picking tobacco near Delhi in southwestern Ontario. It was back-breaking work, 12 hours a day, but he stuck it out for 40 days and 40 nights, emerging with $360. After a short stay in high school to establish his Canadian credentials, he entered the University of Toronto, graduating in 1952, at age 25, with a degree in electrical engineering.

He got jobs with Canadian National Telegraphs and Atlas Radio, then dabbled in a few other alliances. But, after five years of working for other people, the boredom became too much for him and he started his own business. Only months before, he had married his first wife, Linda Gutterson, the daughter of a prominent Toronto family. No one was surprised when he struck out on his own.

While still a student, he and some friends dabbled in an entrepreneurial venture designed to augment their December incomes. They sold Christmas trees and did so well that Munk asked Dominion Stores if he could use their parking lots to sell trees the following year. He had, typically, thought it through. The extra traffic would increase sales at their stores, he told them. He had special signs printed — "if you're going to buy, buy from a student" — adorned with the University of Toronto crest. He hired students and paid them partly by commission and partly by the profit made by the whole project. (Even then, he was structuring his motivation to create teamwork.)

By his third year, he had 17 lots and had turned the project into a sizable business. He bought the trees in the summer, hired several trucks to transport them to Toronto just before Christmas, and lined up a platoon of students to run the logistics. One of the students remembered that several of the trees were a bit scraggly; Munk told him to tell their customers that they filled out once they were inside a warm house. That year, however, there was a huge snowstorm in Toronto two days before Christmas and even the streetcars ground to a halt. No one went out to buy Christmas trees. Munk was left with a very large inventory of unsellable trees and a $2,000 deficit. This was a very large sum of money for an impecunious student in those days, but he paid it off in a year. And he learned at an early age how arbitrary fate can devastate even the best laid plans. It was not the last time it would happen.

Once in business for himself, as Peter Munk Associates, his ambition had something to feed on. He installed very expensive hi-fi components in rich people's homes — burying them in their walls, antique furniture, or cupboards. He soon built up a loyal list of satisfied clients who referred him to new prospects. Sales soon reached C$8,000 a month, which was enough to provide him with a small salary but left a bottom line that hovered on either side of zero. He employed two people — Michael Chojnacki, an electronic technician (later to become vice president of manufacturing in Clairtone) and a secretary, Helen Campbell, one of only four people he has employed as secretaries in more than 40 years.

He wore every hat in the business, and, although his style was already apparent, the polish was still to come. In a typical personalized letter to selected prospects, the courtly Hungarian flavor of his English must have given its recipients a few chuckles.

Dear Sir,

My aim is not to tell you HOW you may have High Fidelity in your home — but rather WHY you should.

Modern living is the rediscovery of the pleasures of living at home. Many of us have found adequate dwellings, a little spare money and some leisure time at our disposal. Home leisure occurs every day, and the home serves as a refuge; it is where the spirit is repaired, refreshed and strengthened against the next day, the next week, the next month.

The best restorative of all is beauty. No beauty can be enjoyed in so much of its fullness in the living room, as that which is met through the ear. There is music to put iron in the soul, music to relax the nerves, music to set feet tapping . . .

Sonic recreation is more kinetic than that enjoyed by the eye . . . The high fidelity requirement is dual. The tonal and dynamic range must be great, so that Paganini's violin is truly a violin, with overtones; so that Poulenc's organ pedals are not wasted; so that Haydn's big bass drum remains big . . .

This is your opportunity which can be both obsessive and delightful. I would like to tell you more about WHY you should have a High Fidelity in your home . . .

All for a mere $2,000. From the very beginning, he set his sights on the first class cabin. Set in elegant type on very expensive paper with ragged edges, the letter still managed to intrigue, despite the gaucheness. But Peter Munk Associates could never create the kind of excitement its founder had in mind. He needed an idea that had serious legs. In David Gilmour, he found the perfect complement for his set of skills and attributes. Together, they could create just such an idea.

Munk's third golden rule:
Work with people whom you respect and who have characteristics you don't have.

"In the history of business, there are probably very few examples of partnerships that have lasted very long," Gilmour says, "because people look for compatibility, by which they mean having very similar characteristics. What happens, however, is that you get two people tending to work over the same ambitions and goals and pretty soon they get frustrated and their egos start coming into play. You get competitive. There can only be one captain to run a ship and when two people fight over the tiller, the ship tends to to-and-fro a bit.

"That was never the case with Peter and me. From the very beginning, I accepted and admired his leadership qualities and his personality and saw that what he needed was space to develop his thinking. I recognized within that space his tremendous leadership qualities and imagination. My father once told me that the wise man listens rather than talks, so I listen and try to absorb ideas. By not getting too close to any given situation emotionally, I can be more objective and more helpful to Peter. I'm there with, perhaps, an objective view — with no axe to grind and no threatened position. So I cannot be persuaded by Peter unless I feel absolutely convinced. One of the key elements to our relationship is the extraordinary degree to which the two of us can enter a room with diametrically opposed views and not leave that room until we're both looking in the same direction."

An objective view of their partnership comes from Bill Birchall, who was to become the third partner a decade and a half later (see Chapter 3) and who has worked more closely with the two of them than anyone else. He says: "David can smell a product and Peter can make it commercially viable. David might not understand how you get to a bottom line, but he always keeps it in focus while he's conceiving a product."

Munk rarely conceives the original germ of an idea, Birchall explains. "Peter is not a cold starter. He picks up very quickly. Give him the germ of an idea, he can build on it. If you ask someone to think outside the box, you can't ask them to also have very tight focus. You would be asking them to have a split personality. If Peter writes a letter, he likes to have a draft to work from."

Munk's genius lies in taking a simple idea, putting it into a global context that places it at the nexus of all the most significant trends of that moment in time, and then sculpting the admixture into a concept of breathtaking grandeur. Like all true entrepreneurs, he is supremely unconcerned about the

41

source of an idea — he'll borrow them from wherever he finds them — but the focus, the grasp, and the reach are all his own.

Like all people with this touch of genius, however, Munk needs a brake to go with his accelerator and, in the early days, Gilmour filled that role. He had the enthusiasm and the willingness to enjoy — indeed, to applaud — Munk's limitless ambition, but he also understood Munk's need for a foil against whom he could argue his concepts and hone them until they were flawless.

This chemistry is only part of the story, however. Gilmour had a much more tangible asset that interested Munk — the extraordinary contacts in the highest circles that he had accumulated through his family and from those heady days traveling around Europe. Gilmour knew how to play them. "I'm more of a front man, meeting people, meeting situations, a part of the formation of a concept," he says. "Peter needed that, so that he had the time to do the hard grind of putting the presentation in the right format. Peter's superb at sussing things out, and at the time I was very useful, as a catalyst, a front man, spearheading certain initiatives."

With his family's social connections, he could walk into the offices of many of the top financiers and businesspeople in North America and Europe — something that Peter Munk simply could not do at that time, as he acknowledged in an interview in 1977: "There are a million David Gilmours without the follow-through of a Peter Munk, just as there are a million Peter Munks without the contacts of a David Gilmour." However, he also sees the human quality of their partnership with the same perspective as Gilmour. "There couldn't be two more different people, in background or values. But there's a chemistry between us that makes it work. Most partnerships break up, either because the deal fails and one blames the other, or because it succeeds and one takes the money and runs. But we started together, failed together, and then went on to build an even bigger success."

The most curious aspect of their partnership, which gave them their sense of destiny, is that not only did their personalities and assets mesh well, but their technical skills were also perfectly complementary. Munk's expertise in electronics and Gilmour's experience with Scandinavian furniture and his sense of design were the perfect combination to take the revolutionary step of putting stereo hi-fi into beautifully finished cabinetry that would blend in with any elegantly furnished room.

It all started one evening, during a raucous party in the condemned Rosedale mansion that Munk and a group of bachelors had rented. Gilmour floated the idea of putting Munk's electronic wizardry into beautiful cabinets and mass marketing them. Munk had been talking about the impending market revolution for high-end hi-fi sets, and he brutally destroyed his friend's idea in his inimitable fashion, reeling off demographic and economic statistics to support his arguments. Statistics, particularly demographics and economics, are not Gilmour's strong suit, so Munk won the battle. But he didn't win the war.

The concept wouldn't go away and a couple of years later, they decided to build a prototype and test the market. It took them six months to build half a dozen units, and, in September 1958, they rented a small room in the Park Plaza and invited 17 buyers from department stores and appliance shops in the Toronto area to view their wares. All 17 placed orders. The pair did not even have to use a hard sell — the beautiful cabinetry and the technical quality of the electronics made for a revolutionary new product. The buyers all knew they would be able to sell them, despite the astronomic price of C$695, which was not far from the cost of a Volkswagen in those days.

Munk and Gilmour must have pinched themselves when they realized that they were on to something beyond their wildest dreams. Within two weeks, the pair had pitched Montreal, then stretched out across Canada — Munk to the east and Gilmour to the west — where the enthusiastic acceptance just continued to gather steam. In an industry where the top-of-the-line models were retailing for C$300 or C$400, their C$695 stereo system sold like hot cakes. In two and a half weeks, they had orders in hand for 82 units. Two months after their launch, they started looking for bigger quarters. Another two months later, in January 1959, Clairtone moved into its new 7,000-square-feet facility. One month later, they got their first orders from the United States. In March, Clairtone won a design award from the National Industrial Design Council. In April — only seven months after the Park Plaza launch — their product was featured in *Canadian Homes and Gardens* and *The Financial Post* ran a big feature on the two young entrepreneurs. The *Post* reported that Clairtone employed 63 people and that Munk and Gilmour planned ten new models in the coming fall.

By the early fall of 1959, one year into their venture, they were averaging sales of C$70,000 a month. In the last four months of 1959, their sales came in at C$412,752. During that year, they sold 700 sets in the United States — about the same number as the entire Canadian radio industry sold in the United States in 1958.

It was a breathtaking launch by any standards — 99.99% of entrepreneurs would have tried to slow down the progress a little to catch their breath, particularly when the inevitable cash crunch started to bite. Not Munk and Gilmour. The first crisis passed when Gilmour, who had just inherited a home from his mother, took out a mortgage and put C$20,000 into the company. They pressed harder on the accelerator.

The second cash crunch was accordingly not long in coming. Revenue Canada became extremely annoyed in February 1960, because the young company was not remitting its sales tax receipts fast enough. The Queen, they said, did not debate terms. They scrambled to find the C$27,000 demanded by the taxman within a 24-hour deadline by collecting some receivables and persuading a buyer at Simpson's in Montreal to take immediate delivery of a large order and issue a check on receipt of the product.

In March 1960, their expansion plans went into overdrive. The federal government selected Clairtone to represent Canadian industry at the huge Ideal Homes Show in Earls Court, London, so they started the search for British partners to manufacture locally. The third cash crunch hit that same month. The company was profitable with a net income of 8.3% of sales, but when sales double every few months, the profits from month A are not enough to pay for double the inventory and double the customer credit in month C. In March 1960, Clairtone's bank loan had soared to C$92,000 and the manager was getting extremely edgy. The company had C$138,000 in inventory and C$105,000 in unpaid client accounts — a working capital requirement of almost a quarter of a million dollars. To finance that, they had C$85,000 in accumulated profits, C$69,000 in delayed payments of their bills, and the bank line of C$92,000.

It was a classic case of overextension that leads almost invariably to bankruptcy. Which is what the two were facing. The banks wouldn't help them any more and Gilmour's best efforts with his father's old friends on Bay Street had met with a solid wall of refusal. Then Ziggy Hahn, who was their accountant then and not yet their vice president of finance, ran into a Toronto promoter named Irving Gould at a party hosted by Gilmour's sister, Shelagh. Gould was intrigued by Hahn's story of the two young men who needed a quarter of a million dollars and agreed to meet the pair at their factory the next morning, a Sunday. He asked a lot of penetrating questions and liked the answers he got, so he offered to put up the money in return for 55% of the company. Munk and Gilmour turned him down. They would not cede control. Two days later, Gould accepted less than 50% and Clairtone signed a deal to go public — an astonishingly brief 18 months after the sale of the first set.

The share issue was done by a firm of investment bankers called N. L. MacNames & Co., who knew Gould well. Gould had taken a shine to the impatient young men and persuaded MacNames to underwrite the issue, earning for his troubles a gift of 50,000 shares from Munk and Gilmour. They raised C$237,000 (net of commissions and legal expenses) by issuing 100,000 shares at C$2.75 each. By that time, the two had put every cent they owned into the company and had to take some money out so that they could live. As part of the deal, they therefore sold some of their shares for almost C$40,000. Having started by putting in C$44,000 to own 100% of the company, the two partners now owned 68% of the shares of a company with a market capitalization of C$1.4 million. And their initial investment had been mostly refunded. Most important of all, the company had some serious cash in its till for the first time.

This was not, of course, an opportunity for Munk and Gilmour to breathe a sigh of relief. It was an occasion to blow even harder into their sails. In the first full year of the business, Clairtone's total sales had been C$311,000. One year later, in the last four months of 1960, sales averaged C$300,000 a month. This was growth enough to impress the most hardened skeptic, but that was no reason for them to slacken their punishing pace. "I work better under pressure," Munk explained many years later. "If I had cash flow problems, I would never have slowed down. No way! Our job was to solve the problem, not take the easy way out."

Munk's fourth golden rule:
Time is short. If you want to achieve much,
you've got to run.

By the end of 1960, the bank debt had soared once again to C$292,000, but it was no longer a serious problem. The price of the Clairtone shares was rising steeply, so Munk and Gilmour were able to use their shares as collateral to provide personal guarantees of the loan. By March 1961, the shares hit C$12, making them each worth more than C$2 million on paper. That was a lot of wealth in 1961.

The rapid success of Clairtone was based on radical thinking and innovative technology. Munk's electronics were state of the art and he invested heavily in research and development from day one. Gilmour's sense of design led him to understand that their sets appealed to women, who liked them as furniture, as much as to men, who liked them for their technology. In a brilliant marketing breakthrough, he told his dealers to pitch the women, not the men. To the dealers' astonishment, it worked. One dealer reported that half of the sets he sold were not even turned on in the showroom.

Munk and Gilmour now realized they could take this company all the way to glory, riches, and fame. At age 33 and 29, respectively, they assumed the more solemn demeanor of international industrialists. In one famous picture that was reproduced in many different publications, they are half facing each other, looking over their shoulders at the camera, unsmiling, determined, confident. Gilmour is tall, looking slightly down his nose, his arms folded to display a large signet ring, serene, supremely elegant, and handsome. Munk is pudgier (he wasn't as lean then as he is today), with the look of a bulldog, his chin stuck out, the merest hint of a frown, his eyes glinting sternly into the camera. This became Clairtone's image. No more the dashing young men, they were now significant manufacturers.

The cash problems never went away, but the momentum of the company now assumed mythical proportions. Munk and Gilmour rode it for all they were worth. Between 1960 and 1963, sales went from C$2 million to almost C$9 million. The company's net income after tax went from C$55,000 to C$300,000. By 1963, 37% of sales were in the United States, where Clairtone products were stocked in all the leading department stores — Bloomingdale's, Macy's, Marshall Fields among them. Clairtone had administration and sales offices in the Time Life building in New York, the Merchandise Marts in Chicago and San Francisco, and the Home Furnishing Mart in Los Angeles. They had sales offices in England, France, Benelux, Switzerland, Germany, and Italy. They had cut a distribution deal with Max Braun, the prestigious German appliance manufacturer.

In July 1962, they opened new 80,000 sq. ft. facilities. It was a media extravaganza, with TV cameras and hoopla galore. The plant was opened by the federal minister of industry, trade & commerce, George Hees, attended by Bob Macaulay, the Ontario minister of economics and development. After the champagne, Munk and Gilmour confided to the two politicians that a retreating stock market had forced Nesbitt Thomson to withdraw its agreement to float a C$1 million debenture for Clairtone — and that the company might fail if the money didn't arrive. Hees agreed to talk to the Governor of the Bank of Canada to see if he could help. It was an unprecedented offer, but Clairtone had become a key component of the government's exhortation to Canadian manufacturers to export more to the United States. A couple of days later, in the office of the governor of the Bank of Canada, Munk told his story. The governor listened and ended the discussion without any comment, but Munk knew how much power he wielded. All the investment banks relied heavily on the Bank of Canada's business in government bond trading. Within days, Nesbitt Thomson called Munk and told him they had changed their minds. The debenture went on sale in September, not a moment too soon — the bank loan was then C$897,000.

It was round about this point that the Clairtone saga took a rather unusual twist. Having started out with the intention of targeting the top 5% or 6% of the population and charging a very high price, Clairtone found the appeal of its product extended further than they had expected. There were a number of reasons for this but one of the most important was that Clairtone had come to represent much more than an audio system. It became a symbol for a new Canada. The company received countless letters from Canadians who had been down to any number of major U.S. cities, including Pittsburgh, Atlanta, Boston, and New York, and had walked into a department store to find their own Clairtones on display. It prompted an unprecedented and uncharacteristic surge of Canadian patriotism. Unwisely, though understandably, the two young men decided to turbocharge their marketing by capitalizing on this phenomenon.

Over the next few years, Munk and Gilmour injected their own personalities into the merchandising program. Advertisements featured pictures of the two, larger than life. Their style of doing business attracted as much attention as the products themselves. They hired Dalton Camp — then a radical new face in the advertising industry — to do their advertising and public relations. They ran a series with a picture of Frank Sinatra and the caption "Listen to Sinatra on Clairtone stereo. Sinatra does." The prime minister, *Playboy*'s Hugh Hefner, and the Beatles all had Clairtone stereos.

When they introduced "Project G" in 1964, it was close to the Second Coming. "Absolutely shocking," the ad blared above that heavyweight picture of the dynamic duo. "Sound like you've never heard before. Clean and big. And realistic as all get out." Project G featured loudspeakers in the shape of two big balls at either end of the cabinet — a design that won countless awards. It was also the first quality stereo system to use solid state electronics. Some of the models had remote controls. There was lots of steak beneath the sizzle, and Munk and Gilmour never thought twice about placing their own heads square across the block.

Over the next few years, Munk became a national figure. (Gilmour, meanwhile, never the one for publicity, had moved to New York in the summer of 1963 to wrestle down the losses in that market.) Munk was on the board of the National Research Council. He spoke to hushed audiences at the Canadian Club. He lectured the intellectually pretentious Couchiching Conference, prescribing solutions to the ills of his adopted country. He lunched with the prime minister. He even thought of running for prime minister.

The Canadian flag was wrapped around his marketing campaign. In his letter to shareholders introducing Project G, Munk wrote, "Only through bold creativity, imagination and strong leadership will Canada enhance her industrial image and achieve lasting success in the markets of the world." The Toronto Stock Exchange monthly magazine carried a picture of the Clairtone assembly line on its cover. Dominating the picture was a banner strung above the heads of the workers: "Make Clairtone sets great because it helps Canada by exporting."

In January 1966, Representative Seymour Halpern made a speech in the U.S. Congress praising Clairtone to the skies, and noting that much of its achievement was due to the vision and ability of the two founders, Mr. Peter Munk and Mr. David Gilmour.

In April 1967, the month when Clairtone glowed brightest, Munk authored a full-page article in *The Financial Post* that cut the financial community up into small pieces in a logical, tightly argued polemic. "The single most prohibitive factor in the current development of a viable Canadian secondary manufacturing industry, capable of mounting a successful export program, is the almost insurmountable difficulty in finding capital . . . The past history of underwritings of young industrial issues has been, on the average, singularly unsuccessful . . ."

He argued that the Americans were taking over precisely the young aggressive companies that Canada needed most badly to build its secondary manufacturing sector, while the "failures, semi-failures, unaggressive and tired firms not coveted for takeover by foreign concerns are the ones most likely to remain with us and become Canada's characteristically ineffective, decaying secondary manufacturing industry . . . The constant international trend toward trade liberalization will eventually erode our current protective tariffs . . . Unless we act now to strengthen financially the Canadian-owned sector of our manufacturing industry, it will be too weak to stand up against the ever-stronger U.S. and European industrial competition and the consequences may be the eventual loss of Canada's very independence."

That month, the price of Clairtone stock hit its all-time peak of C$15. The next month, results for the first quarter of 1967 were released, showing a sharply higher loss of more than C$200,000. Three months later, Munk and Gilmour lost control of Clairtone. Six months later, Munk and Gilmour had been fired by the new government of Nova Scotia, which by then controlled the company.

Munk's fifth golden rule:
Don't give away your destiny. Don't put control into the hands of a body that doesn't have interests aligned with yours. Governments are a good example.

The government connection started happily enough in 1964, when Munk and Gilmour thought they'd died and gone to heaven. Colonel J. C. MacKeen, a director of Industrial Estates Ltd. (IEL), the venture capital arm of the Nova Scotian government, approached Munk and Gilmour secretly in New York with an offer to finance their growth, provided Clairtone moved its production facilities to the province. IEL didn't want any equity, so Munk and Gilmour would retain control. They could hardly believe their ears. After the usual round of detailed negotiations, the province agreed to commit C$8 million for starters, of which C$3.5 million was intended for a huge, spanking new, integrated plant covering seven acres. With cash flow problems about to become a thing of the past, Munk gushed to the media that it was such a fantastic deal, he didn't know why everyone didn't do it.

The plant opened in June 1966, with maximum fanfare. Premier Robert Stanfield pulled the switch that sent the first unit rolling off the assembly line. Among the 1,000 people who applauded the celebratory speeches were John Turner, then a minister without portfolio in Lester Pearson's cabinet; the good congressman from Washington, Seymour Halpern; the lieutenant governor of Nova Scotia; 8 provincial cabinet ministers; 3 university presidents; and 11 directors of IEL, including Frank Sobey, its president, and Bob Manuge, its general manager. The distinguished guests had arrived from Halifax in a special train chartered from CN to whisk them the 100 miles to Stellarton, the home town of Frank Sobey and the new home of Clairtone.

A leading light in the business world, Sobey had his finger in many pies — apart from his duties with IEL, he was mayor of Stellarton and head of the intricate network of businesses surrounding Sobey's Stores, the foundation of his family's immense fortune. The train was a nice touch. A nicer touch was the Lockheed Learstar Munk had bought the month before to ferry dealers and executives into Stellarton from Toronto in twice-weekly flights. This was the life. But the end was already in sight.

In December 1965, just as the construction was getting under way, IEL had agreed to add another C$2 million to the C$8 million it had already committed to Clairtone, on condition that color TVs were added to its product line. Clairtone had no experience in TVs, but the market was just beginning to take off. Munk was predicting sales of C$20 million that year, with the prospect of major increases to come as TV production settled down. His chances of reaching that goal looked good. The Clairtone name had a solid reputation in Canada and the United States, and everyone was predicting a massive surge in retail sales as people dropped black and white for color. In October 1966, General Electric predicted that 70% of households would have color TV by the end of the decade. After sales of 2.7 million units in the United States in 1965, RCA had projected 1966 sales of 5.5 million units, but had reduced that to 4.7 million because of parts shortages.

It just never happened. The demand was slower than everyone expected and every TV manufacturer took it on the chin. RCA, GE, and the other giants could absorb the shock. Clairtone never had a chance. Munk had been gearing up production in anticipation of a surge in sales and, by the end of 1966, was sitting on inventories of almost C$6 million, equivalent to four and a half months' sales. Once again, Clairtone didn't have enough cash flow.

Munk started negotiations with E. F. Hutton to float a debenture in the United States for $2.5 million, but delayed finalizing the deal until profitability improved. He drew a blank at the banks and learned a singularly important lesson in the process. After managing to penetrate the powerful banking bureaucracy to reach the man who had the final say in credit decisions of that scale, he was told, "Remember, Peter, the buck used to stop here. Before IEL if we had pulled the plug and not given you the C$50,000 you needed, we would have been responsible. Today, we have the government. They have C$9 million in your company. Do you think that if our bank says no to you for C$2 million, that the government can let you go down?" In other words, when a government is involved, the private sector feels no compulsion to risk a single penny, because the government's pockets are the deepest of all.

Munk tried everything. He almost persuaded Singer, the sewing-machine conglomerate, to either buy the company or sign an agreement to market its products through its 1,800 dealers worldwide. But, as the banker had explained, IEL scared them off. After arduous negotiations, he won agreement from the government agency to invest another C$2 million in June 1967. The money didn't materialize. Finance Minister Ike Smith wouldn't release the funds. In July, Smith succeeded Robert Stanfield as premier when Stanfield decided to switch to federal politics and run for leader of the Progressive Conservative party. Stanfield had believed in Munk and Gilmour. Smith didn't. In happier days, Smith and Munk had gone to San Francisco to promote the province. Smith's presentation was so boring and uninspiring in Munk's opinion that he had told him, undiplomatically bluntly as ever, that he was a detriment to the mission.

As premier, Smith knew exactly how to handle the situation. He handed over the money on condition that it be used to buy enough shares to put the government in control of the company and that the board of directors fire Munk and Gilmour. By then, however, the prolonged uncertainty over both the marketplace and the government financing had seriously destabilized the company. Suppliers refused credit. Two unions were squabbling over the right to represent the workers. The laid-off coal miners of Stellarton were having difficulty switching to electronic assembly lines. Munk had recently fired the general manager of the plant, who was an old friend — Dam Carel Frederik van Eendenburg, scion of one of the founding families of giant Philips in Holland, and former president of Philips's subsidiary in Canada. Van Eendenburg had quit his job running the Philips subsidiary in Ireland to come to Stellarton, but he had proved too rigid a manager and the workers were close to rebellion. The marvelous woodworking machines, which took raw lumber in at one end and pumped out beautiful cabinets at the other, had terrible quality control. Defective TV sets were being returned in distressing numbers.

Clairtone was paying the price for a critical strategic error in 1961, when it bought the company that had been supplying cabinets. It was the first step down the slippery slope of vertical integration. The intention was clear enough — if they manufactured every part of the final product, they would co-opt the profits being made by their suppliers. Later on, with the Stellarton plant in mind, they decided to integrate the manufacture of the electronic components they had been buying from suppliers. The only trouble with this line of thinking was that they also co-opted the cash flow problems of their suppliers. They lost one of the most critical sources of financing for any business: credit from suppliers. The decision to vertically integrate the manufacturing end of the business may have looked good in the books of the economic nationalists, but it complicated the management of the company and made the whole operation unwieldy. Over the years, Munk had held it all together by sheer force of willpower and an amazing capacity to manage the full range of functions associated with a state-of-the-art manufacturing complex — a marvelous achievement on its own — but added to the breakneck pace of Clairtone's growth, it was unmanageable. The two entrepreneurs just couldn't cope.

It is possible that Munk could have turned Clairtone around over several years, but it was absolutely certain that the Nova Scotian government never would. Under the province's leadership, the company spun horrendously out of control. Shortly before Munk and Gilmour were squeezed out, the half-year results came in showing a loss of C$800,000. The second half of that year was disastrous. Sales for the whole of 1967 were up 14% over 1966, at C$17.6 million — but they came with a loss of C$6.7 million. The province put in the wrong people to turn it around and things rapidly got even worse. Over the following three years (1968–70), total sales were C$25.5 million at a total loss of about C$16 million. When the whole sorry mess was wound down in 1971, the accumulated deficit written off by the province was C$23 million after the sale of all remaining assets.

The debacle was devastating for Munk and Gilmour, financially as well as professionally. In March 1967, they had held slightly less than half the shares of Clairtone between them — which were worth about C$2.5 million then. As the share prices started sliding, they sold about 10% of their holding in July, to net themselves more than C$250,000. The following year, when Munk had lost control of the company and been fired, he was sued by one shareholder, John Adams, who had bought 1,000 shares that same month for prices between C$10 and C$11. Adams claimed Munk had sold his shares when he knew about the damaging half-year results that were not made public until the end of August and that this action contravened the Insider Trading laws of the Ontario Securities Commission that had come into force in June of 1967. Munk argued forcefully that, at the time the shares were sold, other publicly available information gave rise to hope for dramatic improvement in the company's fortunes, contrary to the half-year results. He said he and Gilmour were forced to sell the shares to cover personal debts. It was the first prosecution under the new Insider Trading law and it created quite a stir in the press, but it never went to court. On the advice of his lawyer, Charles Dubin (who subsequently became Chief Justice of Ontario), Munk reluctantly settled the case out of court for about C$22,000, because it would have dragged on for a long time and disrupted the new business venture he was planning. Considering he had earlier turned down an offer to settle the case for part payment of Adams's legal fees, it was a big price to pay.

At the end of 1964, as Clairtone was strumming its way into the hearts of Canadians and the Nova Scotian government was busy unzipping its wallet, the former president of Volvo Canada, Pat Samuel, held a small press conference in Toronto to announce the formation of a new Canadian automobile company, Canadian Motor Industries (CMI). The details were hazy, but it soon emerged that two of the directors of the company were Peter Munk and David Gilmour. Days later, it was revealed that Clairtone was the controlling shareholder, having used C$1 million of the C$8 million it received from Industrial Estates Ltd. to buy 51% of the shares of CMI.

So what was a stereo company doing in the auto industry? If it had been anyone other than Munk, Clairtone would have been laughed off the business pages. But it was the prototype Munk strategy: Diversify while the going is good. His Clairtone stock was rising strongly on the Toronto Stock Exchange, he had money in the bank from IEL (which had agreed to the investment), and he figured that challenging the giants in the stereo equipment business was a risky proposition that couldn't last forever. "I set an objective and when I achieve it, I recognize the time has come to diversify," he says. "We had increased sales to 10,000, then 20,000, and then 40,000 at C$695 . . . The market could not take much more. We were topping out. So I had to find something more sustainable."

The idea of taking on the auto giants originated with Pat Samuel, who was also a big name in Canadian industry in those years. As president of Volvo Canada, he had made a name for himself by increasing his company's market share significantly.

A New Zealander by birth, Samuel emigrated to Canada when the U.S. government decided his tourist visa wasn't appropriate for the jobs he was holding down in Los Angeles and put him on a Greyhound bus to Vancouver. The first job he could get was in the auto business as a used car salesman; it wasn't long before he started his own dealership, marketing sports cars. Soon afterwards the company that owned the franchise to distribute Volvos in Canada hired him to be general manager. The relationship with Volvo wasn't going well at that time and Samuel flew to Stockholm for a big showdown, but he was not successful and Volvo decided to buy back the Canadian franchise. To Samuel's great surprise, however, Volvo asked him to head up the Canadian operation and he accepted with relish, using a brilliant advertising campaign to ratchet up his sales. But he wanted more.

He conceived of the idea that an assembly plant in Canada would establish an even firmer basis for increasing Volvo's market share, because it would be the only foreign car made in Canada — a major selling point in a time of mounting economic nationalism. Another trip to Sweden — this time successful. Not long afterwards, he reached the pinnacle of his career with Volvo when he opened the new plant in Nova Scotia, assembling PKD (Partially Knocked Down) cars, using parts shipped from Sweden. He didn't miss the chance to make it a special event — he flew in the Swedish Crown Prince to officiate and persuaded the Canadian navy to provide two destroyers to give the event some heft. Samuel's lead would be followed by other manufacturers, but only many years later.

His initiative struck a chord with Frank MacMahon, the chairman of Westcoast Transmission, who phoned Samuel and asked him if he would like to start a Canadian auto industry. Samuel said he would, of course, and set off round the world to look at other manufacturers. He was concentrating on the European companies, but an Australian friend told him the Japanese made good cars, so he visited Japan on a whim. At the Isuzu engine factory in Japan, he did a double take when he saw their test bed — 1,200 engines running simultaneously, controlled by a central console that monitored torque, fuel consumption, electrical systems, and emissions. It was technologically way ahead of anything in Detroit. "Jesus," he thought to himself, "what's going to hold these guys back?" He came back to Toronto predicting they would be #3 in North America in ten years. He was much too conservative.

It sounds impossible today, but in 1965, Japan still had a reputation as a cheap manufacturer of shoddy goods. It was still a poor country — its per capita income was $670 compared to $2,652 in Canada. The idea that its cars might compete with General Motors, Ford, and Chrysler was generally considered to be ridiculous. Samuel, however, knew then what dawned on the rest of the world a year later, so he recommended to MacMahon that the Canadian company form an alliance with the Japanese manufacturers, starting with a distribution arrangement and moving into a manufacturing operation once sales were established.

MacMahon liked Samuel's plan and pledged C$50 million in financing. Then Samuel met the financial establishment. MacMahon was a director of the Royal Bank and he asked the bank chairman, Earl McLaughlin, his opinion of the new venture. McLaughlin's bank was, after all, going to co-finance the new company. McLaughlin asked one of his other directors, the president of General Motors, who gave him a brief and powerful response that amounted to a verdict of "ridiculous." The North American car industry was not impressed with Japanese cars in general and the new upstart in particular. End of discussion. MacMahon called Samuel: "I'm going to piss on the fire and walk away," he told him.

When MacMahon left (taking with him the blue-ribbon establishment support that had persuaded the Japanese to go into partnership with CMI in the first place), Samuel turned to Munk, who had by then become a friend, and the two decided the opportunity was too great to pass up. Munk went to see the premier of Nova Scotia, Bob Stanfield, his most important supporter in the province.

"Mr. Stanfield," he pleaded, "we have a chance here to create what the Germans have done in the Ruhr valley — an area of interrelated industrial achievement where one industry feeds on another and it becomes self-generating. If we can get state-of-the-art electronics here, if we can get furniture design here — and North America is exploding with consumer goods — and if we can get car assembly here, within a generation we can build a skill set here that will restore Nova Scotia to where it was 100 years ago, when it was the center of shipbuilding and much of Canadian industry."

Mr. Stanfield could not resist. He added another C\$1 million onto the Clairtone loan and Clairtone became the controlling shareholder in CMI. Samuel pressed on with his plans to build a dealer network. By June 1965, he had reached 48 dealers, which was good but not enough to generate any momentum. Then Studebaker came on the market, looking for a buyer to feed its 1,100 dealers across North America.

Four months later, Munk, Samuel, Harold Egan from IEL, and a team of lawyers and accountants were flying to South Bend, Indiana, to sign a 104-page document to seal the purchase by CMI of the auto manufacturing assets of Studebaker Corp.

The signing ceremony was due on Sunday at 2 p.m. On the Saturday night, Gilmour flew in from the south of France and talked Munk out of it. The next morning, Munk told the assembled team he had changed his mind and the deal was called off. "We're too small," he said.

The deal with Studebaker was extraordinary. CMI would have received all the auto assets for — at most — $1 million payable over five years. At that point, Studebaker was in trouble, but it wasn't bankrupt. It just wanted to get out of the business with a minimum of liability — and its biggest potential liability was its dealer agreement, under which it guaranteed to supply them with cars. Studebaker estimated that lawsuits by car-hungry dealers could cost it up to $40 million, so it had set aside a fund for just that purpose. The $1 million that CMI was paying for the assets would have gone toward any lawsuits that Studebaker dealers might file for failure by CMI to provide them with cars. If CMI took over and kept the dealers supplied, the parent would save $40 million. If there were no lawsuits, CMI would pay nothing for Studebaker. It would get in return 1,100 dealers, $300 million in tools and dies, a factory in Hamilton, Ontario, and the warehouse in South Bend.

Samuel figured he could retool the Studebakers to make them more appealing, but his core strategy was to import Isuzu cars from Japan and market them under the Studebaker marque. There was more. Before the deal with Studebaker materialized, Samuel had negotiated a 20-year agreement with Toyota that gave him the exclusive rights to market Toyotas on the whole eastern seaboard of the United States, plus all of Canada and the Pacific. Toyota could not change its price for the first five years. "They were unsophisticated," Samuel said later. "The total exports of automobiles from Japan that year was probably

8,000. They didn't have much idea of what they were doing and how to do it. So we came along looking like the salvation."

Studebaker would have been the answer to all his problems — it would have given CMI an instant dealer network. "It had mind-blowing potential of international significance," says Munk. "A respected U.S. name allied with Japanese models." When the deal collapsed, however, it was a terrible blow to Samuel because he had abandoned his development of the independent network. He quickly ran into trouble and by March 1966, Munk had to go to Vancouver to negotiate an infusion of money from Mitsui, which owned 30% of the company. He got C$1 million from them, but it cost Clairtone its controlling position and Mitsui gradually moved into the driver's seat, subsequently selling its holding to Toyota, which became the sole owner of CMI.

It was the end of any hope for a Canadian company participating in the incredible Japanese auto boom. Four months later, Samuel quit over a dispute with Harold Egan, and Munk went soon afterwards as his Clairtone empire went into decline. Two years after Samuel was squeezed out and Toyota was firmly in control, CMI's annual profit reached $20 million.

Was Gilmour wrong? Could Munk have become a successful auto mogul? In 1996, Munk reflected that the probability of its succeeding was two-thirds. Gilmour still feels it would have been too much for them at that time. However, he admits it may have been 50–50 if two conditions had prevailed — first, an environment that encouraged the banks to support them, and second, a focused approach with one car model, instead of bringing in two manufacturers from Japan and one from the United States, not to mention other Europeans with whom Samuel was talking. Samuel himself puts his odds at better than even if they could have obtained financing.

The strategy was certainly unconventional, but it was workable because of the timing — Japanese cars were within months of revolutionizing Canadians' and Americans' perspectives on Japanese quality. The biggest problem would have been financing the business when the banks were hostile to the idea. That has never been a problem for Munk, but he was still young and inexperienced. Samuel was one of the very few people in North America at that time who could negotiate successfully with the Japanese. If anyone in Canada could have done it, it was probably those two.

The collapse of Clairtone was as shattering as its rise had been exhilarating. For many, many years afterwards, Peter Munk and Clairtone were synonymous in the mind of the general public, both tainted with lingering suspicions of some kind of wrong-doing, overlaid with a coating of resentful bile. It was only when Barrick started being recognized as an astonishing success story that the odor started to lift. At the time of the Park Plaza reunion in 1989, people familiar with the business world had dropped their negative view of Munk, but to many Canadians who had never heard of Barrick, that evening's celebration of Clairtone would have seemed totally incongruous. For almost two decades after 1968, Munk had to bear the burden of his adopted country's judgment that he was a young braggart who deceived Canadians by giving them a brief moment of euphoria for their country and pride in their potential, then dashing it all by letting it fail. The depth of the sentiment against him mirrored the height of the adulation accorded him when Clairtone was flying high.

He moved his corporate headquarters to London in 1972, at the insistence of his new financial backers, but he never wavered from his resolve to come back to the country he had adopted as a young man of 21. "I feel very good about Canada," he said in London ten years after the collapse. "I love Canada. I feel at home in Canada. I want to settle in Canada. I will settle in Canada. And I will do something important in Canada." Every friend he had and every business associate told him he was crazy to even think about coming back to Canada to try to earn again the respect of Toronto's frowning establishment. But he did.

Munk accepts his share of the blame for Clairtone's collapse. He feels most strongly that the involvement with a government was the biggest mistake. In a 1979 interview, he said: "The combination of our greed and their willingness to hand out money made us too big and we could not cope with it. With the grants, we way overbuilt. This left the company short of cash and vulnerable when sales did not meet expectations. When you deal with government, the normal business criteria don't apply any more."

He also said, "We were in a new plant in a new area, trying to make a new product that was totally unfamiliar to us. Those were bad days. I was desperate." He should have grown more slowly. His and Gilmour's unrelenting commitment to rapid growth was, as much as anything, the root cause of their downfall. He knew the risks, but he would never trim his sails in a gale. "If you want to build a skyscraper higher than anyone else, you're asking for problems. So when I say I want to build the highest building, I'm challenging the fates."

But that obsession for growth gave him something else, too. "We grew fast because we fed on our self-confidence and our success of yesterday. We were always successful, we always overcame our problems, no matter how big they were — and when you come from nothing and grow that fast, you always have problems. And every time we overcame another problem, we became a little more self-confident about our ability to over-come the next one." As he said 21 years later at the Park Plaza Hotel, that self-confidence was all he needed.

That is what made the demise of Clairtone so devastating. He told *Executive Magazine* in December 1978: "There comes a three- or four-month period when you really wonder whether it was all just a fluke and maybe you're going to have to go back and get a job as an engineer with Canadian National Telegraphs (if you can get a job). There's a period when you just do not know whether you can in fact do it again. Then, when spring came, I went up to Georgian Bay where I've had a place since the 1950s. There are no telephones and no radio and the island is always the same. You know that the island is there and that you are going to die one day and that Clairtone goes up and Clairtone goes down but those trees have always been bent that way because the wind bent them, and the rocks have always been the same. You get your perspective back."

It can't have been easy, especially after his first wife left him in the same year he was "kicked out of Clairtone," as he loves to put it. Gilmour said, many years later, that "Peter and I are so fortunate. We have no sense of remorse, career-wise, at all." Whether that's the reason or not, Munk didn't take long to bounce back onto his feet. By September 1968, he was flying full tilt on a new project to transform tourism in the South Pacific. He had embarked on a course that would lead him far away from where he started, but would prove to be even more exhil-arating than Clairtone and a great deal more lucrative. Lucrative enough to allow him to return to Canada eight years later with his head held high, a successful entrepreneur.

3

STRONG FOUNDATIONS BUILT ON SHIFTING SANDS

The Coral Coast of Fiji is a paradise, inhabited by the gentlest, friendliest people on earth. As hosts of a tourist destination, the Fijians must be about as close as you can get to perfection (provided you can learn to slow down to Fiji time). A mixture of Melanesians and Polynesians, they are big, brown, laid back, and always ready with a smile.

There was a time, however, when their reputation was less appealing. For almost all of their history after they first came to these parts 3,500 years ago, the multitude of tribes scattered around the country's 300 islands and 540 islets spent most of their time intriguing to kill each other — and celebrating victory by eating the most distinguished among the vanquished. The cannibalism only stopped shortly after their principal chiefs agreed to put aside their old ways and cede the country to Britain in 1874. To seal the cession of his country to the Great Lady Queen, the warrior King Cakobau, who was the most important chief, or Ratu, gave Her Majesty's representative the one thing he felt she would understand — his favorite war club, known as the blood bather. This, he wanted her to know, was the only law known in Fiji.

The cession ceremony, marked by a semblance of pomp, if not circumstance, was held in the old capital of Levuka, on the island of Ovalau, which is 20 miles from Suva, the "new" capital on the main island of Viti Levu. The rain came down so heavily that day that they had to postpone the signing for a couple of hours.

Fiji may indeed be the embodiment of the romantic South Seas, but it is certainly not all sunshine. On Viti Levu, around Suva in the southeast, the average annual rainfall is 120 inches, permitting only 127 sunny days a year. At the other end of the island, near the international airport at Nadi, the rainfall is less than 70 inches a year, with a dry season during winter, pushing the number of sunny days to 267 a year. Climatically, Viti Levu is two worlds: sunny and parched in the leeward northwest, rainy and lush in the windward southeast. The Coral Coast, where all the tourists go, is the southern coast of Viti Levu, almost 125 miles of gorgeous coral lagoon along the island's belly, from Nadi in the dry west to Suva in the wet east. When tourists talk about the Coral Coast, they are usually talking about the baked 30 miles from Nadi to Sigatoka, where pink skins turn lobster red in less than an hour.

In 1968, David Gilmour flew to Fiji to inspect some property that belonged to him, Munk, Samuel, and another partner. In view of their limited financial circumstances, they were nervous about spending money on the airfare, but someone had to check it out. Gilmour had a friend who was an air stewardess (as they were then called) and she arranged a cheap flight for him. He was visiting Fiji for the first time. They had spent C$250,000 to buy the property in 1964, sight unseen. "We thought of it as an investment for our grandchildren," he says. "Something we put away and didn't spend any time on."

As he stepped out of his car, his shoes sank ominously into the mud. He was, he soon realized, in an isolated swampland. The annual rainfall at what is now Pacific Harbour is 100 inches a year. It isn't as bad as that of Suva, but its 229 sunny days a year still don't match the west island's 267. The road connecting the site to Suva and Nadi was unpaved in both directions. It did not look good. However, he met the minister of labor, Ratu Edward Caucubau, tall, superbly built, with the regal bearing to reflect his long lineage of ancestral chiefs, and Arthur Leys, the leading local lawyer. Gilmour was impressed by the two of them, so he phoned Munk to say they should press ahead and do something with their Fiji property. This singularly unpromising piece of moose pasture thus became the focus of Peter Munk's undivided attention. It became his next project, the one that would pull him out of the Clairtone mud and into the highlands of prosperity and success.

"It was a lousy piece of property," Munk said later. "No one has ever made money in Fiji. And no one knew less about Fiji than I did, believe me — and no one knew less about land development than I did."

There was a very simple reason for picking Fiji as his next project, despite his unpromising qualifications — it was the only asset Munk and Gilmour had salvaged from the wreckage at Clairtone. Munk had no other choice.

Munk's sixth golden rule:
*Play with the hand you're dealt. It's very frustrating to
apply your mind to a different hand.*

The property had come to them as an afterthought in much happier times, when they first met Pat Samuel in the early 1960s. Samuel had been dining with the Munks and Gilmours in 1963 and the talk had turned to vacation destinations for the rich and famous — Lyford Cay in the Bahamas, Acapulco, Monte Carlo, and so on. Samuel was not impressed. "All those places are passé," he said. "The place to be now is the South Pacific. The Japanese are getting rich, the Australians love to travel — and they will all want to go to Fiji, just as the Americans and Europeans now want to go to the Bahamas." At that time, there was a land boom in Bahamas, which was being developed at breakneck pace for rich, lily-skinned northerners in search of sun.

It just so happened, Samuel went on, that he had an option to buy a hotel built on 12 acres of land on the Coral Coast and he assured them it contained the best beach in the world. The only trouble was that he couldn't afford to exercise the option. He suggested that Munk and Gilmour might sell a few of their Clairtone shares and put down the C$200,000 or so required to buy the property.

"Nobody," Munk admitted later, "can sell me like Samuel." They decided to explore the idea further. Samuel took off from Toronto one Friday soon afterwards, flew to Fiji, and drove for five mad hours on the unpaved road to reach Deuba, the closest town to the property. There he filmed the property's lush surroundings and magnificent beach with his 8 mm camera and then took off for another five-hour trip back to the international airport at Nadi. Then back to Toronto to report for work at Volvo on Monday morning. A couple of days later, the three men watched Samuel's movie flickering on the dining room wall at Munk's home.

As a New Zealander, Samuel grew up with the notion that Fiji, only 1,200 miles to the north, was a paradise. He had flown over it during the Second World War and always wanted to return. In the early 1960s, he had taken a vacation and spent a few days in Fiji to rest up on the way home. He found out that a 12-acre beachfront plot was for sale for £800, so he looked around for a good lawyer in Suva. He found Arthur Leys, whom he engaged to arrange the purchase. A few months later, Leys phoned Samuel and told him an American was interested in the land he'd just bought and would he like to sell? Samuel asked what he wanted the property for and Leys told him he wanted to build a vacation home there. Samuel thought for a moment and told Leys he would sell the American 2 acres for £2,000. Leys was shocked because he knew the land wasn't worth that much money — he thought Samuel had overpaid at £800 for the whole 12 acres. But Samuel insisted he make the offer. To Leys' astonishment, the American accepted.

Samuel smelled an opportunity, so he later returned to Fiji to see what else was available. He found that the Beachcomber Hotel was for sale, overlooking another magnificent beach and 12 acres of land. The Beachcomber had been built by an American film producer to house the crew when they were filming an adventure movie called *Captain O'Keefe*, starring Burt Lancaster. When the movie was completed, they sold the building to some Fijians who converted it into a ramshackle hotel that became a favorite calling place for cruise ships in search of local color. Shades of Somerset Maugham. Samuel

71

couldn't afford to buy it outright, so he bought an option to buy. This was the property that he now wanted Munk and Gilmour to buy.

Samuel has had a truly remarkable career, by any standards. Like Munk, he always shot for the stars, but unlike Munk, he seemed to do it for thrills rather than trying to create wealth or build an empire. When he turned 70 in 1995, he said, "For the first 69 years of my life, I lived for wine, women, and song. For the rest of my life, I shall waste my money."

He became a pilot in the Second World War at the age of 17, smuggled into the Royal New Zealand Air Force by his father, a former member of Parliament, who was able to bury his medical records containing his age. At the end of the war, the 20-year-old Samuel was sent off to Singapore with a group of 21 people appointed by the New Zealand government to bring back their prisoners of war. When they got there, there was no transportation, so his commanding officer told him to find some. He found two 34-seater buses and commandeered them for the Royal New Zealand Air Force. The air force didn't need the buses all the time to ferry around its personnel, so he used their down time to help out the local population — he hung a banner on the sides of the buses announcing "Samuel's Services" and rented them out to all comers. The business fizzled when the owners found out where their vehicles had gone, but Samuel managed to escape serious recriminations. It was wartime, after all.

Later, when he left the Air Force, he sailed from New Zealand to Hawaii in a 36-foot ketch. In Honolulu, he ditched his boat and joined some Americans who were sailing to Los Angeles. Once on the mainland, he managed to elude the immigration authorities for many months while he took several illegal jobs, ending up at the Beverly Hills Polo Club, where he met many stars and personalities — including people such as Gary Cooper, Elizabeth Taylor, and Heddy Lamarr, to name just a few.

One of his assignments was to help out Ronald Reagan, whose horse was balking at jumps. Reagan was then the head of the actors' guild and a big man in Hollywood; Samuel, an accomplished rider, soon whipped his horses into shape for him. Reagan came back a week later complaining that Samuel had done a terrible job because they were still balking. Samuel told him the horses jumped very well with him in the saddle, so perhaps the problem was not with the horses, but with the rider. Reagan was not impressed. He doesn't take calls from Samuel when he's in California. Samuel also spent many hours teaching Otto Preminger how to ride. Preminger offered him a job as an assistant director, but the immigration department intervened, putting an end to his film career.

Listening to this soft-spoken man, speaking so slowly that he seems to be weighing every word, it is hard to imagine him taking audacious risks. He moves as he speaks, with deliberation and an understated sense of purpose, his long, pointed nose giving him a bookish look totally at odds with his character. There is no outward sign of flair, no flamboyance; his intellectual machinations are resolutely shielded behind his slightly hooded, inscrutable brown eyes. Yet his whole life is an exuberant statement about savoring everything that life has to offer.

He has a weakness for royals. He worked for a Saudi prince for five years and his love of horses has given him access to British royalty over many years. He treasures his friendship with the Queen Mother, whose signed picture has pride of place on his mantelpiece, and whom he visits whenever he's in London. He is a breeder himself and has acted as an agent for the Queen Mother, buying New Zealand horses for her.

His life has been shaped by adventure and calculated risk-taking, which have taken him into every continent except Africa. Wherever he went, Samuel managed to penetrate the upper echelons of business and politics. He is very proud of what he has done and who he has met, but has the Australasian distaste for bragging. The only hint of his understatement is the wry smile that always lurks at the corners of his mouth, signaling his detached perspective and keen sense of humor. It is perhaps that sense of humor, that ability to look at things from a completely fresh perspective, that drives his amazingly fertile mind, unearthing business opportunities long before just about everyone else. He lacks Munk's focused intensity, however, and freely admits he is at his best creating opportunities, rather than implementing them.

Unlike most other people who became Munk's partners, Samuel resisted becoming a planet around Munk's sun — although he was important to Munk's career, having saved his business from collapse on one occasion with his superb salesmanship. However, he could never become a permanent part of Munk's entourage. He would always lope off in some independent venture before he got too entangled. It hurt Munk, who hates to see a partner or a friend leave him, but it was probably just as well. If Samuel had stayed with Munk, it might have turned him into a poor implementer of his own and other people's plans rather than a creator of opportunities, where he shines.

Samuel's flickering home movie on Munk's dining room wall in 1963 twigged Munk's and Gilmour's interest. They wouldn't sell their Clairtone shares, but they deposited some of them with a bank as collateral and took a loan for close to C$250,000 between them. They didn't even go to Fiji, they just exercised

the option on the Beachcomber, even adding three other properties for another C$50,000, which brought their land holding to
430 acres on the Coral Coast.

Four years later, when the three of them went to Fiji to induce
the birth of Pacific Hotels and Developments on their piece of
swampland, there was not a shred of doubt in their minds that
it would turn out to be an immensely successful business. But
they were the only three people in the whole world who thought
this. Their fourth partner, Mac Hogarth, who had been through
the Clairtone years with them and had contributed to buying the
Fiji properties in 1963–64, couldn't see any prospects for
success, so he dropped out. Howard Beck, a Toronto lawyer
who incorporated the new holding company for the venture
(Southern Pacific Properties), says that he had "major reserva-
tions about the project. I thought that Peter was — I wouldn't
say crazy, but certainly on the road. However, that was my lack
of conception."

It didn't take Munk long to swathe his baby idea in voluminous
blankets of supportive megatrends. He dug up every possible
angle that could improve its chances of success. He chanced
upon a Boeing brochure mentioning that all its Boeing 707s
flying between Asia or North America and the South Pacific had
to stop in Fiji to refuel. This made Fiji part of Boeing's long-
term vision of its world — and that meant a long list of airlines
shared the same vision, including Qantas, Canadian Pacific,
British Airways, Continental, Air New Zealand, Pan Am,
American Airlines, Air India, and others. The map of airline
routes in the South Pacific was visually compelling, with the
spokes of the wheel clearly centered on Fiji at the hub. That
made the resort easy to get to.

Then Munk proved that not only was it easy for tourists to get there, but they also really wanted to go. To his great joy, he found that tourism to Fiji had grown in the previous few years. Only 14,722 tourists visited Fiji in 1961. By 1968, the number had risen to 66,458, led by Australians and Americans. In 1968, there were 1,500 hotel rooms in Fiji, and he forecast (with the support of *The Economist* Intelligence Unit) that 3,500 would be needed by 1973. At the same time, the Japanese were just beginning to spread their wings. Their economic miracle was gathering speed and they were becoming rich. They had money to spend. Munk forecast in 1970 that 2 million visitors from Japan would come to Fiji every year by the end of that decade. Jumbo jets were just beginning to come into service when Pacific Harbour was launched and Munk naturally demonstrated that this would increase traffic enormously, accelerating the growth rate.

The prospects appeared so good to Munk that he decided the 430 acres they already owned were not enough. That's when he discovered Fiji's rather unusual real estate laws. When the Fijian chiefs ceded their country to Britain in 1874, they had already observed the rapacious habits of European settlers and traders, so they insisted that, as part of the deed of cession, 90% of the country's territory be held in permanent trust for the indigenous Fijian people. For a supposedly savage culture, still mired in cannibalism, it was a remarkable exhibition of commercial perspicacity. It didn't take a genius to see that the supply of available Fijian land for development was not unlimited.

Having decided to proceed, the partners went to Fiji to pay a call on the indefatigable Arthur Leys, who introduced them to an East Indian named Lakshman. This unprepossessing man owned 6,000 acres in the Deuba vicinity, adjoining Pacific Harbour's Beachcomber property, and his bargaining skill soon stopped the eager Canadians in their tracks. He was in no hurry to sell and was toying with a price that was several multiples of what Leys had told them was the maximum they should pay. Howard Beck remembers the scene vividly: "We were sitting with Lakshman in some mud hut and I said to Peter, 'We should not do a deal with this guy — he's too smart for both of us.'" Arthur Leys agreed. But Munk had made up his mind.

"Listen," Munk told Lakshman. "You have two choices. You can carry on like you have done for a hundred years or you can become rich by letting me turn this into a paradise that can be sold to the Germans, English, and Americans. You will have the world's richest people playing golf here and all your children can marry rich girls. But I cannot do this if I only have 12 acres and a beach. I need 7,500 acres. You tell me what the fair value is and you give me an option. If I fail, you're back where you were. If I succeed, you guys will all be rich."

Lakshman finally agreed to an option that valued the property at C$372,000. Leys was appalled. "I won't let you exercise this option, Peter," he said. "It's criminal. It's triple what the value is." But Munk had to have the property, because he already knew what he was going to do in Fiji.

Lakshman's 6,000 acres meant that Munk could make his story large enough to attract major finance. Not only was Fiji the hub of the South Pacific, not only was tourism growing there at 25% a year, not only were hotel facilities hopelessly inadequate, but *he* had the biggest block of land on the Coral Coast, where freehold land was extremely hard to come by. It gave him unique leverage. And getting the government onside was a breeze with Leys' connections.

He sat down with the minister of tourism. "Sir, you can have it two ways," he started off in his direct way. "You can have mass tourism, which means you have to put in more and more sewers, because every time your tourist [answers the call of nature], you have to have a system in place to turn it into drinking water again. Or you can go the same way as Switzerland and go for the elite tourist. But you have to be prepared to put in a championship golf course, waterways, and all that — you'll change the map of Fiji — so that people have a reason to come here. I can do all that for you."

The government became a big supporter — and always remained so.

All he had to do then was to transfer his ideas onto paper in the form of a development plan, based on sound engineering principles, and prepare a cash flow forecast with all the associated revenues and costs. His total lack of experience in the field was of no concern.

Munk's seventh golden rule:
You don't need to know the industry you're going into.
If you apply yourself, you can always find the experts.

But he couldn't rely solely on the experts. He still had to craft the basic concept in a way that it would meet his own standards. The cash flow forecast was easy. Roberts Real Estate had just issued a prospectus for its Bahamian development, which it was then taking public. Munk took the prospectus and superimposed it on his Fiji property. He still didn't have a price list, however, so he couldn't do a cash flow. At the time, David Gilmour was in Britain staying with James Hanson, later Lord Hanson, the swashbuckling chief of Hanson PLC and already a powerful force in British industry. Munk got the address of Roberts Real Estate's London sales office and gave it to Gilmour:

"Go down there and tell them you're a rich Canadian who's staying with the Hanson family. Tell them you're interested in a lot." The handsome young Canadian did as he was asked. The salesmen loved his classy look and the Hanson name had their heads spinning with visions of multiple lots and wads of pounds. Pretty soon he had a complete price list.

Munk now had the cost structure and the price list, so he could do a cash flow forecast. "The cost of the infrastructure is nothing on 7,000 acres," he said at the time. "The profit margin is something like 80%. The commissions were 10%. How can we lose?" It was never quite that good, but it was still very good.

Next, he had to have a development plan. He went to the best-known firm in Toronto, Project Planners Ltd., who had done the planning for the site of Expo 67, as well as the Lyford Cay development in the Bahamas. He took Mac Hancock, the managing partner, out to lunch and told him he wanted a master plan just like the one he'd done in Lyford Cay — a golf course, roads, waterways, whatever was necessary. Hancock said it would cost Munk $400,000.

Hancock suspected Munk was on a fishing trip and confirmation was quick to come. "I can't even afford to pay the air tickets for you to go there," Munk told him. "But I'm prepared to give you a percentage of my company. Christ, you have 40 engineers and planning people, your income is great. This way, you can reduce your tax by charging your costs on this project against your income, then get paid in capital gains. [Capital gains were not taxable in those days.] What a wonderful thing for you to save something if I'm successful. You and I are engineers. We both know that if something happens to us, our income is finished. But, if you have equity in a business, you can lose your legs in an accident and still be rich."

It was a classic Munk play. With powerful logic and superb presentation, he paints a picture of great wealth waiting to be harvested at the end of a project — wealth so great that it dwarfs the petty investment he's asking for up front. It's a story as old as time, and its purveyors have failed to deliver all too often, but Munk can make his story come alive like few other people. He does his homework, he has a transparent commitment to do whatever has to be done to achieve his goals, and he understands the hot buttons that motivate people. His "presentations" are a work of art. In 1968, he had yet to demonstrate he could deliver, so he had to rely on his burning intensity and his logic to convey his determination to succeed. Later, when he had established his capacity to deliver, he could rely on his track record to carry his entrepreneurial pitches, but he has never slackened his insistence that his concepts be honed until they are perfect.

Hancock was convinced by the presentation, but he couldn't speak for his partners, so he suggested Munk pitch his proposal to a partners' meeting. Munk went to their elegant third floor offices on Avenue Road and gave them his pitch. "You put out the master plan," he said. "I'll hire away the salesmen who hustle Bahamian land, because it's easier to sell the only project in the South Pacific than one of 20 in the Bahamas. We'll take it public and you guys will all have shares."

Munk gave them the outline of his cash flow projections, but these professionals had worked on many developments and Fiji held no special magic. They had enough work without having to worry about such a distant location being run by a newcomer in the field. Many demurred — but three of the partners, including Hancock, accepted Munk's challenge and agreed to do the job for shares instead of cash. (Some years later, Project Planners went bankrupt when they never got paid for a huge project in Saudi Arabia. The three partners who delivered Munk's master plan in return for shares, however, did well on Munk's little nest egg, which was worth $3 million when they retired.)

Munk now had all the necessary ingredients except for the financing. Land development is very capital intensive. All the costs are up front and it's too risky to finance with debt. Munk figured he needed $4 million equity to get him to the point where revenues would start to flow from land sales. It was a challenge, even for him.

The financing of land development is a weird and wonderful art. Science it is not. Black art, maybe. Certainly, it is infinitely creative, an exercise in conjuring up value by spinning dreams that change people's perceptions of ordinary, glamourless earth. A pedestrian developer may have to give investors 50% of his company in return for $1 million to develop his ten acres, while another might persuade investors to give him $10 million to develop the same plot and they'll be happy to receive only 25% of the company in return. In the first case, the developer's ten acres has been valued at $1 million. In the second, the same land is worth $30 million. The difference lies in the concept — the extent to which the use that is proposed for the land is likely to generate profits for whoever owns it.

There's also the question of location, of course — 100 acres in the Arctic is not going to fetch as much as 100 square yards in New York City — but for land in comparable locations, its value depends on how creative the developer is in finding a way to use that land constructively. Someone who owns swampland that is barely fit for agricultural use will not be able to live the life of Riley on the income it furnishes — no one is ever going to make much money out of the land, so why would they pay much to own it? On the other hand, someone who has assembled a block of that same swampland and obtained government permission to develop it into a dream resort can reasonably claim that the land is worth a great deal more, because the developed land can be resold at a high price, which will generate significant profit to the developer. Then again, if Kim Basinger moves into one of the homes the developer builds, the prices of all the surrounding homes rise and the value of land makes yet another quantum leap. However, it would have to be a highly desirable development to attract Kim Basinger, so it would cost a lot more up front to develop. It's a delicate balance between the up-front development cost and how much the customer is likely to pay for the finished product.

All this is hard enough to gauge for developers who have the cash to finance projects all by themselves. It gets extremely complicated and interesting when developers don't have two cents to rub together. All those real estate wizards of the 1970s and 1980s made money on a very simple premise. They figured that land development meant borrowing $8 for every $10 they invested, watching that $10 double in value almost regardless of what they did with it, paying off the $8 debt and being left with $12 — a profit of 500% on their $2 stake. It worked for almost two decades. They were in the right place at the right time and they never needed to be creative in adding to the value of their land. Many of them duly lost everything when the boom came to an end. The $10 halved instead of doubling, and thereby turned the $2 stake into minus $3.

It's called leverage — but leverage on what? The whole pack of cards still depends on the plot of land at the tip of the inverted pyramid. And here's the reason for this quick review of

Real Estate Investment 101: developers with genius don't depend on a rising market to make their fortunes off leverage. They know that if they can design concepts that create a perception of value, they can build in the leverage on their equity, *before* they have borrowed a cent. The secret — easier said than done, as always — is to buy land from people who see no potential at all in it, create a dazzling concept that fires people's imagination with its potential, then allow other investors to share in making the dream materialize. Only then do they borrow. To continue with the analogy: buy land for 50¢, develop a concept that makes it worth $2.50, bring in partners for $2.50 (they are so excited about the vision, they don't mind paying $2.50 for a half share in land that was bought for 50¢), then go and borrow the last $5. If the market then doubles, that original 50¢ investment becomes $7.50 after paying off the $5 debt — a return of 1,400%. And if the market is cut in half, it's a breakeven instead of minus $3.

The major advantage of this approach is that it is financially conservative — borrowed funds represent only 50% of the development's cost. But it is exceptionally highly leveraged for the developers because they have managed to obtain half the ownership with one-tenth of the investment.

The concept has to be dazzling. And the developers have to be adept at land valuation. They have to be able to prove with irrefutable logic that the concept, all on its own, without turning a single sod, has turned that land into something worth five times what they paid for it — provided they can turn the concept into reality. Because so much depends on a hard-nosed ability to implement the dream effectively, putting a value on undeveloped land is highly subjective — a magical concoction of economic megatrends, commercial acuity, and tight-fisted costing that can translate individual expectations and indulgences into cold, hard cash.

When he started out in the land development business, Munk did not yet understand all these nuances. In fact, he had a great deal of difficulty raising capital. Every underwriter he approached in Toronto gave him the same response: "Well, Jeez, Peter, how can we take this to our board? You're the biggest failure in your own field. Now you want to raise public funds to do hotels and land development in Fiji? It can't be done." Eventually, he persuaded Cochran, Murray, a small brokerage in Toronto, to underwrite the deal and they prepared a prospectus that was cleared by the Ontario Securities Commission in 1969. Just as they were about to launch the issue, however, the Toronto Stock Exchange fell out of bed in a market-wide collapse and Initial Public Offerings (IPOs) became temporarily extinct. He had to find another way.

In the negotiations with Cochran, Murray, the underwriters had made it clear they would have difficulty floating the issue unless Munk had someone on staff with some experience in land development. Munk relayed this to his lawyer, Howard Beck, who knew just the man. Bill Birchall had been the accountant for Roberts Real Estate and had handled most of the negotiations with the underwriters when they went public, but now he wanted to move on. He agreed to fly up to Toronto from the Bahamas if Munk would pay his fare. Munk duly found some money and offered him a job on the spot. It was the beginning of another long partnership.

Bill Birchall ("young Bill" to Munk, then and now) is tall, slim, and extremely handsome. With his mane of silver hair, his healthy, almost unwrinkled face, and the direct gaze of his wide-open brown eyes, Birchall looks as if he doesn't have a care in the world. His breezy manner and brisk British accent add to the sense of being in complete control. Now 53, he's in his second marriage and has three young children whom he adores and who have given him a new lease on life.

Birchall loves numbers the way a writer loves words. Many people use numbers to dazzle or befuddle their listeners, and more than a few accountants use numbers to drain any twitch of humanity from the world they are measuring. Birchall uses numbers to illuminate. He can give fresh insights into familiar situations with the way he presents his numbers. A financial statement is to Birchall what a score sheet is to a composer — he can hear the music in his head. He talks of balance sheets that "sing." He's actually an accomplished musician himself, playing his versions of modern rock, among other genres, on his electric organ to entertain his and his children's friends. He is that mythical creature, the creative accountant, with the added bonus of a remarkable grasp of detail and a memory that is faultless going back a quarter of a century. In interviews given for this book, the memories of some of the participants for events in the 1960s or 1970s were often way out of whack, sometimes hilariously so. But not Birchall's. Every fact he offered checked out with the documents or with other people who were as close or closer than him to the events. He has always been the person who could smell what was going on in the operation — he has even trained himself to read upside down.

Birchall was ideal for Munk. He combines an iron grip on the meaning of numbers with a flair for making them say what he wants them to say. For the decade in the South Seas, Birchall was Munk's point man. He did the things that had to be done. He negotiated the banking arrangements in the long string of crises that peppered their lives until 1977. He checked that everyone did what they had promised to do — and when they didn't keep their promises, he prodded them firmly, but politely, with no possible chance of misunderstanding. He worked incredible hours nailing down the myriad of details that can sink a land development project as quick as a flash. Moreover, in Peter Munk, he found a true kindred spirit. "He is the best untrained accountant I have ever come across," he says. "Accountants like Peter because he is not a volatile, unfocused kind of person. He has a very clear vision from a financial perspective and he's very true to that."

With Birchall in tow, Munk could set about spinning the dreams that would lure the $4 million he needed into his company. The 29-year-old Birchall settled down with his new boss in early 1970 and put together the financial plan for the Fiji project. "It was the longest budgeting process I have ever been through in my life. It took three or four days, but I was impressed by his attention to the larger issues as well as the smaller issues. We put into effect a financial reporting system that prompted the managing director of Jardine Matheson to say a couple of years later that it was as good a financial reporting system as he'd ever seen."

By the end of Pacific Harbour's first year, Munk and his partners had made the assessed value of its swampland balloon dramatically merely by assembling the land, obtaining government approval for the project, and preparing the development plan. In the spring of 1970, Munk hired a firm of land valuation engineers and they came up with a figure of $4 million. He was ready to face the skeptical investment community.

He couldn't use the depressed Toronto market to raise his startup capital, but Gilmour pulled a rabbit out of the hat, as he did for Munk on a number of occasions. He was at a dinner

party given by Gordon White (later Lord White), who was James
Hanson's partner, when the star guest arrived, a man named Jim
Slater. Slater was the whiz kid of finance in those years. His
firm, Slater Walker Securities, had stood the venerable City of
London on its ear with its daring deals and global vision. He was
everywhere, pushing millions of pounds, dollars, deutschmarks,
and francs around the financial centers of the world. And here
he was asking this friend of his friend, a charming young
Canadian who was hiding his desperate need for $4 million,
what he did for a living.

Gilmour displayed his own brand of suave salesmanship,
painting the fabulous prospects of their swampland in a few
deft strokes. He soon made another convert to the cause. Two
weeks later, one of Slater's directors, Simon Pendock, visited the
site with Gilmour and recommended that Slater Walker invest
the necessary $4 million. Slater Walker got 50% of the company
for its $4 million, giving Munk and Gilmour one-half owner-
ship of an $8 million company. As he had paid very little in cash
to put all this together, it's fair to say that Munk's vision, a lot of
toil, and some brilliant salesmanship had multiplied his and
Gilmour's C$300,000 more than 13 times. Not bad for starters.

Soon afterward, Gilmour's sister Shelagh's well-connected
husband gave them another referral — Henry Keswick, who ran
the London office of Jardine Matheson and later became its
chief executive or "taipan." Founded in 1832 by two Scotsmen
whose names are not hard to guess, Jardine Matheson led the
development of Hong Kong from the day it was founded. From
its murky Chinese trading days, it went on to build a global
empire, always the first European company to buy land and open
an office as each Asian country opened its doors to the West. By
1970, it had sales of more than $200 million and hundreds of

subsidiaries and associated companies in 31 countries. Gilmour got only $400,000 out of them, but more substantial investment was to come later. Much more important, however, Munk and Gilmour got David Newbigging, who was then taipan, as a member of their board. It was a connection that was to pay big dividends in the years to come.

The core corporation in the Fiji project was an umbrella company that Munk set up to oversee all the investments he planned to make in the South Seas as he diversified on the back of Pacific Harbour's anticipated success. He called it Southern Pacific Properties (Bahamas) and it became the owner of Pacific Harbour. Jim Slater put his $4 million into SPP in April 1970, and immediately set about finding other investors to share the risk. That was his *modus operandi* — to invest the seed money then spread his risks. Pendock, who was riding herd on the investment for Slater, did the rounds of selected clients and associates of Slater Walker who might be interested. He found some good ones — like J. G. Boswell, an American based in the northwest United States who was expanding into the Pacific and the Peninsular & Oriental Steam Navigation Company (the legendary P&O, which has dominated shipping in the Pacific Ocean for more than a century), whose representative on the SPP board was Lord Geddes. In a matter of months, Munk, Gilmour, and Slater had put together a blue-ribbon board of directors who were in a position to offer them gold-plated credibility and significant assistance in the Fiji project, as well as the necessary cash.

Half a year later, Pendock himself took a substantial stake in SPP by investing £500,000 to buy almost half of Slater Walker's share. At the time, Pendock was in charge of the Slater Walker division that handled portfolio management for its rich clients. He had grown tired of the job, however, and was looking for some excitement. He certainly got that when he quit Slater Walker, joining Munk and partners at the end of 1970.

A year after Slater's initial investment, SPP raised $2\frac{1}{4}$ million by floating a private rights issue of common shares. Apart from the obvious benefit of putting more cash in the till, the rights issue served an even more important purpose — it put a new value on the land, which had barely been touched at that stage. The new shares in SPP were sold at $3.60 each and as there were 5 million shares outstanding after the issue, that valued the whole company at $18 million. One year after deciding to proceed with the development, SPP had raised a total of $6\frac{1}{4}$ million and the intrinsic value of the land (not counting the cash put into the company) had therefore risen to almost $12 million or 40 times the original investment.

"We were surprised at the demand for the plots," says Bill Birchall, "so we increased prices." The cost of construction was also higher than they had planned, but the price increase had a bigger impact than the higher costs, so the profit margin rose significantly. Higher profits meant higher values for the land, and Munk and Birchall lost no time in revaluing their land to reflect the new realities. Those were great days for Pacific Harbour. In the first year and a half of the marketing program, sales consistently came in ahead of budget and the potential seemed limitless.

In July 1970, work started at Pacific Harbour, watched over by a new Munk, resplendent in flashy ties, with curly locks hanging over his ears and wearing a broad, relaxed smile. No more Mr. Industrialist Heavyweight. The attention to detail was just as intense, the drive just as unstoppable, but the style was different — for a while at least.

The dream was pure Munk — an absolutely immense project. Out of that swampland, Phase I took 1,150 acres and massaged them into a garden community, with 49 acres of multiple-dwelling sites, 67 acres of commercial sites, 5 hotels, 2 marinas, 1,300 villas on plots ranging up to $1\frac{1}{2}$ acres, and miles of road-ways — plus an airstrip. He laid down a special telephone system, underground electricity cables, miles of paved access roads, and an 18-hole championship golf course designed by Robert Trent Jones Jr., the best-known golf-course designer in the world. The construction crews had to move 3.6 million cubic yards of soil to dig out four miles of navigable waterways and an 80-acre lake — then they took that soil and piled it onto the golf-course site to raise its level. The $2.75 million hotel that was replacing the old Beachcomber would have the biggest swimming pool in the Southern Hemisphere, with its own island (designed by a leading Toronto architect, Harry Kohl, who also agreed to be paid in shares instead of cash).

"I believe Fiji will develop as one of the playgrounds of the world," Munk told the press on announcement day. "But I'm sure the local character will not change." The plans included picturesque Fijian villages, sports fields, a polo ground, and a beach club. "It will be the Monaco of the South Seas." He told the Fijians his company planned to complete Phase I in three years and spend $50 million in total over the next 20 to 25 years.

Soon afterwards the marketing program slipped into high gear. He hired top salesmen from all over the world, including some who had sold mutual funds for the notorious Investors Overseas Group run by Bernie Cornfeld, who was jailed for fraud. Munk used a technique that has stood him in good stead — every sales office was linked to a prestigious local firm that gave the whole thing credibility. In Britain, his partner was

Knight, Frank & Rutley. In Hong Kong, Jardine Matheson acted for Pacific Harbour. In Australia, Intercapital Investments handled the sales effort. His own salesmen were highly paid on a commission basis — initially 25% including all the overrides, but as low as 18% some years later on. Munk fired them up. One of his best salesmen was Gerald Lancaster: "Peter Munk was the motivator of the whole operation," he says. "The sales force could identify with him. He'd been out there pitching, too. He's a straightforward, truthful guy. Admittedly, he paints a rosy picture, but that's OK. That's what it's all about."

Pretty soon the buyers started flooding in, including some very prestigious names — Prince Victor Emmanuel of Savoy, Prince Juan Carlos of Spain, Count von Bismarck, and Lord Pilkington, chairman of the giant glass manufacturer in the United Kingdom, to name just four. Munk had projected sales of $7 million to $8 million in the first 15 months. It didn't go quite that quickly, but it still went very well indeed — land sales were $4.6 million in 1971 and about $10 million in each of 1972 and 1973. In February of 1974, the Fijian minister of finance, Charles Stinson, told the press: "Pacific Harbour is by far the best development ever to come to Fiji." Phase I finally opened at the end of 1974, one year behind schedule, thanks mostly to a hurricane in November 1972, and a strike. It was a critical success — the development lived up to its promises for beauty and class.

There was no joy in the opening for Munk, Gilmour, and Samuel, however. When Phase I opened, the game was already over. The first oil crisis in November 1973 had precipitated a worldwide recession, which slashed 1974 land sales almost in half. Worse, the increase in the price of fuel hit air travel particularly hard and tourism to Fiji drooped. In what should have been a year of triumph for Pacific Harbour, 1974 was the toughest yet. The company lost $2.8 million. Once again, Munk's enterprise was in desperate shape. In 1975, the recession was even worse and land sales dried up almost completely, falling to about $3.5 million. It would have killed the company had it not been for a life-saving deal pulled off by Pat Samuel, who made a spectacular sale for $3.5 million, thereby enabling the company to eke out a small profit and stay alive for better days.

Samuel sold a half interest in the 6,000 acres that Munk had bought from Lakshman and was holding in reserve for Phase II. The buyer was Taisei Corp., a Japanese construction firm that was part of the huge Fuyo *keiretsu* (a group of allied companies, often with mutual shareholdings), which included companies like Nissan. In the early 1970s, the Japanese were very interested in the South Seas. In fact, one trading company was on the point of signing a major deal with Pacific Harbour when the oil crisis hit, devastating the Japanese economy. It called off the deal in a four-foot long telex that explained the whole history of the Japanese economy and ended by saying the quadrupling of oil prices meant it could not proceed with the deal. Taisei, however, didn't walk away, because at that time, the Japanese government was trying to get more of its private-sector companies doing business outside Japan. It had a system whereby construction companies received "points" for foreign contracts, and each point increased their chances of winning domestic contracts. It still made sense for Taisei to look at Fiji, despite the shattered economies on both countries.

The deal with Taisei probably saved Munk's bacon. Without it, Pacific Harbour would most likely have gone bankrupt, unraveling his carefully constructed diversification program (see next three chapters). At the time, Munk, Gilmour, Samuel, and Birchall all believed they would muddle through somehow, but they were in far greater danger than they realized. A second failure at that point, moreover, would almost certainly have ruined Munk's chances of ever making the breakthrough that eventually led to his enormous success in Barrick.

The Taisei deal can be credited to two factors. The first was that Gilmour was able to help Taisei make some contacts in Egypt, leading to the precious foreign contracts that would earn the points necessary to enhance its domestic business. At the same time that Pacific Harbour was negotiating with Taisei, Gilmour was spearheading SPP's massive project in Egypt that had been personally approved by President Anwar Sadat (more of that in Chapter 5). When Taisei Chairman Koji Minami was introduced to Sadat by Gilmour, the prospects for future foreign contracts seemed bright enough for him. After the meeting, he turned to Gilmour and said, "Now, we sign."

The second factor was Samuel's superb salesmanship. The property had originally cost SPP only C$372,000 and yet he persuaded the hard-nosed Japanese to part with $3.5 million for half of it at a time when the global recession had crushed the land development business, eliminating any prospect of an early realization of its pre-recession value. Samuel understood the Japanese better than most Westerners at that time. He had dealt with them many times since he had first seen their diligence and competence in Isuzu's test bed for engines. He got to know them, partly thanks to his Japanese *amour*, perhaps, and he knew how to negotiate with them. He was comfortable sitting through a whole day negotiating over a single paragraph, because he understood the dynamics. On one occasion, negotiating with Toyota, the Japanese negotiators were being particularly obtuse, so he rose to his feet and read them the telephone directory for an hour or two. He could act inscrutable as well as they could. He understood their mentality.

Munk played no part in the ritual dance. He knew he didn't have Samuel's impassive patience. He also knew that Samuel's courtship of Taisei was hitting all the right buttons. Samuel had escorted Minami and his executives around Fiji, displaying better manners than they were accustomed to seeing in a *geijin*. He had also visited them in Tokyo frequently. Finally, in the boardroom of Taisei's Tokyo headquarters, Samuel nailed down the final details. Toward the end of the meeting, one of the senior directors looked at Samuel and said: "Samuel-san, you are an honorable and an honest man. I have been told that your resort is on the rainy side of the island. Is this true?"

Samuel shrank into his seat. The rainfall had been a delicate issue from the first day. When they were still raising money in 1969, Gilmour had been to see Evelyn Rothchild who was interested enough to send one of his executives out to Fiji to check it out. The minion came back and told Rothchild that the project was very well put together — good design, good planning, good budget, good concept. Except for one thing. It was on the *wrong* side, the rainy side. Rothchild Bank declined to participate. Munk was furious. He told Gilmour he should have said that if he had been able to assemble 7,500 acres on the sunny side, he would not have needed his $4 million. He had always been careful to make it clear in the prospectuses that the resort was in an area of high rainfall — indeed, that was why they had such lush vegetation and their gardens were so beautiful. But still, it was a sensitive point. It was the rainfall that had made their land a swamp in the first place.

Samuel gritted his teeth and answered: "It is true. The resort is on the rainy side."

"Good," the director said. "Japanese people like the rain."

"In that case," Samuel replied, struggling to maintain his inscrutability, "they are going to be absolutely bloody delighted with Pacific Harbour."

The small profit in 1975 that resulted from the Taisei sale turned out to be a blip. From then on, losses soared in the dead Fijian market. The success of a land development project depends on very heavy operating and sales expenses — which peaked at almost $3 million (excluding commissions) in 1973. If the land is not sold quickly, the selling expenses drain away all the profit. That is what happened to Pacific Harbour. All the lots were finally sold, but it took until the end of the decade. By 1978, the accumulated loss at Pacific Harbour was $8.8 million. For the next few years, annual losses continued at somewhere between one-half and three-quarters of a million dollars, until they finally sold the development in 1981 for half a million dollars. The final loss on Pacific Harbour was somewhere in the region of $10 million.

Pacific Harbour was not a failure, however. It was gloriously successful in its first three years and during those years, it became a source of other opportunities that, between them, eventually created far more wealth than would ever have been possible with Pacific Harbour. Those opportunities would never have arisen if Munk, Gilmour, Birchall, and Samuel had not first created Pacific Harbour.

4

TAKEOVER TWO-STEP

From the very beginning, Pacific Harbour was only one part of Munk's total concept. He wanted not simply to develop 6,500 acres in Fiji — he intended to create a tourist and resort *industry* in the South Pacific that would attract rich Americans, Japanese, and Australians (among others) who wished to buy homes, stay in hotels, and generally amuse themselves in the South Pacific. He wanted, as he put it, to do for the Pacific Basin what the Bahamas and the Caribbean had done for the Atlantic Basin. Pacific Harbour alone could not meet those criteria, because developing and selling land is only a short-term business — at a certain point the land is all sold and then it's just a maintenance company. So he had to find other businesses that would give him a solid, permanent base of repeatable profits on which to build his empire. The vehicle for this strategy was Southern Pacific Properties, through which the profits from Pacific Harbour would be funnelled into an array of complementary businesses. From day one, Munk always kept a weather eye open for potential acquisitions to build his permanent empire.

He found that base under his nose, in Fiji. One of the prime markets for Pacific Harbour lots was Fiji itself, so Munk approached all the important organizations on the main island. He had some success — many of the cabinet ministers had homes in Phase I, among them the prime minister. He also targeted local businessmen, one of the more prominent among them being the local manager of one of the four Travelodge Hotels in Fiji. This particular manager was not impressed by the Canadian with the East European accent. He agreed to see Munk, then kept him waiting for two days before dismissing him with haughty disdain and a complete lack of interest.

This is definitely not the way to treat Peter Munk. He decided to take a closer look at the chain. He found, to his astonishment, an octopus with tentacles stretching into islands all over the Pacific — mostly in Australia but scattered from Tasmania and New Zealand to Fiji and Samoa, from Singapore to Papua New Guinea. They had more than 80 hotels.

"They were the big shots," Munk remembers. Their annual sales in 1971 were A$16 million (US$19 million) and net profit after tax was A$1.2 million. The chain had more than doubled in size over the previous six years. Then he checked the chain's stock price and found to his still greater astonishment that the market valued the whole company at the equivalent of one year's revenues. A few months later, in February 1972, the stock price had fallen to 64¢(A), which put a value on the company of

A$12 million. It was an aberration. Admittedly, the bottom line was not healthy — net profit had gone up only 35% over the previous six years, compared to a 138% increase in annual sales — but the assets were worth a lot more than the market was indicating. The hotel industry is subject to strong cycles and the Australians were heading for a cyclical low.

Travelodge fitted perfectly into Munk's long-term strategy for the Pacific Basin and he could afford to buy it. He didn't have the money, but he knew how to get some. Munk had to turn SPP into a public company, quoted on a stock exchange somewhere, and raise money from the public. The timing was perfect. The value of SPP was growing in leaps and bounds as Pacific Harbour's then-promising future unfolded and he knew investors were always eager to invest in a company that was growing strongly.

Munk's eighth golden rule:
*Take your company public when its value is rising
in order to raise more money on the stock market
for diversification.*

Munk drew up a proposal and went to see Jim Slater in London. By then, SPP had moved its head office there at Slater's request. He wanted to keep a close eye on these Canadians who seemed to know no bounds. Slater liked Munk's approach to Travelodge and added a few wrinkles of his own. The plan was to take SPP public through a reverse takeover and then use the public company to raise money on the stock exchange.

The idea of a reverse takeover is simple. The owner of the private company buys control of a very small publicly quoted company, then makes that company buy the (much bigger) private company that the owner wants to take public. To finance this purchase, the small public company issues its own shares — and it has to issue so many shares that the owner of the private company gains control of the public company, which now owns the formerly private company. The advantage of a reverse takeover is that it avoids the necessity of preparing a prospectus for an initial public offering (IPO), which can cost hundreds of thousands of dollars and take up months of management time.

By the time the plan of action was agreed upon, Munk was in a frantic hurry to approach Travelodge to make a bid for a controlling interest. He has infinite patience when the timing is not right, but once he has made up his mind to proceed, he steamrollers everything in his path. The share price of Travelodge was at record lows and he wanted to strike immediately. He did not want to wait until his own public company was in a position to raise money by issuing shares to the public — he couldn't be sure when the market conditions might be right — so he and Slater agreed to an arrangement whereby Slater Walker would advance enough cash to buy the controlling stake. The loan could then be repaid out of the proceeds of the public issue, to be underwritten by Slater Walker as soon as market conditions were favorable.

The concept was simple enough, but the details were tricky, especially the terms of the cash advance and the price that would be attached to SPP when it was taken over by the public company. Jim Slater agreed to buy a small public company on the Hong Kong Stock Exchange and asked Munk to go to Hong Kong to negotiate the cash advance and the percentage splits in the reverse takeover — in other words, how the shares in the public company (after the reverse takeover) would be divided between Slater Walker and the shareholders in the private company.

Munk, Pat Samuel, and Simon Pendock rented a hotel suite in Hong Kong, where they met with two executives from Slater Walker. The negotiations soon got very tough. Slater Walker drove a harder bargain than Munk wanted. He felt they (who were, after all, part owners of SPP) were not offering SPP fair value for its Fiji development. His forceful logic was to no avail. They refused to budge. Exasperated, he lost his temper and stormed into the adjoining bedroom, refusing to talk any further. The deal was off, he announced savagely.

While he was fuming in the bedroom, Samuel and Pendock caucused in a corner of the suite and decided they had to salvage the negotiations. They went back to the table without Munk and struck a deal with Slater Walker. Next morning, over breakfast, they told Munk what they had done and said he had to accept it. Munk lives and dies by the sword of logic, and he listened to the hard facts that Samuel and Pendock laid before him. The deal was too important to miss for the sake of a few percentage points in the Hong Kong company, they told him. As he has done so often, before and since, he embraced their logic because he couldn't refute it. The deal was on.

Slater Walker instructed an affiliated company, Haw Par Brothers International, to buy a controlling interest in a small company on the Hong Kong Stock Exchange. Haw Par found King Fung Development Co., which had $10\frac{1}{4}$ million shares outstanding, trading at about 35¢,[1] and bought 65% of its outstanding shares for $2.35 million. King Fung had gone public only a few months before and its main asset was a complex containing shops and office premises.

---

[1] All the figures quoted for the Hong Kong stock market have been converted into U.S. dollars at the rate of exchange in July 1972: US$1 = HK$5.66

The new directors of King Fung then did the reverse takeover of SPP (Bahamas) — they bought SPP by issuing 70 million of King Fung's shares to the owners of SPP in return for their company. The deal was done in March 1972, and three months later the new directors changed the name of King Fung to Southern Pacific Properties, to complete the process. Munk's group (which included his key partners plus Slater Walker, Jardine Matheson, P&O, and J. G. Boswell) had controlled two-thirds of the private company. Now they controlled 57.5% of a public company that had been trading at about 35¢ in February, giving it a market valuation of $28 million. Better still, Haw Par committed itself to sell the building complex owned by King Fung for $4.4 million, giving King Fung some extra cash to buy into new opportunities.

Within weeks of the reverse takeover, King Fung's shares started rising dramatically, hitting $1 immediately after the deal was announced at the beginning of March, then going on to a high of $1.41 in May. "We were the flavor of the month," says Bill Birchall. "They were very impressed with our financial backers — P&O, Jardine Matheson, Boswell, and company."

At its high point, Munk controlled a public company with a market valuation of $113 million. Clairtone was beginning to look like small potatoes. The thrill didn't last long, however. The stock price immediately started drifting downward — to $1.06 at the end of July, 95¢ at the end of August, then steadily on down to a low of 57¢ halfway through November. It then recovered to 75¢ early in the new year of 1973, only to resume its decline down to its original price of 35¢ at the end of 1973, a victim of the Middle Eastern oil crisis, which battered the price for the next few years as SPP absorbed the shocks of the devastating recession in the travel and resort business.

Munk couldn't go to the market for more funds within weeks of the reverse takeover, partly because he was already preoccupied with the bid to take over Travelodge, and partly because the stock was just too volatile to price it properly. He did the next best thing, however. In May 1972, when the price of SPP's shares (still officially called King Fung) valued the company at more than $100 million, Munk made his successful bid for Travelodge. When the dust settled, he had bought 54.8% of the company at a cost of 16\frac{1}{2}$ million in cash and 4 million shares of SPP.

Three months later, in August, SPP duly floated its rights issue on the Hong Kong exchange[2] to raise $17.9 million — more than enough to repay the cash advance for the Travelodge acquisition. SPP never raised money on the Hong Kong Stock Exchange again, because its share price soon fell below the value of its assets, and no one sells part of their assets if the buyer is not willing to pay more than they are worth. In those brief five months, however, SPP had achieved its objective to raise the money to buy a majority shareholding of Travelodge.

Although the timing on the issue was flawless, Munk and his partners still learned an important lesson from it. They set the price for the issue at HK$5.40 in the middle of a steady decline in the stock price. The price had stuck at about HK$5.40 for a few weeks just before the issue, but it didn't have any upward momentum and HK$5.40 was at the top of the range of recent trading. As a result, the issue was not snapped up by Hong Kong investors and Slater Walker was left holding some of the shares it couldn't sell. That caused some frostbite between Munk and his most important investor.

---

[2] They sold 18.7 million shares at HK$5.40 or 95¢ (U.S.).

Munk's ninth golden rule:
Always leave something on the table in a public issue.
If you push for the last penny, it may hurt you
the next time around.

In two and a half years, Munk had transformed his and Gilmour's C$300,000 into the makings of the business empire he sought to build. He managed a successful, half-completed major international resort in Fiji and he controlled half of the biggest hotel chain in the South Pacific. Or so it seemed that summer of 1972. In fact, his control of Travelodge was an illusion that was to cause him great grief.

When Munk first decided to target it, Travelodge was an impregnable fortress, way out of the reach of any foreigner, let alone the then-unknown Munk. At that time, Australians were generally antagonistic to any attempt by foreign interests to buy control of one of their high-profile companies and they had the tools to make their bias stick — principally a government that was prepared to legislate or regulate anything that wasn't going the way it wanted. There had recently been a public outcry, led by the politicians, who forced ITT, the giant U.S.-based conglomerate, to abandon its bid for an Australian food-processing company called Frozen Foods Ltd. There had even been a great deal of controversy over the desire of TNT, a huge Australian-based transportation company, to take over Ansett, a regional airline.

TNT was founded by Sir Peter Abeles, who was a resident of Australia, but he was considered to be foreign by some Australians because he didn't live there year round. His second home in Switzerland, however, did not detract from his being one of Australia's most successful entrepreneurs, a friend and business partner of Rupert Murdoch and a companion to many powerful politicians. By a curious coincidence, Abeles, who is Hungarian, knew Munk when he was still a boy and their lives were still linked. Munk's stepfather had been secretary/assistant to Abeles' father in Vienna after the war and Abeles' wife was a passenger with Munk on the trainload of several hundred Jews who paid the Nazis a huge ransom in 1944 to be allowed to leave Hungary for Switzerland.

For Munk to have any hope at all of navigating the treacherous shallows of Australian political infighting, he had to have the enthusiastic and wholehearted support of the chairman and managing director of Travelodge, Alan Greenway. Normally, that would have been unthinkable. Only two years previously, Greenway had been described in the newspapers as having a "fetish" about foreign ownership. He planned to put Travelodge out of reach of foreign bidders. "If we run faster, we will be more difficult to catch. That is why we have set targets for some pretty high profits in the next few years, so we will be invulnerable to unwanted suitors."

By 1972, however, as his profits sagged, Greenway was singing a different tune. His debt had soared, and he was beginning to get nervous. He wasn't desperate for cash, but he knew that he couldn't raise capital on the Australian markets in a cyclical downturn. His margin for error was evaporating and his vulnerability to a change in economic conditions was becoming uncomfortable. He would never support a complete takeover, but he might support the right kind of new partner. He was ready to listen to an approach from Munk. Both men believed that Travelodge's financial difficulties were a temporary problem — but they expected diametrically opposite outcomes from the association.

Munk initially had a great deal of respect for Greenway. He had, after all, had a remarkable career — one that matched and, in some respects, surpassed what Munk had tried to do with Clairtone. In fact, the two had much in common, although their personalities were chalk and cheese. Against Munk's ebullience, Greenway is reserved; against Munk's intense intimacy, Greenway is formal and somewhat withdrawn. Where Munk is emotional and volatile, Greenway is phlegmatic and suppresses his feelings until he explodes. Greenway is short and somewhat stocky, with little "presence." When Munk walks into a room, he effortlessly engages everyone in the room. Greenway waits for people to come to him, hesitant to reach out and initiate contact. In the early 1970s, the Aussies liked outrageous people, but not characters like Munk, who epitomized the "tall poppy" — a person who stands out and appears to think he is better than others.

Overall, Greenway gives the impression of a devoted, hardworking executive who tries, with all his might, to do the right thing. Courteous and soft-spoken, he speaks with a slow, but still clipped, Australian accent and very rarely smiles. He is also very clever. He was, at the time, something of an Australian hero — one of the first to lead Australian businessmen onto the world scene. He was the only Australian director of Trust Houses Forte, the most prestigious hotel chain in Britain. His reputation as a strong-willed man was amply earned in the way he ran Travelodge, yet he never appeared to be pushy in public. There was almost nothing in his public persona to suggest the harddriving, aggressive ambition that put him at the top of the heap in the Australian tourism industry. Having been the boss from a very young age, he was not accustomed to competing for the right to make decisions in "his" business and when he had to start dealing with Munk's fluid torrent of tightly argued strategies, he could barely cope — he was not effective in articulating his point of view and generally retreated into silence or the assertion that Munk did not understand the industry. Like so many executives who reach the top of large organizations, his sense of his own power was derived principally from the position he occupied. His sense of ownership of the hotel chain was based on his having built it up into a national icon, not on the very few shares he owned. He demanded from his executives the respect that his office deserved, and enjoyed a remarkable loyalty from Travelodge employees long after he was gone.

His career up to 1972 had indeed been remarkable. He was born the same year as Munk, in 1927, in Wollongong, 30 miles south of Sydney. He left school at 14 to work as a clerk in the local Water Board, then joined the Royal Australian Navy as an ordinary seaman at the age of 16. After the Second World War, he went back to school on a veteran's ticket, and spent two years in law school but never got a degree. A decade later, he had scraped together enough cash to buy the liquor license for a small pub in Cooyal, 170 miles northwest of Sydney on the edge of the arid outback.

"It was all I could afford," he said later. "It had mud walls three feet thick, no running water or electricity and one kerosene-lit guest room, which I wouldn't have wished my worst enemy to stay in. In fact, only one person did stay there in the two years I ran it." That guest, it turns out, checked in for three nights, but fled after one. The bar trade prospered, however, and he soon sold the license, taking a vendor mortgage (which was never paid), and moved on to Goulburn, 62 miles into the mountains from his seaside birthplace. He managed the local Grand Hotel there for a while, then persuaded the owners to sell the hotel and buy the local motel, which he ran. He had seized the trend that was then just starting to transform the Australian accommodation industry — families packing their kids into the station wagon and traveling all over the country, staying at small, inexpensive motels. The owners then brought in other investors to build three more motels, before taking the company public in 1959 with Greenway as their managing director. He started adding motels at a furious rate, reaching gross revenues of A$4.4 million after only three years. His concept was ambitious. He wanted to blanket the country with his motels, so that every guest checking out of one Travelodge could book into another one 250 miles down the road for the next night. It worked. He was on his trajectory to destiny.

In 1967, he became chairman of the company as well as managing director and in 1969 he became chairman of the Australian Tourist Commission. In *The Australian* in 1968, he was referred to as "one of Australia's recognized authorities on travel and accommodation." He had arrived. But he didn't stop there. He wanted to break into the international big leagues.

He had entered in 1966 a joint venture with the Trust Houses group from Britain to develop a series of large hotels in major centers. The same year, he teamed up with Montreal-based Power Corp., whose president then was Maurice Strong, who bought $3 million of convertible notes, which Power Corp. later converted into 1.2 million shares. (Power Corp. sold the shares at a profit two years later when Strong moved on to his next challenge.) In 1968, Travelodge Australia became a significant shareholder in U.S.-based Travelodge International Inc., which had 400 motels and 21,000 rooms. Greenway was appointed chairman of the U.S. chain and the Australian company was given the contract to manage the chain.

The papers loved him. He was "Australia's first takeover operator in the U.S.A." In fact, however, the U.S. link was tenuous. Greenway's Travelodge had only 21% of the holding company, which owned 28% of the motel chain, so his investment was minimal — but the former owner of Travelodge International, Scott King, liked Greenway and gave him a sweet deal. King had first met Greenway when he decided to visit the Australian company that was using his Travelodge name without his permission (but quite legally). The two hit it off and when he wanted to retire, King made sure Greenway was involved in the group that bought his controlling shareholding. The other shareholders in the holding company were some of the best names in the world — Trust Houses, Western International Hotels Co., and some powerful merchant banking firms, like Schroder Rockefeller & Co. The president of Schroder Rockefeller was James Wolfensohn, who is now president of the World Bank. Wolfensohn had introduced Strong to Greenway and was a director of Travelodge for some years. It was heady stuff, and perhaps a bit too much for Greenway at the time. "I get into environments where I still feel like a country boy," he told *The Australian* in 1970. "Amongst those Wall Street and London brokers and bankers — career men in their field — although I enjoy it, I feel like a new boy."

He was more at home in his motels, where his reputation went from strength to strength. In 1970, Roy Winegardner, a top executive with Holiday Inns in the United States (and later its chairman), said he came to Australia to study the Travelodge operation, which was described to him as "the best motel and restaurant management group in the world."

The next year, Greenway signed an agreement with Mitsubishi to develop a chain of hotels in Japan. The Japanese said they preferred to deal with the Australians rather than the Americans, because the Australians managed to preserve the personal touch. Shortly afterwards, he signed another agreement with Indonesia's minister of economic affairs, His Highness Sultan Hamengku Buwono, to develop hotels and tourism throughout Indonesia.

It was hardly surprising that Greenway regarded Munk as a small-time operator of marginal importance, stuck away in Fiji, with no presence in the hotel business. (Pacific Harbour did not run its own Beachcomber Hotel — it signed a contract with American Airlines to run it on its behalf.)

By the spring of 1972, however, the hotel business was in the early stages of a radical transformation. The motel-hopping family car trips were falling out of favor. Australians were now going to Europe, Japan, and western United States, and they were seeing much better hotels. They now wanted more prestigious hotels back home and they didn't mind spending some money to get superior surroundings and service. Travelodge owned a string of "Ma & Pa" motels, which started to see their business decline.

In that environment, Greenway had a serious problem: The chain had grown so large that it was becoming impossible to manage all those little units effectively. The Ma and Pa motels with 20 or 30 rooms were acquired when Travelodge bought Caravilla Motels, and Greenway had instituted a disposal program to sell them off. This was not enough, however. There were still a lot of motels bigger than Ma and Pa motels, but too small for a chain like Travelodge to manage effectively.

He then had to choose between upgrading these smaller motels to meet the emerging market or selling them to small companies that could manage them effectively. It was an awful dilemma. He didn't have the cash to upgrade them and he couldn't bear to sell any of them to raise the cash he needed. Having scrimped and scratched his way to prominence by consolidating the accommodation industry in Australia, buying up tiny motels scattered all across the vast continent, these small units were in his blood. Although he knew what he had to do, he couldn't shake off his roots so easily and the process was much too slow. By the time Munk came on the scene, they were a significant annual drain on the chain's profitability.

Instead, Greenway chose to leap into the upscale market by borrowing to buy more hotels. He had already bought the Parkroyal chain from the Rockman family in Melbourne, which was a better class of hotel than anything he had previously owned. His biggest problem in the upscale market, however, was difficulty in raising his tariffs to a level where he could earn a reasonable return on his investment. Inflation was taking a heavy toll on the Australian economy and Greenway, who had by then become the industry leader, was afraid that higher room rates would devastate his occupancy rates. Consequently, although the new hotels helped his image, they did nothing for the bottom line.

So he shelved his expansion plans in Australia and turned his head to international ventures. Besides signing the agreement with Mitsubishi, he joined a partnership to build a new luxury hotel in Tahiti. James Wolfensohn had approached Greenway to invest in some prime land owned by the Jesuits with a view to building a hotel. He asked Greenway to manage the hotel and promised to find the necessary financing. Travelodge bought 17% of the hotel and its construction subsidiary, T. H. O'Connor, was given the contract to build it. Both deals might have been strokes of genius in better times, but these were not good times — and Travelodge had, in both cases, taken on huge potential liabilities in the midst of a rapidly deteriorating economic situation.

The third of Greenway's ill-fated deals in 1972 was the contract he signed to manage the Boulevard Hotel in Sydney, the first five-star hotel to be built there in many years. The developer who built the Boulevard outmaneuvered Travelodge, which agreed to an annual rent that was much too expensive, earning the right to lose a lot of money every year for a quarter of a century.

The declining profitability of his motels and hotels, combined with the high cost of moving into more upscale properties, had the inevitable effect of hammering his profit margins. Profit before tax and depreciation was 15.7% of gross revenue in the year ending June 1971, compared to 21.3% three years earlier — and as the year-end approached in 1972, margins had slipped still further to 9.5%. Long-term debt was A$17 million, compared to A$7.5 million four years previously. It wasn't a matter of survival yet, but the trend was alarming.

His shareholders, meanwhile, were staying away from the stock in droves. Between August 1970 and February 1972, the stock slid relentlessly from A$1.75 to 64¢. At that level, there was no way he could raise funds on the stock exchange. He had to find a partner. So, when Munk sounded him out, Greenway agreed — "a little too readily," he said later — to negotiate a deal.

The real bait in Munk's proposal was the shareholders behind him. P&O was the biggest shipping company in the world and a very big tourist operator in the South Pacific, with a large office in Sydney. Jardine Matheson was the leading trading company on the Asian side of the Pacific. Slater Walker was the most dynamic investment bank in the Commonwealth. Any one of these companies would have been a marvelous addition to Greenway's expanding stable of partners. Munk understood this clearly and, although he could not make commitments on behalf of his investors, he implied that SPP could lead these investors into the arms of an amorous Travelodge.

"I thought I was smart enough," Greenway said 23 years later, "to get him to use his connections with Jardine Matheson, P&O, and so on, so that they would joint-venture with us like Trust Houses Forte. [Trust Houses had merged with Forte to form Trust Houses Forte, which had continued the Trust Houses association with Travelodge.] We would form a company in which they were the shareholders and Travelodge was the vehicle that would become a mother hotel company worldwide." In other words, he thought he could create his own relationship with P&O and Jardine Matheson. Then, once economic conditions turned around, he would buy Munk's shares back. He believed that Munk needed him desperately because his Fiji development was on the ropes and short of cash. He also knew he needed Munk, but he did not regard him as an opponent worthy of much more than cursory attention.

As soon as the two men started talking, Travelodge stock started moving up. In March, the board cut the half-year dividend to 4% from 6%, but the stock still edged up to 72¢(A). It didn't make a lot of sense. The prospects were not improving enough to justify a rising stock price. Then in May, there was a flurry of trading that pushed the price to A$1.02. It turned out that Sir Charles Forte was the buyer. As chairman of Trust Houses Forte, he sat on the Travelodge board and through the purchases on the open market, he increased his stake in Travelodge to 12.3%. Forte had previously agreed to notify Greenway of any stock purchases he proposed to make, but did not do so in this case, causing a small tiff. The more important effect of this play, however, was its impact on Munk. He was beginning to get nervous over how much he would have to pay. He had to have the company. It was perfect for his long-term strategy. He was not going to let it out of his grasp whatever the cost.

As his adviser for the takeover bid, Munk hired David Hoare, the managing director of Ord-BT, the Australian subsidiary of Bankers Trust. Although its parent was huge, Ord-BT was still a little company in 1972 and only one year old. Hoare was last on Munk's list of interviews to select a banking adviser and he asked Hoare to meet him in the Wentworth Hotel at 9:30 one Friday evening. Hoare was a little surprised at the timing — although he later grew accustomed to what he called Munk and Gilmour's "drawing-room management style" (they never seemed to meet around a desk). Munk was ensconced in the largest suite in the hotel, accompanied by Birchall, Gilmour, and a few other key employees. Halfway through the meeting, Munk asked if Hoare would like some dinner. Hoare thanked him and accepted. A short while later, the eight people present trouped into the adjoining dining room where each place setting had a covered silver platter. They removed the covers to reveal one club sandwich for each diner.

Hoare's task was to navigate the bid through all the shoals of opposition in government, Travelodge, and the SPP board. Munk's SPP shareholders were not at all sure this investment was a good idea. They were expecting a dividend policy from Munk and did not want all their profits ploughed back into expansion. Munk successfully turned them around with the full force of his persuasive powers, with a little help from Hoare.

Meanwhile, Hoare was engaged with Munk and Birchall in their due diligence — checking Travelodge's books to make sure that everything was as Greenway said it was. Through these negotiations, Hoare was kept busy putting all the necessary legal and financial documents in order and Munk was virtually living in his office. "He kept dashing into my office and asking me if it would help if he phoned someone, or did something," remembers Hoare. "He had just come here from skiing in Switzerland and he had twisted his knee, so he was hobbling about with a stick. Nothing was going fast enough for Peter. He was an absolute pest. Finally, I gave him a supply of papers and magazines and locked him in the boardroom. It was the only way I could get on with processing the work."

Munk's biggest problem was that the price of Travelodge had risen so dramatically that he was being forced into offering a higher price than he had intended. The net tangible assets of Travelodge were valued at 96¢(A) per share,[3] so anything above that would be paying more than the shares were officially worth — which would create opposition to the deal from his own shareholders in SPP, especially since profits were sliding in Travelodge. To make a higher price palatable, he had to demonstrate that the assets were worth more than 96¢(A) — which called for a land valuation, a technique that Greenway's financial people had yet to explore. But Greenway had given Munk enough information to do a land valuation himself. As part of the due diligence process, Munk had received a series of financial projections for the chain prepared by David Block, a highly respected accountant in Sydney. These projections, as is normal for any putative seller, may reasonably have been described as looking on the bright side. Using these projections, Munk, Birchall, and Hoare applied the art of land valuation learned in the Fiji project and found that the Travelodge land and buildings, adjusted for the yields that might be expected from improved financial management,

---

[3] This is a measure of the excess of the company's assets over its debt, based on the cost of buying the assets. It is usually a conservative measure of the value of the company.

came up with a value of A$1.53 per share. This, then, was the price they offered to Travelodge shareholders when they announced the bid in May. The bid was conditional on approval of the Travelodge board, whose directors solemnly pondered its merits and declared it to be inadequate but suggested they would settle for A$1.55.

Although everyone felt this was an extremely generous offer — it was double the price at which the stock had been trading three months previously — Munk told the press, perhaps more for the benefit of his own shareholders, that it was a bargain at the price. Ultimately, he was right — it was very cheap. But at the time, it was so far over the market price that it was universally considered to have been a steal for the lucky shareholders who sold to Munk. Indeed, the shareholders might have been miffed if Greenway had deprived them of the opportunity of selling half their shares at such a large premium.

"He wanted the company so badly that he would have paid almost anything to get it," Greenway says. Munk would never argue with that but his perspective is a lot different, because he was going to pay for the Travelodge shares by issuing SPP shares in Hong Kong. "The money I paid was a function of my share price for the Fiji operation, because I paid in paper — and the stock went crazy in Hong Kong. The announcement of the Travelodge bid sent the shares to $1.40. If my [SPP] shares moved from 70¢ to 85¢, it more than compensated for paying A$1.80 instead of A$1.55 for Travelodge. It was a strategic move, to maintain the momentum of the company [SPP]."

Munk's tenth golden rule:
If an acquisition is strategically right,
don't worry about price.

The biggest danger in paying such a high price was that his own directors might have condemned him for being irresponsible. Munk had an answer all ready, however. In the 1972 accounts for SPP, he showed HK$39.7 million for goodwill (the premium of the price he paid over the book value of the assets purchased, as shown in the annual report) and noted that a revaluation performed by Jones, Lang, Wootton, chartered land surveyors, had calculated that the replacement cost of certain of the Travelodge assets was HK$39.3 million higher than the stated value of those assets. The net effect on the balance sheet was a negligible A$400,000. Munk was to become one of Jones, Lang, Wootton's best clients in the following few years.

The takeover still had to be approved by the government, however. Although Australia had not formally established a foreign investment review board, the government had the power to block takeovers — and Travelodge was certainly the kind of company that would catch the eye of the "pollies." No problem. Greenway flew to Canberra with Hoare. Together, they visited the prime minister, the leader of the Opposition, the leaders of two of the three parties in the Senate, and the deputy secretary of the Treasury. Greenway supported the takeover enthusiastically and came away with a green light from the federal government.

Munk, meanwhile, was doing his bit to spread sweetness and light. He told the staff that the offer was conditional on the entire management team staying with the company. He was quoted in the press beneath a picture of him smiling broadly: "I want the company's management, not its bricks and mortar." He described Greenway's team as having the finest expertise of its kind in the Southern Hemisphere and suggested that one of the reasons the takeover would benefit Australia was SPP's ability to attract investor funds from its travel industry and financier connections. "I was sucking up to Greenway," he acknowledges with a smile. He also provided Greenway with two "comforters," both of which would come back to haunt him. First of all, he agreed not to increase his holding beyond 50%, leaving Greenway in charge, and limiting SPP to only one seat on Travelodge's nine-man board of directors. The second condition that Munk signed was a guarantee that Greenway would receive certain financial benefits if he should ever be squeezed out of the company and that Munk would not vote against the majority of the board in elections to the board of directors until 1977.

When he signed these documents and made his statements, Munk believed he would be able to work constructively with Greenway: "I really wanted to bet on him," he said "I thought this guy was a genius." However, he also knew that he would not be content with 50% forever. As Hoare remarked later, "Munk is not a guy who co-exists easily with anyone else at the same level." His decision to go for only 50% reflected a realistic assessment of his chances of getting a total takeover approved by the government in power. Greenway would never have supported a complete takeover and he had close ties with the government at that time. He thought he could win Greenway over with time and the force of his own salesmanship.

It is highly unlikely the partnership between these two men would ever have worked, but Greenway certainly set the tone early on by making it clear he didn't attach any importance to Munk. In the 1972 annual report, the change in ownership rated three paragraphs on page three of the Chairman's report to the shareholders. Furthermore, Greenway instructed his staff to give its majority shareholder exactly the same information as the other directors — no more, no less. Every request for additional information from Munk or Birchall was referred to Greenway and usually refused. SPP, Greenway insisted, was just another director. He was running the show, always had done, always would do.

Initially, it was not a major problem. SPP had no one in Sydney and they were operating on the assumption that Greenway regarded them as cooperative partners. Munk returned to England after he had toured the Travelodge offices to tell the staff how much confidence he had in them, instructing Birchall to be supportive wherever possible. "It was clear the company didn't have any financial capability, after building hotels here, there, and everywhere," says Birchall. "We tried to use our contacts with P&O and Jardine Matheson to bring them management contracts."

Three months later, however, Greenway grabbed their attention when his board eliminated the dividend completely. The annual dividend had been running at A$1.2 million, so SPP would have received about A$600,000 (or $725,000) — which would have been very useful, considering SPP's galloping consumption of capital at the time. Munk would have preferred, to put it mildly, to have cut Travelodge expenses and continued with the dividend. To this day, some of the people who were with SPP believe Greenway did it out of spite, which he denies. It is more likely that he did it because he needed the A$1.2 million pretty badly himself and he felt he had this powerful group of investors behind him who would insulate him from the negative market reaction to cutting the dividend.

Munk's investors, however, were not interested in helping Travelodge through its difficult patch. They were still dubious about the investment. "They were shareholders of mine," Munk says, "but they wouldn't give me an extra buck." Greenway's assumptions about the benefits that SPP would bring him were seriously off base. It wasn't a devastating problem, however, as Travelodge's finances improved slightly and Munk and his partners were so preoccupied with Pacific Harbour that Travelodge did not demand their urgent attention. But Greenway's high-handedness had eroded Munk's belief that he could talk him into becoming part of his team.

The simmering animosity finally boiled over when the results were announced for the year ending June 1973. Not only did the directors refuse to pay a dividend, but the profit margins had worsened. David Block's forecast a year earlier that dividends would be reinstated proved to be a pipe dream. Worse still, Greenway continued to pursue his program of rapid expansion against all the advice that Munk and his board offered him.

Munk was furious. He felt he had been "had." He commissioned a report by outside consultants that reviewed operations for the previous five years and demonstrated with crushing directness how the financial circumstances of Travelodge had deteriorated during that period. Fixed assets were up 139%, long-term loans were up 248%, and gross revenues were up 72%; but return on capital, net profits per room, and earnings per share were all down 50%. He presented his report to the Travelodge board in November 1973, recommending that Greenway relinquish his position of managing director and that a new chief executive be hired to run the chain.

The board of directors — Greenway men all — acknowledged the problems they were facing but declined the invitation to fire Greenway. From that moment, it was all-out war between the two chief executives, consummate salesmen both.

"I thought he was doing a brilliant job when I bought the

company," Munk says. "I didn't realize it was a sinkhole of a company. He was a brilliant salesman. He could sell me. He used to talk about the Australian accommodation industry and how it was his life. Who would have thought that this guy had totally lost control? He couldn't pay dividends. They were in development, they wanted to build more hotels. They couldn't make it on 40 or 50 and they were just building more, just taking on more debt. And when he got to 50, he'd have wanted 54."

The same month, the oil crisis hit the world and everything changed. The cash flow in Fiji collapsed and tourism in Australia evaporated. Interest rates soared north. Australia was being run by Gough Whitlam's Labor government, a wild and woolly administration that wreaked havoc on the economy and precipitated a major constitutional crisis.

It could hardly have come at a worse time for Munk. Construction costs in Fiji were 50% higher than he had budgeted and, although sales had gone well up to the end of 1973, he had not unloaded all the lots and sales now fell to almost nothing. He had to take drastic action, so he decided to move the administrative offices of SPP — meaning Birchall and Roger Kirby, another accountant who had been hired to help out Birchall — from London to Sydney. (Kirby would become managing director of Travelodge four years later.) Birchall immediately sliced the spending plans drastically although he couldn't stop it completely as Munk was committed to finishing the infrastructure program. To make matters worse, Pacific Harbour had to use some of its scarce resources to finance the clients who were putting down only a quarter of the price and paying the balance over seven years. Within weeks of arriving in Australia, Birchall told Munk he had completed his forecast for Pacific Harbour in 1974 — he anticipated a negative cash flow of $2.6 million.

As the recession of 1974 bit deeper, many clients found it difficult to keep up their payments and Pacific Harbour had a serious collection problem. By the end of 1974, whether they knew it or not, SPP was sliding into insolvency. Pacific Harbour limped through 1974, all systems shut down and husbanding resources obsessively. They were under a lot of pressure.

For the next three years, Birchall and Kirby wore out the sidewalks between their offices and those of their bankers — including any new banker who would let them in the door to hear their pitch. In a feat of remarkable ingenuity, financial acumen, dogged persistence, and plain old-fashioned stamina, the two accountants wheedled the bankers into keeping SPP alive until the cash started to flow in 1978. Birchall made his financial accounts jump through hoops as he never had before, extracting ounces of optimism from tons of doom, building a lasting relationship with the financial community in Sydney.

They had their moments of high farce. SPP's Travelodge shares were deposited with its banks as collateral for loans and as the price of the shares kept falling, the banks kept coming back to Birchall asking for more collateral. Every square inch of property they owned was in hock. Once, when Citibank came to them with a demand for more collateral, Kirby discovered that they had pledged only part of the golf course in Fiji — so they offered Citibank the fourth and ninth holes as additional security. The bank was not amused. As interest rates soared and property companies collapsed all around them, there was scant sympathy for their problems.

The whole group was now fighting for its life and its owners began to pursue divergent strategies. Early in 1974, Slater Walker Securities had failed spectacularly, along with many others in the secondary banking industry. As part of the winding up, its shares in SPP were sold in May to P&O, whose holding thereby rose to 34% of the outstanding shares of SPP. A month later, P&O offered to buy all the remaining shares of SPP at a price of 35¢. This represented a comfortable premium over the market price and above the 31¢ that it had paid for the Slater Walker holding. P&O's directors said they would proceed with the offer only if it was supported by the SPP board. Munk turned them down, saying he wouldn't sell for less than 44¢. He went to see Sir Charles Forte to ask him to support his refusal of the offer. "I told him that P&O was stealing the company from us," Munk says. "So the bid failed. It was the first time in 110 years the company had failed in a bid."

When he told Birchall, Samuel, and a couple of other directors what he had done, they were appalled. They told him they would be foolish not to accept the offer. They would be getting a million or so dollars each, which looked very good to them considering how gloomy the outlook was.

"I couldn't see the wood for the trees," Birchall remembers. "I was very depressed."

Munk argued against them: "I would have walked away with $2 million, which was completely unacceptable," he said emphatically afterwards. But he accepted their consensus and went back to P&O saying the board wanted to accept the offer after all. The financial director, Oliver Brooks, told Munk he was sorry but P&O had closed the book on the offer. It was no longer available. Another remarkable piece of luck, particularly as Brooks stayed on the SPP board and continued to give the company the benefit of his astute advice.

Greenway had his own watershed in 1974. The initiatives he had taken to move upscale had sent his costs spiraling, while the recession put a tight lid on his revenues. He had lost almost all his financial room to maneuver.

The first hotel in the proposed chain with Mitsubishi was the Narita hotel, at the site of the new international airport outside Tokyo. Twenty years later, it was a very successful hotel; 1974, however, was a different matter. While the airport was being built, local community groups decided it was encroaching on agricultural land and picketed the site, halting all construction. The hotel was almost completed by 1974, but there was no end in sight to the political standoff over the airport, so it could not open. An empty hotel is an expensive hotel. Admittedly, Mitsubishi was financing the hemorrhaging, but Travelodge was ultimately on the hook for one half of the mounting liabilities — and their financing agreement ended in 1976. There was no way that Travelodge could find enough money in the following two years to pick up its 50% of that accumulated deficit, so Greenway was relying on Mitsubishi to extend the financing arrangement.

As for the Boulevard that Greenway had been so keen to add to his "system," the ruinous leasehold agreement he had signed with the owners of the property was costing Travelodge a base rate of A$750,000 plus 15% of the gross revenues over A$2.5 million. The owners had built the hotel without consulting hotel designers, so it was in a bad location with a design poorly suited to a hotel operation. There was no possibility whatsoever that Travelodge could make enough money to cover the lease. The chain lost almost A$500,000 every year. "It was a mistake," Greenway acknowledges now.

The Tahiti Beachcomber, which started out as an investment but became totally owned in 1978, was another heavy loser for Travelodge, its occupancy languishing at rates as low as 30% when it opened in 1974. It is a magnificent site, but no one went there. It was off the airline routes, and the French navy had decamped, taking with it an important chunk of Tahiti's economy. The hotel was losing money at an alarming rate and Greenway stepped in with an unsecured advance. In the year ending June 1974, this advance totaled A\$670,000, but a year later it had ballooned to A\$2.9 million — at a time when Travelodge (which then owned only 17% of the Tahiti hotel) had suspended dividends and was strapped for cash itself.

Greenway's eyes were fixed on his long-term vision and he wasn't watching the proliferation of potholes at his feet. Even his staff was nervous about the continued rush for growth. "We would argue against some of his expansion plans," says Doug Stewart, who was then his marketing general manager. "If he couldn't think of a good argument to support his own position, he would just say that it was an investment for the future — and then go ahead and do it."

Another, not quite as senior, added: "The people around Alan were scared of him — and many of them still are, to this day. The hotel business is very hierarchical and if you're the boss, you have the power of the admiral."

Of course, that's not how Greenway saw it. "You create something that will have a sense of value; you don't create it as a vehicle to make money. We were in the hospitality service industry. That was my raison d'être. I was worrying about 8,000 or 9,000 guests a night. Were they comfortable? Were they being given service and would they come back again? And the 5,000 employees doing it. I knew we had to make profits, but we were a patient investor with a service-industry mentality, as opposed to a property mentality. Munk and Birchall were interested in financial gymnastics. We were poles apart. We were never ever on the same page."

Greenway felt that the chain was in a minor trough and that if he could tough out the next few years, he would emerge triumphant as the head of a worldwide chain of quality hotels. "Mitsubishi had indicated they were happy to renegotiate our deal — with me, not Peter. The managing director of the Mitsubishi Trading Co., Bunichero Tanabe, came to me and said, 'I am ashamed. We're suffering because the hotel hasn't opened. We need an extension of time, so let's sweat it out together — we will provide the funds.'"

Munk saw this kind of talk as wishful thinking, and it enraged him. And Greenway's insouciance only made it worse, at a time when Munk had slammed the lid on his own plans in Fiji, when he had had to suffer the indignity of Kirby reprimanding him for spending £5,000 which wasn't in the budget, and when he was even forced to fly economy class on his frequent trips from London to Fiji and Australia. "His office walls were covered with pictures of hotel inaugurations with governors and prime ministers and presidents. He had a silver trowel for laying foundation stones . . . Well, screw the growth. If you can't make money with 40 hotels, why the hell would you build 60? The key is to make money and reward the shareholders who, after all, own the business."

Greenway was impervious to his arguments, insisting that Munk didn't understand the hotel business. "Peter said I was poor at financial administration — which is something I have never claimed to be good at. I had good financial people around me. I was the visionary. I was minding the shop. They [SPP] were playing Monopoly money."

Greenway might have been right, but Travelodge would have unraveled very quickly if he was wrong. From Munk's perspective, it was totally irresponsible not to take evasive action, and he was not shy in telling Greenway how he felt. But Greenway refused to accept advice from a man who had no experience in the hotel industry and who thought that Greenway was so bad at his job he should be fired. He did more than just ignore Munk's advice, however. He counterattacked. He was also on the SPP board and he told the directors that they should not listen to this emotional and erratic Hungarian.

"Greenway was no fool," Birchall remembers. "He's an extremely intelligent and clever person, but he didn't have many cards to play. The one card he could play was, 'Peter Munk knows nothing about the accommodation industry, he knows nothing about Australia. The place is run by unions in Australia and only I know how to deal with unions. I am the chairman of the Australian Tourist Commission. How can you give any credit to what he says?'"

Greenway had to be careful, however, because he didn't want to alienate his potential investors, so he tried to isolate Munk, suggesting that SPP's business plan was good but Munk could never implement it. It very nearly worked. J. G. Boswell decided he was fed up with the whole thing and wanted out. But the other directors decided to appoint a committee to study the feud. The chairman of the subcommittee was Bob Rose, who ran the P&O operation in Australia, and he came down firmly on Munk's side.

They were now even. Each had tried unsuccessfully to depose the other. But Greenway still didn't understand the danger he was in, because he always underestimated his adversary. In particular, he never appreciated the extent of Munk's fury over his continued opulent lifestyle despite the precarious situation of his company.

As a national leader in tourism and recreation, Greenway had acquired a high profile as the sponsor of yacht races all over the country (Australia is boat mad, so it is a prominent sport). Munk is not averse to a bit of glamour himself and the sight of Greenway presiding over these festivities rubbed the salt a bit deeper in the wound of his relative poverty.

Then there was the art collection. Greenway had started the Travelodge art collection some years previously, when he bought a hotel in Melbourne and discovered that the original art on the hotel walls was worth almost as much as the price he paid for the hotel. He decided to put prints on the wall and display the originals in the company art collection. He started a national competition with an annual prize of A$10,000. In return for the prize, the artist ceded reproduction rights to Travelodge — so Greenway could have prints made and hang them on the walls of his hotels. He was very proud of the art collection, which had cost Travelodge A$200,000 by 1974. It represented a major contribution to the cultural life of Australia. For Munk it was a disgraceful waste of scarce funds.

Finally, Travelodge had bought Greenway a beautiful house in Rose Bay, in the prestigious eastern suburbs of Sydney. The house was rebuilt for the chairman, at Travelodge's expense. It was right on the waterfront, with its own docking facilities, and had a beautiful view of the bay and the opera house. The house cost A$450,000 and Greenway's rent was A$10,000 a year below the market price for a house of that caliber. Every day that Greenway remained in that house, Munk's anger mounted. Keeping the house was not a demonstration of brotherly solidarity with his cash-starved "controlling" shareholder, whose promised dividend had been discontinued months after he invested in the company.

As Greenway tried to maintain his corporate image while his

financial foundations crumbled, Munk saw only that his biggest contribution to cutting costs was to eliminate the dividend. His profit margin was still in a free fall, having reached 8.9% in the year ended June 1974, on its way down to 5.9% the following year. But revenues had risen strongly, enabling the company to pay down some debt and ease the cash situation somewhat. Still, the directors of Travelodge opted to withhold dividends.

By the end of 1974, the relationship between the two men had deteriorated to the point where it had become abusive. Memories are a bit vague on this period. Greenway doesn't remember any antagonism and feels there were very few confrontations. The SPP people, however, remember 1974 and 1975 as a period of high drama and shouting matches. Roger Kirby, who got on quite well with both men, may be a more dispassionate observer than most: "Munk and Greenway had some shocking rows on the phone. Greenway's got a hide like a rhinoceros — he couldn't care less."

Greenway, of course, knew the relationship wasn't going smoothly, and it is possible he was so busy trying to "mind the store" that he was oblivious to the volcanic anger that was boiling up in Munk. However, Munk is not normally diffident in expressing his views and feelings, so it is difficult to imagine him being anything other than direct and aggressive with his concerns. Whether Greenway knew it or not, there is absolutely no doubt about Munk's feelings. He was livid with rage. Mark Johnson, one of his advisers, says he had to act as a go-between for the two men[4] and has few happy memories about the process: "Greenway could get surly under pressure and very defensive. Munk would get emotional. It wasn't fun. It was

---

[4] Greenway does not recall this at all.

128

very nasty by the standards of the time. Very pressurized."

Munk eventually decided that if he couldn't get Greenway's board to restore dividend payments, he had to find another way of getting some money into Pacific Harbour from Travelodge's somewhat healthier cash flow. At an SPP board meeting in Fiji, he suggested to Greenway that perhaps Travelodge should put some money into SPP.

Greenway's response was immediate. "I had always believed Peter Munk invested in Travelodge to obtain respectability," he says. "This was the first indication I had that he wanted money as well as respectability. He had promised to provide financial support through the aegis of his investors and he then turned round and said, 'Hey, you fund us.' Well, I was pretty forthright. I told them they were whistling in the wind. They saw that I regarded them as a shareholder in Travelodge. I was not a cash cow for them. I declared that we were not there to help them, we were our own company."

Twenty-three years later, he added: "I know now that I painted a target on my chest at that meeting."

Maybe, but the immediate result was that Munk gave up. He put his Travelodge shares up for sale. He tried everything to hype the price of the SPP stock in Hong Kong, to no avail. He retained Donaldson, Lufkin & Jenrette Securities Corp., who tried to sell the block of shares to American Express, among others, with the help of the sons of Gough Whitlam and David Niven. No luck. No one was interested. Greenway became enthusiastic about helping Munk for the first time in months and offered to introduce him to several potential buyers, including Qantas. All the time, Travelodge shares were still sliding, headed toward their ultimate low of 24¢.

Munk realized that selling his Travelodge shares was not an

option. To rescue his devastated empire, he had to find a new project that would generate enough cash to enable him to spread a bit of it around in his other holdings. He embarked on a period of frenetic activity in search of deals. When David Hoare visited the SPP offices in London, he came away bemused. "Lord knows what they were doing. On with the next great deal. I think he was busy looking to add value in different ways. I would say, 'I don't like the smell of it — it's going to get in trouble.' Eighty minutes later, he'd say, 'You're right,' then he'd change it all around. 'We'll put so-and-so in as managing director . . .' He just didn't stop."

Munk got into some bizarre situations. He bought a copra plantation on a small island in the Solomon Islands — it didn't work out as a resort, because the seas were infested with sharks, but he sold it at a profit later as a copra plantation. He also visited New Zealand Prime Minister Robert Muldoon to try to exercise an option on some beautiful beach property in the northern tip of the North Island. Samuel had taken out the option on the property some years earlier but had agreed to contribute it to SPP, provided it be returned to him if the company didn't use it. Munk turned the full force of his charm on "Piggy" Muldoon, but the prime minister was impervious. "We don't need your development, Mr. Munk," he told him, "and we don't need you." Munk canceled the option in disgust, to Samuel's dismay.

Once again, however, Gilmour came to the rescue by opening the necessary doors for Munk. He had met some Egyptians at a party in England and told them about the hotel chain SPP owned. They were interested in developing Egypt for tourism and asked if SPP would be interested in working with the government. It was the start of another mega-dream that soon involved the president of Egypt and some wealthy Arabs who had grown rich on the oil prices that had destroyed Pacific Harbour (see next chapter). Munk had found the money source he needed.

Meanwhile, Kirby had been busy in Sydney. He befriended a woman in the accounting department of Travelodge and persuaded her to become his secret informant, feeding him information about how the company was run. The information should have been freely available to SPP, but it wasn't. Not only did Birchall and Kirby now know how Greenway was keeping his books, but they found out where the major opportunities lay for reducing losses. Between the two of them, they began to acquire an understanding of how to make money in the hotel business in general and in Travelodge specifically.

With this knowledge in hand and an Arab investor in mind, Munk's path was clear. As he wrote in a memorandum to Birchall some months later: "[Since SPP acquired half of the hotel], Travelodge has paid no dividends and its current annual operational cash flow is about $7 million, a level which has been kept constant for the past 5 years. Of this $7 million, about $3 million is spent on servicing existing debts, leaving the balance for overheads unrelated to hotel operations and profits." He proposed a series of corrective measures that would raise the cash flow available to SPP to $21 million a year.

In April 1975, he decided to go for 100% ownership and fire Greenway. That would enable him to put into action the measures that would turn Travelodge around, and it would allow him to get his hands on Travelodge's cash flow to relieve Pacific Harbour's cash difficulties.

Peter Munk went calling again on David Hoare, who had by this time become a director of Travelodge — not officially as a representative for SPP, but clearly on Munk's side. They decided it was feasible to bid for the balance of the shares. Hoare felt they could overcome any political opposition that Greenway might stir up against them, because the erratic Labor government of Gough Whitlam had been defeated and the new Conservative government was more likely to be amenable to powerful economic arguments, which Munk knew he could generate.

Munk also added some new advisers — Mark Johnson and Peter McGovern of Hill, Samuel of Australia. Johnson and McGovern put together the top-secret campaign code-named Slingshot. The code name for Travelodge was Target and SPP was, of course, Slingshot. A potential partner in the takeover (Qantas) was Arrow. The campaign plan had detailed flow-charts, showing all the major decision points, along with the advantages and disadvantages of each available option for that decision. It was thorough. Greenway never stood a chance.

The Slingshot team checked with the banks to see if a change in management would affect their loans to the company. Travelodge's general manager, finance, George Haines, had been trying unsuccessfully since March 1975 to negotiate the renewal of a A$12 million loan from the Commonwealth Trading Bank that expired in March 1976. It was by no means certain that he would conclude the negotiations successfully. The bank was still balking at renewing the loan even after the company accepted a series of covenants limiting its actions — and if Commonwealth didn't renew, no other bank would touch Travelodge. The bank told Johnson and McGovern it would make its decision on the basis of the financial circumstances, not on the beauty of the faces in the executive suite.

The team also went to Canberra to ascertain if the government would challenge the deal because of the foreign ownership.

The reception was favorable, even though no guarantees could be given. They took advice on the legal ramifications of breaking the various agreements Munk had signed with Greenway. All the potential problems they identified were found to be manageable. Munk was ready for battle.

But first he had to convince his own board, which, since it regarded the investment in Travelodge as dubious in the first place, was unlikely to be enthusiastic about throwing still more money at it. He argued his point forcefully with them and they responded that they would prefer it if he just rode out the storm. Eventually, he found out what the key triggers were for them — they would go along with him if he didn't ask them for more money and if he got the balance of the shares at a really good price.

Munk's eleventh golden rule:
Look for partners who will argue with you, because it disciplines your thinking and enables you to pick up negatives that you yourself may overlook.

Munk was confident he could raise the money he needed from his new Arab sources. The negotiations with the Egyptians had turned up a ripening relationship with Adnan Khashoggi, the famous (or notorious) Saudi trader who made hundreds of millions of dollars in commissions on sales by his American clients to Saudi agencies. Khashoggi had already indicated he was favorably disposed to letting Munk use his money to buy the rest of Travelodge. As for the price of the deal, the stock was bumping along in the 20s and the 30s, at best, so he knew it was not going to take a lot of money.

His only significant hurdle was therefore Greenway, who

could be counted on to raise a stink if Munk made the offer while he was still chairman of the company. He therefore decided on a two-step strategy: first he would remove Greenway from the board; then — with his hands on all the levers at Travelodge — he would get approval from his board to take the company private. Munk and his team narrowed their focus to Travelodge's Annual General Meeting on October 30, 1975, which the Slingshot team decided was the only time to take control of the board and fire Greenway.

Greenway would still be difficult to dislodge, because he was in firm control of his board. However, the deteriorating situation in the company had weakened his position with the independent directors, albeit not seriously at that point. He had also lost one of his staunchest allies when Lord Crowther died in 1972. He had been chairman of Trust Houses when they first invested in Travelodge and he became a mentor to Greenway. When Trust Houses merged with Forte in 1970, Crowther became chairman of the combined company after a bitter fight with Sir Charles Forte, who never forgave him — or his supporters. Crowther asked Greenway to sit on their board, giving him access to an international five-star operation.

Sir Charles Forte took over from Crowther on the boards of both Trust Houses Forte and Travelodge. He never really liked Greenway, whom he saw as a Crowther supporter, and thought that Crowther had allowed Travelodge to benefit disproportionately in their joint venture, from which Travelodge was pulling down hefty annual management fees. The switch didn't change Greenway's control of the board, but his position was eroding.

As Munk, Hoare, Johnson, and McGovern surveyed the Travelodge board in September 1975, they calculated that out of the ten directors, SPP had only two representatives (Munk and

Samuel). Greenway could count on four — an employee, a former owner of some properties that Travelodge had bought, the head of a Travelodge subsidiary, and Greenway himself. The last four were supposedly independent. Two of them, Sir Arthur George and Bill Thompson, an independent financial executive, had traditionally voted with Greenway; the other two, Sir Charles Forte from Trust Houses Forte, and Norman Jones, his Sydney representative, were known to be unhappy with Greenway, but had supported him in the past. Six to two against Munk, with two more undecided.

At a special board meeting on October 9, Greenway informed his directors that the financial situation was worsening and he tabled a plan to turn it around. At Munk's urging, the directors rejected the plan. They told him that the cuts in expenses were insufficient as his profits still came out worse than budget, even after the cuts. They pointed out that the cuts in overhead were designed primarily to preserve the status quo — marketing costs were to be cut by 38%, while the executive costs (Greenway and his deputy) were to be cut by 10%, when the opposite should have been the case. They also told him that the drastic revisions to the budget less than three months into the new year caused them to question the integrity of the financial forecasts.

Munk cabled Forte in London and told him what he thought about the way Travelodge was being run. He also told him that he had "reluctantly" decided he had to take responsibility for protecting his investment and fire Greenway. He found a sympathetic listener. Forte indicated he would go along with him, buttressed by a very strong letter from Norman Jones, who detested Greenway and supported Munk. Six to four against Munk.

To stand a chance of removing Greenway, Munk had to sway

at least one of the other two independents, Sir Arthur George and Bill Thompson, to balance the two camps in the board at five to five. Then he planned to use the juggernaut of his persuasiveness to finesse Greenway out of a job. George was a Greek immigrant who had done well in business as a lawyer and developer and was a highly respected businessman in Sydney. For many years, he used to play a regular game of poker with three other men — Sir Peter Abeles, Sir Paul Strasser, and Sir Rob Askin, the premier of New South Wales. The three businessmen had all made their mark and were wealthy men in 1975.

Munk now called on Abeles and asked him to have a word with Sir Arthur George, explaining what a good man Munk was and how he only wanted to help the company. Abeles obliged and George swung over to Munk's side.

Five to five, evenly balanced and ready for a showdown. Munk could not guarantee to carry the board, but he had at least neutralized it — and he knew he could vote his 58% of the shares to carry the change in control at the Annual General Meeting. His strategy was therefore to propose that Bill Birchall be made a director, to replace Thompson, who was retiring in rotation and was therefore up for re-election. This strategy contravened the agreement Munk had signed with Greenway in 1972, promising not to vote for a change in the composition of the board before 1977, but he had found a legal loophole.[5]

On October 17, Munk set about implementing his plan. He wrote a letter to Thompson explaining what he was going to do and saying it was nothing personal — he just happened to be

---

[5] SPP had created a holding company between itself and Travelodge, so technically, SPP wasn't voting for a change in the composition of the board — the company voting for a new board was SPP's subsidiary, which was not part of the agreement signed with Greenway.

chosen because he was going off the board by rotation. He indicated that everyone would much prefer to keep Thompson and have Ken Bailey, Greenway's deputy, give his place to Birchall. He also called a meeting with Greenway, at which he told him he was going to nominate Birchall as a director to replace Thompson. Greenway, naturally, objected furiously. But he knew Munk was now mounting his second assault on his job.

Both of them then scurried to the federal government in Canberra, to union headquarters, and to the banks. Greenway spent the whole of the following week in Canberra, lobbying the politicians — but ignoring the bureaucrats in Treasury, who supported SPP. Some of the "pollies" supported Greenway, but most went for Munk's argument. He had prepared a superb presentation with graphs and tables, showing how jobs would be lost and the economy would suffer if Travelodge wasn't turned around. "It's up to you guys," he told them. "You can have it Australian and bankrupt or you can have it foreign and employing 4,000 Australians in a healthy growing company. I can only tell you — because I am the major shareholder — I hate to say it, but I am the loser if you louse it up. This company will be bankrupt."

It was a masterful exercise in hard logic. He showed anyone who would listen how the profit per room under management had fallen from A$500 in 1966 to A$151 in 1973 and A$0 in 1975, when the hotel group barely broke even, because almost the entire net profit had been earned by the construction subsidiary. Meanwhile corporate overheads had risen from A$2.3 million in 1973 to A$2.8 million in 1974 and A$3.3 million in 1975. The construction cost of the Tahiti hotel was almost 50% over budget and Greenway had given the 17%-owned hotel an unsecured advance of A$2.9 million, which they were unlikely to recover in view of the appalling losses in the hotel's first year. The Boulevard was losing A\$475,000 a year and it would cost Travelodge A\$1 million to buy out its lease. And on and on. Greenway called it "a demolition job on the man who built the company."

Munk had been working on the minister of labour for some time, giving him free weekends in Fiji, so he was sensitive to Munk's point of view and advised the union leaders to listen to him. Despite Greenway's conviction that only he could carry the unions, Munk won over their leaders. Greenway had lost any hope of mobilizing public support against Munk.

Munk's twelfth golden rule:
Life is about meeting objectives. Sometimes your objectives cross other people's. Then you have to fight — and you fight to win. What's the point of fighting if you don't win?

The directors of Travelodge had consistently supported Greenway over the years, but the outside directors were finally beginning to get nervous at the deteriorating financial state of the company — particularly the failure to negotiate a renewal of the loan from the Commonwealth Trading Bank. Under the power of Munk's devastating analysis, George and Thompson succumbed. The two men and Michael Sinclair, the former owner of some of the chain's properties, put together a motion for the board meeting on October 29, the day before the Annual General Meeting. They proposed, among other things, that Greenway and Bailey resign from their executive positions but Greenway continue as a nonexecutive chairman. Birchall was to go on the board's slate of proposed directors in Bailey's place. With seven people committed to this motion — although Greenway was still unaware of it — the result was now certain. But the deed still had to be done.

Munk knew it would be messy. He had two directors who were potential heart-attack victims. Sir Arthur George had a history of heart palpitations and Norman Jones was, although he may not have known it then, dying of heart disease (he died four months later). Munk arranged to have two doctors on hand, in case the passions of the board meeting precipitated any heart attacks. On October 29, Sir Arthur George presented his motion, which stunned Greenway, who was outwardly calm, but in a state of shock. The independent directors didn't lift a finger for Greenway, and the motion soon passed. Then the discussion started on what compensation should be paid to Greenway and his departing executives and the temperature rose rapidly. Munk was playing hardball — he didn't see why he should reward someone for incompetence. Greenway had a written agreement, however. Sir Arthur George got extremely agitated and had to leave the room with palpitations. Birchall was shaking. ("He hates confrontation," says Munk.) Eventually, Samuel, who thought Greenway was being treated too roughly, proposed an amount and everyone agreed. Then they got down to the business of how to handle the announcement of the changes.

For Greenway, the whole thing came as a complete shock. As Samuel was to remark much later: "He regarded the SPP guys as a bunch of fleas climbing the back leg of an elephant with intent to rape."

Greenway was especially stunned that his supporters did not respond vigorously to Munk's onslaught. "It never occurred to me that they could be so ruthless," he said nearly a quarter of a century later. "I thought there were people around the table who would say, 'Hey, this guy's brought us to this stage, he's never let us down, we've trusted him, we'll go along with him.' It was a character assassination."

He had never even lobbied his board for support. "I never believed that I might be ousted. I knew things were uncomfortable and I knew talks had been taking place, but I was naive. I believed that my performance would speak for itself. When the Munks of this world are out there pushing, striving, politicking, I was sitting back saying 'I know what the facts are here. I know what's true and surely everyone else knows and surely at the end of the day, it will out.' The real reason is that I was not part of the establishment. I was from the wrong side of the tracks. I didn't even finish high school."

Samuel, who had always got on with Greenway, comments laconically: "He never understood the depth of Peter's ability."

The next day, the Annual General Meeting took place in the Rushcutter Travelodge and the TV cameras were out in force. The press had been alerted that there was going to be a big change in the company. To be admitted to the meeting, the shareholders had to show ID at the door. Greenway gave his chairman's report, which he had written before he knew he was being fired, which gave the meeting an air of unreality. At the end of his report, however, he told his shareholders that he had always believed the roles of chairman and managing director should be separated, so he wanted to announce that he was resigning as managing director, but would remain as chairman. Travelodge had been Alan Greenway's whole life. He broke down and wept on the podium, along with some of his colleagues, as he thanked his loyal employees for their support and wished them well.

The tension was palpable. When Greenway asked if there were any questions, a lady in the audience asked him why Travelodge didn't give their guests a good deal, like they did in South Africa. "Here, it costs almost the same if there's one person or two in the room. In South Africa, they are more reasonable." The tension evaporated in a ripple of exhausted laughter and the meeting adjourned.

Later that day, Greenway resigned as chairman, although it wasn't announced for another month.

The two men were soon confronting each other again in court. Greenway sued to get the retirement benefits he was promised in one of the "comfort" letters that Munk had signed in 1972. Munk sued to evict Greenway from the house in Rose Bay. Munk withdrew his suit when he found out Greenway had already left and Greenway got his package after two years of legal wrangling. Greenway went to live in the United States, where he has been successful as a hotelier and investor.

Two months after the Annual General Meeting, Sir Arthur George and Michael Sinclair resigned from the board.

Twenty years later, Greenway reflected: "I don't feel resentment. I sleep comfortably at night. Munk probably sleeps comfortably at night, but I sleep more comfortably. I realize I was naive."

Munk, as usual, wasted no time or energy reflecting on the events of that month. He had too many other fish to fry. Egypt needed his attention, and Pacific Harbour was still in dire straits. That evening, he started work on the grueling road of taking Travelodge private. He still had to restructure Travelodge to crank up its cash flow and he had to nail down the financing from Khashoggi.

5

THE ARAB
CONNECTION

I n the winter of 1974, far removed from the anguish and
drama of Southern Pacific Properties, David Gilmour was
doing what he does best — cruising the social scene
frequented by the international business and political elite. He
happened to meet an Egyptian at a dinner party in London. Not
just any Egyptian, of course, but Ashraf Marwan, an assistant
to the President of Egypt, Anwar Sadat. In the post-prandial
chatter, someone asked him what he did for a living so he told
them about the Fiji resort and Travelodge, the largest hotel
chain in the Southern Hemisphere. Marwan was intrigued.

"Couldn't you do the same thing in Egypt?" he asked.

"Well, yes. Certainly," replied Gilmour. "Anything can be
done." After some careful dancing around the subject, Gilmour

elaborated on the philosophy of the Fiji development. "Countries that do not have adequate infrastructure make a terrible mistake by going after numbers in their tourist promotion. Without the infrastructure, all you can offer is bed and breakfast. As a result, the average stay is only three or four days and the tourists don't leave much of their money behind."

Marwan was even more intrigued. This was exactly the trap the Egyptians had fallen into. Before Egypt fell under the sway of the Russians, tourists used to stay in the country an average of 20 days. Since the Egyptian government started modeling its tourist promotion on Bulgaria and Romania, both of which went for big numbers, the average stay of tourists had dropped to 6 days.

"What are you doing this weekend?" he asked Gilmour.

"Well, I'm going to the country, but I could postpone it."

"Would you, please? Come down to Egypt and I'll get you an audience with President Sadat."

Gilmour phoned Munk in great excitement the next day and was met with amused skepticism. It seemed just too good to be true, especially in a country that had been a Russian satellite for 20 years. "Go if you like," he told Gilmour, "but I'm not paying for the airfare."

Gilmour was fuming, but he was determined to go. There was no way he was going to miss the opportunity of meeting Sadat. So he bought his own ticket and went that weekend. In Cairo, he was met by Marwan and taken to his office at one o'clock in the morning. A few minutes later, Marwan was on the phone to the minister for construction, Osman Ahmed Osman, who dropped in to see them both at 1:30 a.m. Osman had been in charge of building the Aswan dam, Egypt's biggest project since the pyramids, and he listened with great interest to Marwan's idea that SPP might repeat in Egypt what it had built in Fiji.

He assured Gilmour that he would arrange for the necessary infrastructure to be delivered to the front gate of any tourist development SPP might build in Egypt — the electricity, the paved roads, the water, and the necessary transportation. Gilmour was rocking on his heels. He knew now that these people were serious. He didn't meet Sadat that trip, but he did on his second trip. Within a month, he had SPP's architects and designers working on a master plan and SPP was paying for his airline tickets.

Slightly more than three years later, Anwar Sadat finalized the sale to SPP of the rights to develop the plateau adjacent to the pyramids of Giza — the most spectacular ancient monuments in the world. It was a dream project — super-Fiji in a country with unending sunshine, next to a matchless destination. In the bleak despondency brought on by Pacific Harbour and Travelodge in 1974 and 1975, the Pyramids Oasis project provided the only splash of hope and opportunity for Munk, Gilmour, and Birchall, who quickly got sucked into the vortex of excitement and excruciating delicacy of Egyptian politics.

A small picture in a simple frame has pride of place in Peter Munk's office. It shows the president of Egypt with Munk and Gilmour on their knees, poring over their plans for their project. To this day, both of them are immensely proud of their relationship with Anwar Sadat. His enthusiasm, his understanding of his country's need for change, and his willingness to make radical decisions to power that process of change were not dissimilar to Munk's and Gilmour's approach to life, although he was painting on a much bigger canvas. His global vision and his down-to-earth personality earned him their lasting, unabashed admiration.

Sadat will be remembered, of course, for the way he changed the course of history by starting the peace process with Menachem Begin — paying for it with his own life when he was assassinated in 1981. But he was equally courageous and innovative in his attempt to decentralize, diversify, and modernize the Egyptian economy. He never really made much progress in that initiative, however, despite his valiant efforts.

Sadat faced two challenges in modernizing the chronically lethargic Egyptian economy — the Islamic fundamentalists, who wanted to suppress any form of modernization, and the stultifying bureaucracy, which was paralyzed to the point that it was incapable of embracing *any* change, let alone modernization. After 2,000 years of external rule, followed by King Farouk's corruption and Gamal Abdel Nasser's 20 years of Communist-inspired leadership, the Egyptian bureaucracy was a great deal more interested in avoiding mistakes than in improving anything. If he was to effect any change, Sadat had no choice but to take the bull by the horns and ram through his innovations, over the heads of the countless vested interests that stood to suffer from change.

In 1973, he announced his "open door" policy, which was aimed at encouraging foreign investors to come to Egypt by offering them favorable terms. One of the first major projects under these new rules was SPP's Pyramids Oasis project. With its daring imagination, the project held out the prospect of transforming the Egyptian tourist industry and sending a welcoming signal to Western visitors and investors alike. It also defiantly challenged the entire Egyptian economic establishment. Not only was the development company firmly under the control of foreigners, but its location on the doorstep of the most magnificent treasures of antiquity, just outside the Cairo city limits, rubbed salt into the wound of Egypt's inability to capitalize on its priceless assets. Sadat knew the risks and he put his personal prestige behind the project, granting it a special exemption from the normal planning procedures and shepherding it through the bureaucracy until it was approved by a vote in the National Assembly.

It was an extraordinary accomplishment for SPP to land this contract, considering it was less than a year after Egypt's traumatic war with Israel in October 1973 and SPP was run by a Jew. The Pyramids Oasis was an ambitious megaproject, with an estimated price tag of $500 million. Over a period of ten years, they planned to develop 2,500 acres into a spectacular luxury resort destination. It would incorporate 6,000 luxury villas and 5,500 apartments, all designed in the idiom of Egyptian culture. They also planned a hotel and convention center, linked to a communications satellite, and a fully equipped medical center. Its recreational facilities were to include riding stables, tennis courts, gardens, parks, nightclubs, casinos, restaurants, and a golf course, designed by Robert Trent Jones Jr. in the shape of an ankh, the ancient symbol of life. Visitors to Cairo would be able to see the resort from the sky as their planes came in to land, indelibly marked by the bright green of the golf-course ankh. It was a breathtaking conception.

Starting from the first meeting that Gilmour had with Ashraf Marwan in early 1974, it took SPP only three and a half years to move the project to the point where the first power shovel dug into the desert sand. That might seem like a long time in the context of Pacific Harbour Developments, which took about two years, but it was faster than the speed of light in Egypt's bureaucracy. As Birchall remarks drily: "The Arabs are quick to sign, but very slow to close."

The agreement in principle was signed at the end of 1974, the master plan was presented in early 1976, formal approval was obtained in April 1976, surveying took a year, then final approvals and the Ministerial decree were issued in June of 1977. It was a masterly display of a relentless focus on keeping the negotiations on track with a bureaucracy that never stopped looking for detours.

Munk's thirteenth golden rule:
If you focus, you win.

Munk's determination, focus, and ability to get things done persuaded a number of very wealthy Arabs that they could trust him with their money. His performance on the Pyramids Oasis project delivered to him the source of funds that pulled him out of the quagmire in the South Pacific and propelled him into Barrick. "The Arabs appreciated Munk because he knows how to make money," Birchall says.

The project was led by Gilmour, who lived for nothing else for a frenetic four years. It wasn't easy. He doesn't have Munk's iron constitution. "I used to get anemic dysentery," he remembers. "I should have been on intravenous feeding. I'd go to meetings with Sadat and I'd be hanging onto both sides of the chair. If I'd let go, I would have fallen off the chair. I finally found the secret. Take two ounces of whiskey before you go out to dinner. It lines your stomach."

A few months after work actually started at the Pyramids Oasis in November 1977, President Sadat paid his brief, historic visit across the eastern border to Prime Minister Menachem Begin. While the long-term effects of this action were profound, the short-term consequence was a violent chorus of opposition from many Egyptians (most particularly the Islamic fundamentalists) and the Russians, who were still smarting from their being kicked out of Egypt by Sadat. He now had to reap the whirlwind he had sowed over the previous decade.

In 1971, he had introduced a limited multi-party system (which forbade Islamic fundamentalists and Communists to form parties) and two years later, he had lifted censorship from the print media. These two freedoms were now used to the hilt against him. However, it was still illegal to criticize the president — a measure he had added to keep freedom of speech within reasonable bounds. The infinitely supple Egyptians therefore needed a surrogate target through which they could indirectly attack the president. SPP, it turned out, was ideal. Not only was it controlled by foreigners, but it was closely associated with Sadat, who had made it clear he backed it personally. By the end of 1977, the attacks were so fierce and so widespread that SPP knew it was going to be tough.

Three months after Sadat's trip to Jerusalem, the cash flow to the Pyramids Oasis was frozen. Three months after that, the project was canceled by Sadat, timed to coincide with his announcement of a series of measures restricting political activity. Only three weeks before announcing the cancellation, as he grappled with food riots over his raising the price of bread, he had told *Time* magazine that the Pyramids Oasis project was one of his top priorities.

The cancellation of the Pyramids Oasis had nothing to do with economics. The company had poured $8 million into new infrastructure. Sales of the villas and apartments were going very well — they had already taken in $7.5 million in down payments for 400 building sites. SPP had found, as expected, that rich Arabs throughout the Middle East were mourning the loss of their former playground in Beirut, and they were flocking to buy villas in the Oasis project. When sales opened for Egyptians, there was a line of buyers that stretched all the way around one Cairo block, waiting to hand over their money.

The cancellation was strictly political. In the final analysis, it died in a tidal wave of lies, innuendo, and jealousy. There was the antiquities professor at the University of Cairo, Dr. Nemat Fouad, who wrote a book called *The Venture of Pyramids Oasis: The Most Dangerous Aggression Against Egypt*. She said the site had great potential for antiquities, suggesting in one rather wild flight of imagination there may be whole cities beneath the plateau. Respected Egyptologists pointed out that the plateau for the development was higher than the plateau of the Giza pyramids, so ancient cities would never have been permitted there. Fouad also suggested, with an equal disdain for facts, that the small artificial lake in the golf course might leak and undermine the foundations of the pyramids. SPP sued Fouad for defamation, but the Egyptian court found in her favor. David Gilmour notes sadly that perhaps he should have hired Fouad's daughter when she tried to get a job at the site.

Another former friend who turned enemy was the Sabri family, owners of The Black Tent, the best-known nightclub in the nearby shanty town that was due to be removed to make way for the Pyramids Oasis. Cairenes loved the dozens of nightclubs in the shanty town because it was on a plateau above the Nile and a bit cooler — and they could do things there they couldn't do in town. The Black Tent's cash flow was reputed to be $1 million a day. The SPP people all used to go there and enjoy the owner's hospitality: "We were treated like royalty," Birchall says. "We got the best sheep's eyes and the belly dancers sat in our laps." Gilmour tried everything to find them a substitute location within the development, without success. "I was naive," he says. "I didn't realize that giving him a nice legitimate theater in the middle of the project would cramp his style."

Underlying everything was the xenophobic aftertaste of the British and French ownership of the Suez Canal, which was remembered in a kind of mantra. The political right wing didn't like foreign investors under any conditions and the extreme left didn't like capitalists — it wanted to go back to Nasser's socialism. And the fundamentalists hated anything Sadat supported. Nothing would ever change their views.

It is conceivable that Gilmour could have managed the project better to forestall the criticism. Indeed at least one of his colleagues felt he had too many hotheads in his team who were unable to deal with the diplomatic subtleties of Egyptian politics. Gilmour himself, not normally a man who shows his emotions, let the frustration get through to him sometimes. Once he picked up a board member by the lapels and threw him across the boardroom table. The hapless man had failed to achieve his goal of clearing the way for the project through the local bureaucracy.

"With all the lies, the nonsense, and the delays, we suddenly realized we were trapped in concrete," Gilmour says, the pain still obvious in his voice 20 years later. "The more the publicity built, the louder the hue and cry, the worse their fear became until it froze them and they became obstructionist."

In the end, it was not the power of any one of the opponents that killed the project, but the absence of supporters. Even though the president of the country was their most fervent supporter, they just ran out of people who were prepared to stand up to the vested interests, the stifling bureaucracy, the mendacious press, and the devious politicians.

When Sadat told them how sorry he was to have been forced to cancel the project, he told them to seek compensation. "There's no one person in the government who can sign a check for compensation," he told them. "You will have to sue us." Against the advice of all his friends, who told him he was throwing good money after bad, Munk pursued the Egyptian government relentlessly through international courts for 12 years before he won a settlement of $18 million. After legal expenses of $9 million, that netted the company $9 million. It meant they weren't out of pocket from the project, but it didn't substitute for the profits they would have made. Still, it gave him some satisfaction and the continuing respect of his Arab investors, who knew just what it took to win a lawsuit like that.

"If it had been a success, it would have been the thing I was most proud of," Gilmour says now, looking back. "Not necessarily the most rewarding financially — but I always fancied myself as David of Arabia! My father had been there in the First World War and volunteered after the war. It was the right sort of thing to do at that stage — the romance of doing something in your life that is great for the people, for the country."

In a report he wrote in April 1977, he said: "The political and economic risks are such that only keen students of the area still recognize the huge potential . . . Virtually every hotel company in the world has arrived in Cairo full of eager anticipation, only to depart months later, disillusioned and frustrated." Sometimes, you just get carried away.

Would he ever go back?

"Never, never. It will never be done."

Despite its ultimate failure, the Egyptian project played a crucial role in the success of Munk's business ventures. Had it not been for the mouth-watering prospects of the Pyramids Oasis, would Munk have been able to resist P&O's offer in 1974 to buy out him and his partners? Surprisingly, the Egyptian project also gave a welcome fillip to SPP's relationship with its main banker, Commonwealth Trading Bank. Birchall had, at first, been very nervous about how the bank would react to SPP's taking on a $500 million project in an unstable Third World country at a time when the company was scrambling to stay afloat. As soon as he knew the announcement was imminent, he went to Commonwealth Bank and told them the bad news. To his enormous relief, the banker was enthusiastic — he thought it would be a boon for SPP.

The project also had a high profile internationally and Munk and Gilmour got a lot of press. They also started meeting a lot of wealthy Arabs. One of the Arabs Gilmour met in 1974 was Adnan Khashoggi, who had a much higher profile than either of them.

Adnan Khashoggi is no stereotypical Bedouin. There is nothing hawk-nosed, lean, and flinty about this charming man. He has wide-set, soft brown eyes that sparkle under the longest eyelashes known to mankind, and a broad smile, never far away from his moustachioed lips. His supple mind, finely attuned to the infinite flexibility required of an accomplished trader, speaks more of generosity and gentleness than of the stoic endurance that suffuses the legendary weather-beaten Bedouin face.

This atypical Arab managed to bridge the gap between Arab and Western cultures to become the most spectacularly successful salesman in the 1970s. With an annual income of about $80 million, give or take a few million here and there, he earned a reputation as the leading playboy of the Western world. He was reputed to own 11 houses around the globe, including a magnificent condominium in New York, elegant properties in London, a chic apartment in Paris, and palatial homes in Lebanon, Riyadh, and several other places. He owned a magnificent yacht, the *Nabila,* anchored at Cannes, and, on the slightest whim, he flitted around the world in his own customized DC8, fitted out in extraordinary luxury as a second home and office. He loves his food and appreciates perfect presentation, so he employed French chefs on his yacht, at home, and even on his plane. It was only appropriate that he should acquire the nickname of the "jet-propelled Bedouin," since he spent an average of 80 hours a month in the air.

This kind of wealth inevitably attracted an enormous entourage of hangers-on, who managed to pick clean every scrap of surplus cash from his annual feast of commissions. Wherever he went, there were swarms of gorgeous women around him and legions of attentive men, bursting with brilliant ideas on how he could spend money in their direction. It was too much for many Westerners, who thought it was a dreadful circus. But it was just fine for Munk and Gilmour, who kept away from the entourage and saw the generous and charming man underneath all the wealth. Both of them hold an enormous amount of affection for Adnan Khashoggi to this day.

"He is a lovely guy," says Gilmour. "He's fascinating, very charming. You can see how he was one of the great salesmen of the world because he was larger than life. He could just charm the birds off the trees. I've seen him in households where he was a hit with little children, beautiful women, and big businessmen. He could just make you feel so good."

Khashoggi's holding company, Triad Holding Corp., owned more than 50 companies in an incredible array of industries, countries, and projects. The company was reputed at that time to be worth $400 million and it included Saudi dealerships for

Chrysler, Dodge, and Fiat, a ranch in Arizona, a meat packing firm in Brazil, a manufacturer of heavy-duty off-road vehicles based in the United States, a gypsum plant in Saudi Arabia, a California bank (Security National Bank), a furniture manufacturing plant in Lebanon, and a myriad of consulting and professional firms dealing with everything from interior design to the design of petro-chemical plants, from restaurants to insurance for international trade, from project management to venture capital.

In addition, when Gilmour first met him in the mid-1970s, Khashoggi was engaged in promoting three massive projects. He was putting together a $600 million world trade center in Egypt that would include hotels, a new pyramid, and scores of other goodies. He had also put together a plan to develop the Sudan, funded by $200 million drawn from 33 banks in Europe and the United States and guaranteed by the Saudi central bank. The projects he was contemplating in Sudan included sugar production, a textiles industry, mineral extraction, a cement plant, and a million-acre ranch for 100,000 head of beef. Finally, he also initiated a $250 million industrial park in Salt Lake City.

Khashoggi's approach to business was a remarkably good fit with Munk's. As his personal assistant, Bob Shaheen, remarked: "Mr. Khashoggi believes that anything is possible if one can only find the right way to do it; he has the gift of persuading others to see it. Through his understanding of people and by his knowledge of business, his enthusiasm and plausibility, he can persuade even the most skeptical to share his vision. And he has the ability to delegate responsibility."

Unlike many Arabs who grew wealthy in that decade, Khashoggi did not earn his money from oil. His father was the first Western-trained medical doctor in Saudi Arabia and became the personal physician to King Ibn Saud. He sent his son Adnan off to be educated in the United States, but when Adnan arrived in Colorado to start his petroleum engineering studies, there was a howling blizzard, so he switched out of engineering and moved to southern California where he enrolled in Chico State College. He never graduated because he quickly became embroiled in business.

His father used to send him an allowance of $5,000 a month and Khashoggi decided to invest it instead of spending it. He bought a dump truck, which he sold at a much higher price. This enabled him to buy three dump trucks, which he sold for even more, and so on. The Arabs are, above all else, traders, and Adnan Khashoggi was a star even in that competitive environment. Not long afterwards, he earned a $6 million commission on the sale of a fleet of trucks to a Saudi government agency and he knew he had found his niche. He acted mostly for large American firms and used his contacts in Saudi Arabia to gain entrée into the right offices, where he could apply his superb salesmanship. The Arabs were trying to figure out how to cope with the flash flood of money pouring into their countries, and he stood ready to help them buy lots of "toys" — mostly armaments, but also trinkets like Lockheed TriStar commercial aircraft. He became so successful that it didn't take long for a backlash to build up. When he earned a commission of $45 million from Northrop on a $4 billion sale of armaments to the Saudi Army, the American politicians started complaining. The newspapers picked up the theme and soon he was typecast as the billionaire arms dealer. No charge against him ever stuck and his name was cleared of the innuendos, but he never shook off the smell of that surge of bad publicity.

It's one thing to make money. It is quite another to keep it.

In the second department, Khashoggi quickly developed some serious problems. He hired McKinsey & Co. to look at Triad, then hired John Thompson to implement their recommendations. Thompson told the press: "The company had grown enormously and in doing so had failed to build in certain necessary business tools — financial management and control tools. Our objectives were becoming so diverse we were almost operating as a whole mass of separate islands and there was a danger of losing sight of our original aims. We felt we had to build in a higher degree of corporate professionalism. Our decision-making cycle was getting too long, for example, and in an opportunistic-style company, this can mean catastrophe." In other words, the company was completely out of control.

The consequences of his style and risk-taking were inevitable. In the late 1980s, his whole empire started to crumble. In 1989, he was even put in jail in New York on a charge of fraud in collusion with Imelda Marcos (from which he was acquitted) and Munk had to write a check for $5 million to get him released on bail. He had Munk's vision, but the lure of hedonism aboard the *Nabila* ensured he would never have the focus to manage his investments successfully.

All this grief had not yet reared its head, however, when Khashoggi was getting to know Munk and Gilmour in 1975. That year, he was still a star. Feature articles on him had appeared in *Time, Newsweek, Business Week*, the *New York Times*, and the *Wall Street Journal*. NBC did a 30-minute special on him. Eighty million dollars a year was rolling in and the sky was the limit. He appeared to be the living embodiment of available investment capital for a cash-starved Western world.

On one occasion, he asked Munk to be with him in his apartment in New York when the chairman of Chrysler Corp., Lee

Iacocca, came visiting. Chrysler was in serious trouble and Iacocca was looking desperately for a private investor with $300 million or $400 million spare cash to rescue the company. Khashoggi was a prime candidate as he already had a Chrysler dealership. Iacocca came with his senior financial executive and a senator from Michigan to make his pitch.

"There were just the two of us and the three of them in Adnan's library in the Olympic Towers," Munk remembers. "It was a very dramatic and powerful presentation, which only Lee Iacocca could make."

Afterwards, Khashoggi asked Munk what he thought he should say, because he didn't want to get involved. "I don't have the money," he said, sitting in his palatial paradise high above the streets of New York.

"Tell him," said Munk, "that really you are a man from the Middle East and Chrysler is motherhood in America. Tell him 'It's ridiculous, unacceptable for me, just a mere man of the desert, to have the cheek to come forward and be involved controlling this priceless gem of America.'" Khashoggi liked the advice and told Iacocca that it would be humiliating and unacceptable for the United States to have one of its major car makers controlled by a Saudi.

Iacocca listened carefully. "Well," he said, "what if the president of the United States himself told you that you were welcome as an investor in one of our great companies?"

Khashoggi looked puzzled.

"May I borrow the phone?"

Khashoggi assented and Iacocca called his secretary and asked her to patch him through to the White House. The phone was answered within seconds.

"Jimmy," he said. "Now I wanna introduce you on the phone

to the most charming man. I think you heard me mention I was coming to visit him. Would you please tell him, Mr. President, he's very welcome to take as much of Chrysler as he'd care to?"

Iacocca handed the phone to Khashoggi whose rolling brown eyes were looking reproachfully at Munk. Jimmy Carter backed up Iacocca all the way and Khashoggi had to endure the embarrassment of turning down Iacocca's request despite the intervention of the most powerful man on earth. It would have been the best investment he ever made. The shares were going for $3 each and he would have had additional options at the same price for three years. He would have been able to maintain his lifestyle for the rest of his life on that investment alone.

When Khashoggi met Gilmour, he was immediately interested in the Egyptian project. He told Gilmour that he had made all his money in the United States and in other countries outside the Middle East. Now he wanted to plough some of it back into the Middle East. Egypt sounded good to him. SPP was then in the process of creating a new, wholly owned subsidiary called SPP (Middle East), which was to be the vehicle for SPP's investment in the project. The project itself was to be implemented by a company called the Egyptian Tourist Development Company (ETDC), which was given all the development rights. SPP (ME) owned 60% of ETDC, while the other 40% was owned by a government tourism agency. Toward the end of 1974, Triad signed a commitment to invest $5 million in SPP (ME). That agreement was important in giving the project legitimacy in the eyes of potential Arab investors, and Gilmour pursued other potential sources of money aggressively, including His Royal Highness Prince Nawaf Ben Abdul-Aziz, a brother of King Saud and a former minister of finance.

As with every deal concluded with Arabs, however, it is a long and tortuous road between signing an agreement in principle and receiving the money. Consummate traders that they are, the Arabs are adept at wringing out the last ounce of advantage in their deals, and they are quite content to string out the bargaining — which they enjoy anyway — for months, while they circle around the deal to ensure that its substance and perception are consistent with their own needs and feelings, even if it means killing the deal in the process. It can be a battle just to get signatures on final documents when all the details have been resolved. Gilmour painfully remembers the times he went to Saudi Arabia to perform the ceremonial signing of a concluded agreement and was made to cool his heels in some antechamber for two weeks by Prince Nawaf. It would have been a loss of face for His Royal Highness to acknowledge the exigencies of the schedules of visiting Westerners.

Negotiating with the Arabs is an art that tests Western values to their outer limits. For Westerners, the process is a test of patience that is physically draining and endlessly supple intellectually. It requires an unusually high level of energy, a commodity with which Munk is generously endowed.

Munk's fourteenth golden rule:
Don't give up.

As the Khashoggi negotiations dragged on, Munk changed his strategy. He had always intended to sell part of SPP (ME) to an Arab investor. (Indeed, part of the agreement in principle signed with Khashoggi in 1974 specifically mentioned other investors in SPP [ME]). During 1975, Munk gained confidence that Khashoggi wasn't the only investor who was likely to put his money in SPP (ME).

The Saudi Arabians were especially keen to invest in the development of Egypt, because they felt that by going to war with Israel in 1973, Egypt had been the principal catalyst in causing the price of oil to quadruple. They figured that investing in Egypt was a way of repaying the favor that Egypt had done them. Most Saudis, however, were not interested in SPP's South Pacific assets — it was too far away and foreign to their historical preoccupations. Khashoggi was a little different. He wasn't bound by his roots. He prided himself on being able to think like a Westerner when he was in the West and like an Arab when he was in the Middle East. Because he is such a man of the world, Munk and Gilmour began to think that they might be able to divert his investment away from SPP (ME), which appeared to have adequate prospects for funding, and into the parent company, which desperately needed cash.

Khashoggi's advisers weren't interested, however, and they dug in their heels. They would put the money only into the company that was directly and solely concerned with the Egyptian project. There was another problem — in order to avoid dilution of the existing shareholders, Munk wanted Khashoggi to invest in SPP at a price way above the price at which its shares were trading on the stock market. He explained to them that the price of SPP shares on the Hong Kong Stock Exchange was totally unrealistic and did not reflect the real value of the company. In its most recent annual report, SPP had shown that each share was backed by net tangible assets of HK$2.34 — but the stock market was valuing the shares much, much lower, having dropped the price to a low of 45¢(HK) toward the end of 1975. Munk couldn't ask Khashoggi to pay the full asset value per share, but he wanted a price at least partway toward the asset value. This boggled the minds of the professional advisers (Khashoggi himself rarely got involved) but Munk persisted, giving them an education on how land and buildings were valued. He did not budge from his contention that HK$1.50 was a fair price when the market was trading at 50¢(HK).

The advisers looked over SPP's calculations very carefully. "It was the most thorough due diligence I have ever seen," says Birchall. "They looked at everything — the management, the accounts, the operations." Birchall welcomed the small army of accountants and lawyers and stuck to his guns, explaining how the property was valued on the basis of the money they were going to make from it. On the basis of their *real* expectations, he demonstrated, the valuation was extremely conservative.

By the time the negotiations were coming to a conclusion in late 1975, SPP had gained management control of Travelodge and they could talk up their prospects even higher, despite the inadequate cash flow in the short term. Still Khashoggi's people balked.

At the same time, Gilmour was close to getting signatures from Prince Nawaf and his brother, Prince Fawaz bin Abdul-Aziz, the governor of Mecca province, who were on the point of offering to pay $8.75 million for 25% of SPP (ME). Negotiations were also well under way to sell another 10% of the company to other Arab investors, which would reduce SPP's stake in SPP (ME) to 65% by the end of 1976. This was more than Munk needed — in fact, it enabled him to withdraw the $2 million SPP had invested in the company, so the company's investment was reduced to almost nothing. Munk was more determined than ever to lure Khashoggi into SPP because he knew that Khashoggi's money was the only money that he had any chance of attracting into the parent company.

In late 1975, he decided to turn the full force of his own salesmanship on the super salesman himself. He chose to do it in London, where he could showcase some of his prestigious connections. P&O was still a valued shareholder after its bid for SPP had been rejected, even if the new chairman, Lord Inchcape, was less fond of Munk's approach to business than his predecessor on SPP's board, Lord Geddes, had been. Munk thought a lunch in P&O's august 200-year-old head office would impress on Khashoggi just how desirable it was to sit as a director on the board of SPP rather than SPP (ME). He also needed to pacify Lord Inchcape who had initially resisted Munk's plan to bring in Khashoggi as a shareholder. Inchcape had backed down only when Munk threatened to sue him for obstructing his efforts to protect their company's best interests. Now Munk told him that if they handled Khashoggi right, they would get him to pay 10¢ more for the stock they issued him. Inchcape agreed to have Munk and Khashoggi for lunch.

"I knew that if we were late for this meeting, the P&O directors wouldn't wait for us and it would seriously harm the relationship," Munk remembers. "It was already remarkable that they should have a Jew and an Arab together in their dining room. I knew that Khashoggi was notoriously late — he rarely got up before noon. So I went to his townhouse and banged on the door at 11 o'clock to make sure we got there on time."

The P&O dining room is magnificent, redolent of the proud history of the company — and it duly had its effect on Khashoggi. Inchcape was still skeptical, however. P&O had been dealing with the Arabs for more than 100 years and they knew them very well. He told Munk he would never get a single dollar out of them. He was not alone in his thinking — many of Munk's associates thought it unwise to go into partnership with Khashoggi, whose reputation as a shady arms dealer gave some of them, as one put it, "the creeps." Munk had no such qualms.

As Khashoggi started to waver on Munk's insistence that he invest in the parent company, his advisers hammered Munk on the price issue. They refused to accept the logic of paying three times the market value for a stock. When the deal came to the point where it was within days of collapsing, Khashoggi decided to get involved himself. He called a meeting of both sides in his London townhouse, which was on Upper Brook St., just around the corner from the American embassy. They met in his meeting room around his magnificent table.

"There were 12 of them and 6 of us," says Munk. "Adnan asked what the status was and they said there was no agreement on the price. So he asked me to leave the room with him."

They walked down a long corridor lined with many doors. Khashoggi popped his head into several rooms, which had various secretaries and employees hard at work, until he found an empty one he could use. It was sparsely furnished with only two iron beds — presumably a bedroom for the bodyguards.

"We sat facing each other on the beds, our faces a foot away," Munk remembers. "He put his hand on my leg and asked for my pen and a piece of paper. He asked me a series of questions, writing down the answer to each one: 'How many shares does P&O own? How many does Trust Houses Forte own?' And so on down the list." The total came to 150 million, counting the 40 million that Munk was proposing to sell to Khashoggi.

Khashoggi was calculating the impact on each shareholder of the next revaluation of the properties, particularly those of Travelodge, where Munk was planning a write-down on the problem properties equivalent to about 10% of the total net assets of Travelodge. This would cause each shareholder to lose about 10% of the value of their SPP shares. Khashoggi was contemplating buying 40 million shares at HK$1.50, for a total investment of HK$60 million. Munk's personal holdings were worth about HK$10 million. Their respective losses with a 10% devaluation would be HK$6 million and HK$1 million.

"Now," said Khashoggi, "if you issue me 40 million shares for a dollar and a half, then after the revaluation I lose 6 million dollars. You lose 1 million." He went down the whole list of shareholders. "Now, if we price the shares at a dollar, and I put 2 million dollars into a Swiss bank account in your name, then you have a net gain of 1 million and I lose only 4 million." The other shareholders were protected regardless, because Khashoggi was still buying his shares at way above the market price. "Now tell me where I have made a mistake. Is my arithmetic right?"

Munk was stunned. He didn't know what to say. He said he couldn't possibly do it. "I told him that our cultures were completely different and in my culture this would be impossible to do when I was negotiating on behalf of the company which employed me."

Khashoggi told Munk to think about it and he said he would. They went back into the room, Khashoggi holding Munk's hand, and he announced that there were matters to reflect on and the meeting would reconvene the next day at the same time. The next morning Munk said he had not changed his mind, so Khashoggi told his advisers to go ahead with the deal at Munk's price — with two provisos: Munk and Gilmour would be tied to the management of the money (if they left SPP, the money would be withdrawn); and the money had to be spent on Egypt, even if it was placed in the parent company.

"I think he gained enormous respect for me then," says Munk. "He knew that in any future dealings with me, he would know that I would be absolutely straight with him and would protect his interest as a shareholder."

Even then, there was one last haggle, which lowered the price to HK$1.31 and raised the number of shares to 44 million. After legal expenses, the deal swelled SPP's coffers by $11.8 million and gave Khashoggi a 29% interest in the company. If Munk had settled for a price close to the market, Khashoggi would have been given 115 million shares for the same amount, which would have given him just over 50% of the total shares. Alternatively, by giving him 29% of the company at the market price, SPP would have netted only $4.3 million.

It was some feat to persuade the world's most famous salesman to pay triple the market rate for his shares. It took Munk a whole year to wear down the wall of resistance in Khashoggi's camp, but it made all the difference strategically. If he had settled for a lower price, Khashoggi would have owned half of SPP and Munk would not have been in a position to demand that he should retain management control despite Khashoggi's much greater cash contribution. With Khashoggi as a minority shareholder, Munk had the freedom to do as he saw best in rationalizing Travelodge operations to multiply its cash flow — and he had enough new cash to take Travelodge private.

6

BREAKTHROUGH

Within days of ousting Alan Greenway to take management control of Travelodge, Peter Munk started putting his turnaround strategy into effect. Part of that strategy was privatizing the company, but the timing for that was determined by the glacial progress of the negotiations with Adnan Khashoggi. In the meantime, the changes to the way Travelodge was run couldn't wait.

The strategy was never articulated as a grand plan. Rather, he went at the changes that would bring the biggest benefits most quickly. The top priority was unloading the marginal hotels that had been targeted for disposal many months previously by Greenway (at the urging of Munk and other directors), but which were being sold at a snail's pace. Munk immediately put that program into high gear, setting specific targets for the prices they should fetch and the rate at which they should be sold. The poor profit margins of these hotels meant that their disposal did not damage the bottom line, while the proceeds from the sales made an important dent in the debt burden. He identified 35 hotels that he wanted out of the chain, even if the property market was depressed — and he put Pat Samuel on commission to ride herd on the program.

The second immediate priority was to invigorate the lackluster management in the chain. One of the principal reasons for the low caliber of many hotel managers was that Greenway's head office had expropriated their power to control their own properties. Inevitably, because the head office people who were making all the decisions were far away from the scene of the action, they became secretive, freezing the managers out of the information loop. "The hotel managers really didn't know what was going on," Birchall says. "They were looking over their shoulders. We got rid of a whole layer of middle management in head office that was totally self-serving. We had to get to the hotel manager. He was the guy who was getting people to come back. We recognized that to get a new face [hotel guest] was going to be extremely difficult, but to get repeat business, that was what it was all about. We had to go to the point of sale."

Munk was a decade ahead of his time. This philosophy was at the heart of a complete restructuring of the hotel management. Alan Greenway had employed 149 people in his head office. Munk let 38 go. The 10 employees in the group development department were no longer needed after they junked the silver trowel, which had been used for the ceremonial first dig in new developments. He also eliminated one of the three senior management positions, tightened up the 33-person marketing department, and slashed the numbers in the 22-person operations department, through which the hotel managers had reported to Greenway. These measures reduced the total cost of head office from A$3.2 million in 1975 to an annual rate of A$2.4 million — a saving of A$800,000.

The person who carried the SPP banner in implementing the new operating style was Roger Kirby, the accountant who had been working with Birchall since 1973. He switched from SPP to Travelodge immediately after Greenway was displaced, taking over George Haines's job as general manager of finance, while Haines rose to chief general manager because he represented continuity to the independent directors — and Munk needed him while his own people became familiar with the operation. The problem, however, was that Haines was still loyal to Greenway. He did not defy Munk, but neither did he initiate anything without being directly asked to do so.

Uncharacteristically, Munk did not fire him. Instead he put in Kirby below him to build on the foundations he had laid with his insider's information over the previous year and develop a complete picture of the chain's operations. "Kirby was a wonderful guy," Munk says. "He wasn't taken in by the bull of the Australian accommodation industry. While he was monitoring our investment, for that year and a half, being an accountant, he identified many of the problems — declining room rates, new hotels — so he gave me the ammunition to know how to turn things around."

With Big Daddy no longer holding their hands in Sydney, some of the managers were not up to the new approach and it was crucial to know quickly who could cope with the Munk philosophy and who couldn't. Munk took it upon himself to find out — and his task was unwittingly made a lot easier by

Greenway, who had gone to some trouble to keep Munk out of the picture among the staff at Travelodge. When Munk took control, the employees did not even recognize him. He used that to his advantage. Every weekend toward the end of 1975, he and Melanie would go to one of the Travelodge hotels.

"I went out under a different name," he says. "Every weekend, we went to a different place. I rented a car. I'd check in as Mr. Smith. That's how I saw Australia — Adelaide, Perth, Darwin, Brisbane. And I stayed there for the weekend as Mr. Smith. I went down to the cafeteria and listened and made notes. It was very simple. When I go as the chairman, everyone sucks up to you. I would never find out what the service is like for the average Joe. But you do find out if you go there as Mr. Smith for the weekend and you ask for room service — or you're checking in or you're checking out. Some of the hotels were spectacular — they really catered, they understood what service was all about. Some of the hotels were lousy, so these managers were changed." He didn't let George Haines and Roger Kirby know what he was doing. He didn't even tell Bill Birchall — he just quietly made sure the managers were changed.

The other side of that coin was to motivate the managers who stayed. Birchall explains Munk's method: "You've got to give them authority, responsibility, and the corresponding remuneration. So, these guys who had no authority to change room rates . . . to change a menu . . . or to even blow their nose were given authority. Some couldn't take it, of course, but most did. The result was that in about 12 months, a guy who had been making $25,000 a year was making $40,000 a year and looking forward to making $50,000 next year. This was exciting. And it was starting to rub off, but you couldn't do it en masse, you couldn't drag them all into one room and do it, like that. You made it work at a couple of properties. Then you exposed other people to those properties and what you were doing to make it work."

For the first time in their careers, the hotel managers had targets — targets that were monitored and enforced under Munk's active leadership. Haines couldn't articulate the vision or set the targets, but he implemented Munk's wishes professionally. As Samuel observed: "SPP provided the imagination — those glimpses of future prospects that George Haines and his people would never have seen."

Munk's fifteenth golden rule:
Leaders should compensate for other people's weaknesses,
and draw on their strengths.

Munk was particularly concerned that hotel managers have the power to discount rates if they felt it was appropriate. Under Greenway, each hotel had a fixed room rate and if a manager wanted to offer a discount to persuade a guest to stay at his hotel, he had to phone head office for permission. Munk wanted his managers to make a judgment when someone walked in toward the end of the day. If the guest looked wealthy, he wanted the manager to quote the full rate. If he looked like a "shopper," he should offer a discount, so that the room would pull in some revenue instead of sitting empty that night. He hammered his senior executives to make the organization supportive of hotel managers who discounted selectively. It was a major change for a group of people for whom discounting had always been a lose–lose situation — they got the blame if revenue suffered, head office got the credit if occupancy improved.

To check on the progress in his initiative to give more power to the managers, Munk was not averse to visiting a few managers (again without telling his top management), pouring them full of beer, and asking them to tell him if head office was supporting their making decisions for themselves. Head office wasn't happy at being second-guessed, but nobody tried to sabotage the delegating process.

Travelodge was, in fact, something of a new experience for Munk. In all his business endeavors up to that point, he had started the business himself, which gave him an intimate knowledge about every tiny detail and wrinkle in the organization. Even in Fiji, where he delegated a lot of the day-to-day management when he moved his office to London, he knew the operation so well that he could deal personally with any problem — and he could smell out emerging problems before they even happened. In Travelodge, the organization had been built by someone else and he had no experience in the hotel business. It also had 3,000 employees whom he could never hope to get to know. It was his first big business.

Wisely, he did not try to reproduce in Travelodge the leadership style he had used early in his career. In the months immediately following his takeover from Greenway, he was deeply involved in the turnaround — apart from his sorties into the "field" to take the pulse of his hotel operations, he was also active in the financial community. During this period, he lived in Sydney, renting a magnificent home on Point Piper in the fashionable eastern suburbs (and paying for it out of his own pocket). He and Melanie were something of a star couple on the social scene, where his contacts with such leaders as Sir Peter Abeles in the business and financial communities gave him an easy entrée to the elite. However, he never really took to Australia or the Australians. For one thing, he wasn't interested in Australian sports, which disqualified him from any serious friendship with most of the sports-mad Aussies. Also, his global interests and European temperament did not resonate with down-to-earth cobbers. So it was no great surprise when he decided to move his family back to London once his changes were starting to work their way through the system — he was getting progressively less and less involved in the details of the turnaround and his constant presence was not essential.

Once he moved from Sydney, his visits became increasingly infrequent. The air trip around the world was hard on him physically. "He would only reluctantly go to Australia for meetings," says Pat Samuel, who was then deputy chairman of Travelodge and the senior man on the spot. "He preferred to stay in England. He didn't like traveling — it used to upset him for days, physically and mentally. His management was done more by telephone than it was by personal meetings."

The combination of his London base and his managerial distance from the Travelodge trenches meant Munk had to learn a whole new style of managing and leading. Because he was not always on the spot to exert the enormous power of his personality when the need arose, he had to make use of the limited time he spent in Australia to initiate strategic changes with such clarity and force that they would be correctly implemented without his persistent supervision. In the five years between taking management control of the chain and selling it, he felt his way into his new role, making a lot of mistakes on the way, as he developed the *modus operandi* that he carried into Barrick Gold with Bob Smith some years later.

If Peter Munk brings one thing to the art of leadership, it is focus. He has the energy and the will to align every fiber in his body in the direction of his chosen objective — and nothing will shake him loose. He says it best himself: "My kids could have fallen off a mountain, my mother could have died, but if I'm fighting for something, I'm totally unaware. That's all I think about when I dream, I sleep, I think, when I get up in the morning. When I go to a party, that's all I think about. So I'm good at focusing."

He learned in Clairtone that he had the capacity to lead a group of people into displaying the same kind of dedication that he himself possesses. He demonstrated in Fiji, against insuperable odds, that he could repeat the trick. By sheer force of personality, he holds his entire management team almost obsessively focused on their clearly articulated objectives. But it is important to understand that Munk's own focus is quite different from his partners' and employees' focus. For one thing, it is much more short-lived and much more intense. He beams his focus on his management team to align them with his goal, then he moves on, leaving the team to sustain the intensity of their focus while they strive to achieve the objective. He is then free to allow his mind to range over innumerable other, unrelated business opportunities.

Pat Samuel remembers that, for many years, Munk was fond of telling him: "Don't carry a briefcase full of different deals. Concentrate on one deal and do it well." But Munk never followed and never intended to follow his own advice. His secret is that he carries two briefcases — one for his single, principal objective, and another, like Pat Samuel's, stuffed with potential opportunities. At any one point of time, he gives the principal objective everything that it needs in terms of his time, energy, and imagination. But he has such prodigious energy that no one focus can ever use it all up — so the surplus energy goes to the second briefcase. He can handle them all. He is, in fact, anything but focused.

It's a style that takes some getting used to. "Peter would arrive [from London] and run around using one of his great talents, which is his personality, to resolve various problems," says Mark Johnson of Hill, Samuel. "He was here for a month, all guns blazing, wanting to get a variety of things done and then going off onto something else. You would get a couple of phone calls after he'd left, then it would tail off until he got back, because then it was in Bill's hands."

For this approach to work, Munk needs high-fidelity amplifiers to broadcast his vision. He can succeed only to the extent that he has trustworthy managers who are more consistent than he is and who can carry his message into the furthest recesses of the organization. They are the people who must take his focus and make it happen. It follows that picking the right amplifiers is crucial to his success, but most of Munk's friends acknowledge that this is one area where his performance has been spotty. He has often made less-than-wise choices of people for senior executive jobs. Sometimes he has leaned toward people who shared his penchant for dreaming big or who told him what he wanted to hear. Other times, he has chosen people whose personalities he liked. The eternal optimist, he has always wanted to believe the best of the people he works with.

In one case, he liked the look of a graphic artist who had graduated from Cambridge University and he appointed him sales manager to report to the marketing manager at a salary 50% higher than his boss's. He also tried twice to hire an operations director to report to Kirby without consulting Kirby — one of them quit before he took up his duties and the other was finessed into a lesser job by Kirby. "He kept foisting the wrong people on me," Kirby comments without any sign of rancor.

However, Munk's fallibility in so critical an area is not the problem it might be assumed to be — he is so quick to realize he has made a mistake that he corrects it before any damage is done. His optimism does not live on in the face of evidence to the contrary, and he pays the unfortunate executive handsomely for what he considers to be his own mistake. Of course, there have also been a lot of excellent choices between the mistakes. Over the years, he has steadily accumulated a powerful team of amplifiers who are in perfect tune with him. In the Travelodge years, however, he was still early in his learning curve, although he did encourage Bill Birchall to step in to provide the necessary, steady consistency that complemented his strategic focus. And his record has improved with experience.

Birchall was never a manager in Travelodge. He modulated, sustained, and amplified Munk's leadership, but he never became embroiled in the day-to-day management of the chain. That was left to George Haines initially, then later Roger Kirby, although neither of them ever graduated into Munk's inner circle of amplifiers. Even when Kirby became managing director, Munk never gave him authority over the operations director. Kirby suffered the inevitable consequences in his relationship with his vice president, but the process was so open, he could never take umbrage. Munk is simply not governed by the conventions of management.

"Of all the people I've worked for, I probably liked him the best," Kirby says. "He would be the most persuasive, the strongest, and most logical. He's also the one with the least background and experience in managerial training. He had no conception of structured management, how you've got to play the game. You can't move around the ranks of managers like that. If you've got layers of managers, you move through the layers — otherwise, you destroy the whole function. He didn't accept that. And why should he?"

Indeed. Munk makes no apology for his approach, which is the essence of entrepreneurship. He is not a steady-as-she-goes manager. If he was, he would never have achieved as much as he has. Consistency is a prison as much as a solid foundation, which is why the best MBA graduates are rarely entrepreneurial.

"He's fine for short periods, to fix it," says David Hoare, a banker who is more attuned to conventional management, "but not long term. If it didn't work, he'd kick it. That's not a criticism. Peter's contribution is made in a leadership way. He came here, lent moral support and commitment and that's important. That's part of the leading bit as opposed to the supervising."

"In terms of working for him," says Mark Johnson of Hill, Samuel, "he's the most fun. I can't think of a client who was more fun, because he was so energetic. And because he wanted to motivate you to do your best for him, he would flatter you outrageously and encourage you. He wasn't one of these surly, nasty clients who attempts to flog you. His method is to encourage and hype you up, to communicate his own enthusiasm. But he was not a people management person. Roger Kirby had various ups and downs and Bill Birchall had ups and downs. However, he's deft at picking up on people's hot buttons very quickly. The best thing about Peter would be his strategic success."

Munk understands perfectly where he can make his most effective contribution. "I was very involved with strategy," he says. "That was my job. It wasn't David's [Gilmour's] or Bill's [Birchall's] — it was *my* job. That's all I do. I don't keep books. I get bored with balance sheets, unless, of course, something goes wrong. But the details . . ."

Even that's not entirely true, however. He doesn't often get involved in the implementation of his strategies, but he monitors monthly results very closely. He was — and still is — a glutton for information. Sitting in his office in London, he could put his finger on any aspect of the operation at will. "We gave him very detailed monthly statements," Kirby says. "It was usually Bill who would raise the queries, but quite often it would be Munk. 'Have you sold this, have you sold that? Why is that figure different?' In Kirby's monthly reports to Munk, there were five pages of statistics and information on each hotel, showing every conceivable cost, down to the laundry.

He was a tiger if he had set a target and the responsible executive's progress wasn't fast enough for him. Many times, Kirby was awoken in the middle of the night by a call from London, demanding to know why he hadn't sold more of the small hotels. Kirby would have to fumble in the dark, trying to find his packet of cigarettes and his summary sheet of the status of the program, as he struggled to give coherent replies to Munk's interrogation. He finally developed, for exactly this kind of occasion, a half-page crib-sheet that summarized the current status of the whole program for all 35 hotels that were on the block.

Besides his gradual accumulation of effective amplifiers for his message, Munk developed another technique to penetrate into the furthest recesses of Travelodge with his vision of how he would like the company to run: speeches. In Clairtone and Pacific Harbour, he had spread the gospel through direct contact with his employees, but he couldn't possibly do it for Travelodge's 3,000 employees from his base in London. He had to replace his technique of leading by example with his own special brand of leadership — by speeches and philosophical exhortation. "He used to speak on the phone a lot," Kirby remembered years later. "Not on the boring, managerial side of it. But on the philosophical side." His speeches have become a major part of his leadership, much admired by all his employees. He doesn't try to impart information in them. He imparts spirit. Just as he leveraged his C$300,000 purchase of Fiji swampland 40 times, so he leverages his brief contacts with his employees by infusing them with a spirit that changes their lives and points them on a path that will ensure success for Munk's company — and for themselves. Success is creating wealth.

Peter Munk is a quite extraordinary orator — to a single listener or to a crowd of a thousand. His inspiring rhetoric invariably focuses on one of two subjects — human values and wealth creation. He does it in such a way that his listeners seem to be able to draw inspiration from it — an insight into how they can personally do their job better, so that they can contribute to the leader's vision. It's almost mystical. How do you make clean toilet bowls seem important to the financial survival and prosperity of a hotel chain? Munk knew how:

"We had 50-odd hotels and the difference between breaking even and losing money and making money was unbelievable," he says today. "Each and every hotel had maybe ten departments — the bartender, the guy who supervises the ladies who clean the toilet bowls, the guy who negotiates the turning on and turning off of the air conditioning, and so on. Each of those guys has an eight-hour shift. You just multiply that — 20 shifts a day for 50 hotels for 365 days a year." The arithmetic is powerful. If each one of those department heads saved $1 per shift, the bottom line would improve by $365,000 a year.

"The bartender can just pour — he doesn't care. It comes to millions and millions of dollars. It is for management to be able to talk to those guys, to give them the knowledge that, God, they can make a difference with their eight-hour shift. When they talk to a customer, or when they don't look when they pour a drink, or when the cleaning lady pours too much cleaning material when she cleans the bowl. If you add it up in a cumulative sense, it can make a company that can go forward and buy another hotel and grow so that everybody benefits — or we can shrink, we can get taken over and we lose our jobs and we end up becoming losers. Why not be part of a winning team? Then you can make a difference. You feel better making a difference: (a) You feel better because you are on the winning team; (b) You feel better because you have contributed. Everybody wants to contribute. We all want to be part of the success . . ."

Munk's sixteenth golden rule:
People are motivated by much more than money.
You just cannot be humdrum. There has to be a joy in
achieving objectives, a joy in creating wealth,
a joy in making properties better.

In speeches to thousands and in small meetings, inside the company and outside, to senior executives and to the lowliest employee, Munk never tires of spreading his gospel. His unabashed commitment to wealth creation, allied with his insistence on focus, makes for a powerful message. It's intensely personal. It's not a packaged version of "personnel management" enunciated by the latest management theory. Every employee who hears the message feels it is intended for him or her personally. They feel they have had a private conversation with him, no matter how many other people were there.

The transformation of Travelodge was well on its way when the Khashoggi deal finally went through in May 1976. The same month, SPP had a board meeting at which Munk sought approval for his plan to bid for the 42% of the Travelodge shares that SPP did not already own. Among those present at the meeting were Charles Dunn, an executive in Triad Holdings, and Essam Khashoggi, Adnan's brother, who usually represented his interests with Munk. In his report, Munk told the board that in the six months he had been in control, he had already made progress in relieving the financial pressure on Travelodge. The program to dispose of unprofitable properties had already netted the company more than $6 million, which had been used to reduce the crippling debt burden. He had also made drastic cutbacks to overhead expenses, reducing head office staff by 25%.

Travelodge was also able to pass a major test by renewing the $11 million loan from Commonwealth Trading Bank in March 1976 — a feat that might not have been possible without the improved cash situation. "The first thing we did when we took control was we asked to have lunch with the bankers," Birchall recounts. "We said, 'We're going to repay you and this is how we're going to repay you.' And we repaid them ahead of time. That bank, the Commonwealth Trading Bank, was ready from there on in to provide us with whatever we wanted. It's not complicated. Greenway had been running the business, frankly, in an irresponsible financial manner. He had bank debts for which he had no plan of either repaying or renewing."

Haines gave the board a generally positive report on the hotel group's activities, forecasting that profit before tax and extraordinary items would rise to A$1.3 million from A$0.8 million the previous year, with most of the improvement coming from the reduction in head office overhead expenses. He cautioned that the situation continued to be serious at the three problem hotels — Narita Airport in Japan, the Beachcomber Hotel in Tahiti, and The Boulevard in Sydney.

Before agreeing to the acquisition of the remaining Travelodge shares, Essam Khashoggi asked for an analysis of the financial implications of the decision. Birchall burned the midnight oil, working till 3 a.m. to prepare the financial projections. He estimated that the A$4 million required to buy out the minority shareholders would deliver a return on investment of 62% p.a. over the following five years. This assumed a price of 48¢(A) for the minority shares. Moreover, the takeover would not need any funds from SPP. Munk proposed to finance the cost of buying the shares with a bank loan secured by a Certificate of Deposit for A$4 million, which would be provided by the Khashoggi money that had just been invested in SPP. Once the takeover was complete, Munk proposed to have Travelodge take over the loan, so that Khashoggi's money could be returned to SPP or SPP (ME) by the middle of 1977. The board duly gave its approval for the takeover and two months later SPP announced its bid for the minority shares in Travelodge at a price of 40¢(A).

It was an extremely aggressive price. The net assets per share in the last annual report had been A$1.20, but the share was trading at 28¢(A) to 32¢(A) shortly before the offer was announced. The market price is an important indicator of a company's value, but Munk had always argued — and continues to argue — that the true value of a company has little to do with the market price. In this case, the market was his strongest argument, which he used to the hilt, but there was an uproar anyway over the low price being offered the Travelodge shareholders. The newspapers had a field day, complaining that he was stealing the chain from Australian shareholders.

Munk's view was simple. "We went with 40¢ only because that was the lowest price we felt we could get away with. If we could have got away with 30¢, we would have tried 30¢. If it had been 50¢, we would have bid 50¢. We had to get the assets, because we had to get the cash flow. We had to start selling the properties and get the cash into our company, so it didn't matter how much we paid for them — we had to get the assets."

The battle turned out to be a great deal tougher than he may have anticipated. He had all his ducks lined up, however. He was able to paint a convincing picture of the chain as being in the most desperate straits — not so much in danger of failure, as in a position where profits were unlikely to improve for many years and vast sums of money would have to be poured into it to revive it. He outlined some of the problems — particularly the three problem hotels — and said: "We do not think that Travelodge has the resources itself to cope with even a limited set of these problems or to meet the cash requirements which may arise from them. We believe it is essential for SPP to be in a position to give its full support, both managerial and financial, to overcome these problems. It cannot do this effectively, or indeed equitably as between minority and majority shareholders, unless it holds 100% of the stock."

As the weeks wore on, the position of the Travelodge board became apparent. In general, its directors put the worst possible face on all its most intractable problems. They pointed out that the company was liable for A$3.6 million of guarantees in respect of the Narita Airport hotel. They noted that the Tahiti hotel was in serious trouble and suggested that Travelodge could not be certain it would recover the A$3.3 million it had advanced the hotel in equity and loans. The continuing losses from the self-inflicted wound that was the management contract at The Boulevard would reduce annual profits by several hundred thousand dollars a year for another 20-odd years.

There were other, equally serious, problems that the directors did not mention publicly, although Munk and his advisers certainly discussed them with the government. Under Greenway's stewardship, Haines had followed a very aggressive accounting policy of capitalizing the startup expenses[1] of new hotels. This had the effect of increasing profits in the year or two immediately after the hotel opened, in return for reducing profits by the same total amount over the following 15 years.

Also, more than half of the rooms that Travelodge managed were in joint ventures with other hotel groups, the most important being the 14 hotels it owned jointly with Trust Houses Forte. Travelodge had been carrying these properties in its books as investments equal to whatever amount of cash they had put into the joint ventures. The subsidiaries that owned these hotels, however, had borrowed a lot of money, and although Travelodge guaranteed the loans, it had not incorporated these loans into its balance sheet. It's called off-balance-sheet financing and is fine when everything is going smoothly, but it represents a huge contingent liability when things go wrong. The best example was the investment in the Tahiti Beachcomber Hotel, which Travelodge carried in its books as an investment of A$216,000,

---

[1] Essentially, it works like this. Money that goes to building a hotel is counted as an investment and is shown on the balance sheet as an asset. Money that goes on operating expenses does not appear on the balance sheet as an asset but is subtracted from revenues in the calculation of net profit. When a new hotel is built, all the money spent (including interest on money borrowed to build the hotel) is counted as an investment up to the point the hotel opens for business; after that point, all the money spent is counted as an expense. The trick is knowing when a hotel has opened. Is it open the day it takes its first guest? Or the day that it starts operating normally at average occupancy rates? Those two days can be up to a year apart. If the second approach is used (as was the case in Travelodge), then the "investment" is proportionately greater and most of the revenues in the new hotel's first year of operations go straight to the bottom line, without having to be used to pay for the expenses which have been capitalized. This makes profits significantly higher. After the first year, however, the capitalized costs have to be written off over the next 15 years, so that the boost to profits in year one is taken back in equal installments over the next 14 years.

despite significant loans and other liabilities built up by the hotel.

The annual report for the year ending June 1976 was released in September, when the 40¢(A) offer was still being hotly contested. All the problems that SPP had referred to throughout the takeover campaign were reflected in savage write-downs in the balance sheet. The net effect was a loss for that year of A$3.4 million instead of the profit of A$1.3 million that Haines had forecast one month before the year-end. Munk wrote off almost A$3 million for the Tahiti hotel and more than A$1 million on other guarantees and expenses (mainly the capitalized expenses that should have been operating expenses); he also incorporated into the accounts most of the losses in joint ventures that had previously been excluded (mainly the Narita Airport hotel). It was all totally truthful, but it was about as gloomy a picture of Travelodge as it was possible to envision.

The minority shareholders, in a case like this, would normally look to the board of directors for advice on their best course of action. Munk, however — as chairman of the company that was bidding for their shares — could not represent the minority shareholders in assessing if his bid was fair, so he asked David Hoare (who was not employed by SPP but had been retained by the company since 1972) to chair a subcommittee of "independent" directors to advise the shareholders on the bid. This potential conflict of interest wouldn't be tolerated today, but no one thought it worth even a comment in 1976. Hoare then hired Price Waterhouse to determine if the bid was fair and the accounting firm came back saying it was indeed "fair and reasonable."

In valuing the company, Price Waterhouse had the choice of using the cash value of the properties if the chain were liquidated

Canada's star industrialists from Clairtone, Peter Munk (left) and David Gilmour, in the mid-1960s.

Nova Scotia Premier Robert Stanfield (left) and Munk at the opening of Clairtone's new plant in Stellarton, N.S., in 1966.

Frank Sinatra and Tuesday Weld relaxing with a Clairtone G-7. "Listen to Sinatra on Clairtone stereo. Sinatra does."

Jim Slater, the founder and driving force behind Slater Walker Securities, which provided the critical $4 million to get Munk going in his Fiji venture in 1969.

Munk and the governor general of Fiji, Ratu Penia, at the opening of Pacific Harbour in 1974.

Egyptian President Anwar Sadat (right) with Munk (left) and David Gilmour (foreground) discussing the plans for the Pyramids Oasis resort project in 1975.

Gilmour (right) at the signing ceremony in 1976 to welcome Prince Nawaf Ben Abdul-Aziz as a new investor in Southern Pacific Properties. Prince Nawaf is a brother of the Saudi king, a former finance minister, and a long-standing, loyal investor in Munk's businesses.

Adnan Khashoggi with Munk and Gilmour at the Toronto Stock Exchange in 1982.

Munk addressing the 1976 annual meeting of Southern Pacific Properties Limited. On his right is Bill Birchall, and on his left Adnan Khashoggi.

Munk making one of his patented presentations to a group in Fiji in 1976. On his left is Adnan Khashoggi, and on his right the prime minister of Fiji, Sir Ratu Mara.

Admiring an artist's drawing of a new Travelodge to be constructed in Waikiki in 1968 are Lord Crowther, chairman of Trust Houses Forte and Travelodge Australia (left), Scott King, Travelodge U.S. chairman, and Alan Greenway, managing director of Travelodge Australia.

The handshake that saved Munk's business in 1975. Because Gilmour (left) introduced Koji Minami, chairman of the Taisei Corp. (center), to Egyptian President Anwar Sadat, Minami signed a deal buying half of Southern Pacific Properties' unused land holdings for $3.5 million.

Pat Samuel (left), Munk, and Gilmour in the Southern Pacific Hotel Corp.'s London office in the late 1970s.

Peter Munk and Bob Smith: the partnership that made Barrick great.

Bob Smith and one of the 190-ton trucks that haul ore from the pitface at Goldstrike.

Bill Birchall, the man who paid his dues in the South Pacific to become part of Munk's inner core of trusted partners.

Dr. Brian Meikle (left) and Bob Smith underground at the Camflo mine in the 1970s. These two men were the mining geniuses behind Barrick, along with Alan Hill and Dit Holt.

Munk conferring with Greg Wilkins, president of Trizec Corp.

Barrick Gold's International Advisory Board in 1995. Standing: Andronico Luksic (left), Vernon Jordan, Howard Baker, Dr. Karl Otto Pöhl, Paul Desmarais, José Rohm, Bob Smith. Seated: Munk, Brian Mulroney, George Bush (honorary senior adviser).

Munk meeting the premier of China, Li Peng (right), with Paul Desmarais and Brian Mulroney in 1994.

Peter and Melanie Munk on safari in East
Africa with David Wynne-Morgan.

On the slopes: Munk skiing in
the Swiss Alps.

Munk (third from left) with the present and former Canadian prime ministers
(except for Joe Clark), at a ceremony for the National Archives sponsored by the
Horsham Corporation, Munk's holding company.

immediately (an asset valuation approach) or calculating the discounted value of the future earnings of Travelodge (a discounted cash flow approach). Normally, the assets per share would be the measure for the first approach — or about A$1.20 a share against SPP's offer of 40¢(A). Price Waterhouse said, however, the asset-per-share approach was not viable, because the chain would never achieve that value if it were liquidated in the economic conditions prevailing at that time. The accountants said that selling all its properties would depress the market for hotels so severely that it would amount to a fire sale. Also, liquidating the chain would trigger all the guarantees in the joint ventures, which would have to be paid out of the proceeds from selling the properties. Overall, Price Waterhouse concluded, net proceeds from a liquidation of the assets worth A$1.20 per share would produce less than 40¢(A) a share.

In view of this conclusion, Price Waterhouse said, they had to value the company as a "going concern," using discounted cash flow. When its accountants valued the properties on the basis of projected income over the next ten years or so, they found that the existing problems were unlikely to be solved in the "foreseeable future," so annual profits would continue at a very low level. Price Waterhouse pointed out that Trust Houses Forte had expressed an interest in dissolving its partnership with Travelodge and suggested that the management contract might then be lost. The outlook for "sustainable future earnings" was so poor, the firm concluded, that A$8 million, or 40¢(A) a share, would be a fair price.

The finance editor of *The Australian* thought the consultants seemed "to be acting more for SPP when they say that 40¢ is fair." He was not alone in his view. A group of shareholders who did not want to sell at 40¢(A) mounted a legal challenge to the valuation, which outraged Price Waterhouse. However, the disputing shareholders had almost no chance of winning their case, and they soon dropped it. The basis for the valuation was incontestable — and the projections were supportable even if highly subjective. Nonetheless, the Price Waterhouse valuation presented an extraordinarily gloomy perspective of the prospects for Travelodge. As it turned out, the net profit the following year was A$936,000, and in the subsequent 18 months to the end of 1978, net profit came in at A$6.3 million.

Mark Johnson of Hill, Samuel was actively involved in these financial Olympics: "If one went back and looked at the rigor of the analysis of the data that was presented to the world at large, either indirectly by media interviews or directly by letters to shareholders, I'm not suggesting any untruths, but the degree of rigor about it was several shades different from what the world requires today. On both sides. Peter was wanting to stress the negative in the public mind — and Greenway was gilding the lily in the early stages. I don't recollect a deliberate campaign to depress the price. There was a campaign to let the world know what was actually here. If there'd been a deliberate campaign to mislead the market, we would not have been involved."

While this battle was being fought in the business pages of the Australian press, Munk pitched all the key constituencies to gather support. The foreign takeover legislation was not a big problem, as it turned out. The government had passed legislation in 1974 governing foreign takeovers and had specifically exempted companies in which foreign companies held more than 40%, so SPP didn't legally have to get permission, because it already owned 58%. However, the climate in Australia made it wise to reassure the politicians they were not making a mistake in letting it pass. Hoare spent a lot of time explaining to federal politicians and their bureaucrats how off-balance-sheet financing worked and how it could put the parent company at risk of default. Munk also did his part, doing a road show with graphs and tables that demonstrated the consequences for employment if the chain was allowed to continue on its present course. He also spent time with the unions, which were key to the implementation of his turnaround plans. One of the major problems with the company in the mid-1970s was the high wage settlements, which squeezed profit margins at a time when it was difficult to raise prices.

Munk and Hoare won over the politicians and union leaders, but the shareholder opposition continued, forcing SPP to extend the deadline for acceptance of its offer from October 20 to November 11, then again to December 12. The target for acceptance was 90% of the minority shares, because that would give SPP the right to force the balance to sell. At the original deadline, only 53% of the minority shareholders had accepted the offer. By October 27, at a rowdy Annual General Meeting, that number had risen to only 54% and Hoare argued down a dissident shareholder who wanted to know why the price wasn't equal to the asset backing for the shares. By November 3, 70% had accepted, and then the opposition finally dwindled away. By December 12, Roger Kirby was able to send a cable to Munk in London saying: "Travelodge acceptances now over 90%. Please give us something more challenging next year."

For the second time in the space of a little more than a year, Munk had nailed his colors to the mast and stuck to his guns with extraordinary determination. Just as he had never budged from his price to Khashoggi, so he never budged from his price for Travelodge, despite the powerful arguments against him.

The first 58% of Travelodge cost SPP A$16 million and the

final 42% cost it A$3.3 million, for a total of A$19.3 million. If Munk had paid the asset value per share of Travelodge each time, the total price would have been A$20.7 million. Four years later, he had quadrupled the value of the company after a spectacular four-year turnaround that changed the whole industry in Australia.

As the corrective measures applied to Travelodge began to take effect, the turnaround gathered steam. Two years after the bloodbath at the 1975 Annual General Meeting, debt had been reduced by A$9 million, from A$24.7 million to A$15.6 million; annual interest charges were down more than A$1 million to A$2 million from A$3.2 million. Trading profit, before extraordinary items, had almost tripled to A$2.2 million from A$770,000.

The three problem hotels were less tractable, but they, too, were attacked with typical vigor. Pat Samuel exercised his highly developed grasp of the Japanese character, negotiating Travelodge's way out of the partnership with Mitsubishi at a satisfactory price. From 1976, the partnership was no longer hidden in off-balance-sheet accounts, so the empty hotel was showing its full annual loss of A$900,000 a year in its books. So extricating Travelodge from the Narita debacle had a big impact on the profit, even if it did remove an enormous long-term opportunity.

Munk tried everything to mitigate the hemorrhaging at The Boulevard, with little success. He tried to sell the lease to Qantas, offering inducements totaling A$2.3 million, but they decided against it. Two years later, The Boulevard would still be losing about A$300,000 a year. The Tahiti Beachcomber was put up for sale, but there were no takers (an extraordinary piece of luck as they discovered). In 1978, the Tahiti problem was solved when, out of the blue, Qantas decided to include a stopover in Tahiti in its flight schedules. Overnight, tourism boomed and occupancies soared in the Beachcomber — pushing net profit to A$1 million a year, compared to a loss of several hundred thousand dollars a year previously.

There was a fourth problem that had been recognized at the time of the takeover, but had not received much publicity. Trust Houses Forte had signaled its desire to end its partnership with Travelodge in early 1976. It offered SPP a choice. Either SPP could take over Trust Houses Forte's loan guarantees or THF would take over management of the joint venture hotels from Travelodge. It was a painful dilemma. Travelodge earned revenues of A$800,000 a year from the 14 hotels it co-owned with THF — plus another A$500,000 in another 14 hotels where Travelodge and THF were partners with other groups. If Trust Houses Forte took over management, not only would Travelodge lose a significant source of revenue, but it would also have a new and powerful competitor in the South Pacific market.

Munk persuaded THF to hold off its decision for a year, while he got Travelodge's finances in better shape. In July of the following year, 1977, THF announced it was definitely severing the relationship. Kirby had already discussed the financial ramifications of buying out THF and obtained the bankers' support for the deal, so Munk asked him to fly to London to meet Sir Charles Forte with him. Munk offered Forte A$6.7 million for THF's holdings in all 28 hotels where Travelodge owned less than 100%. Forte was a bit surprised at the offer — the investment was carried in his books at about A$4 million and he made no effort to hide his skepticism that SPP would be able to raise the finance, but he accepted the offer, expecting perhaps to pick up the properties when SPP defaulted later. He even agreed to let SPP pay off A$3 million of the purchase price over the following three years. The deal closed in March 1978. The extra profits from those hotels paid off the purchase price within two years.

As the Trust Houses Forte negotiations were moving toward closure, Munk began to turn his mind to the pathetic performance of SPP's stock on the Hong Kong Stock Exchange. P&O had indicated they wanted to sell their 24% of the company — the shares were in the doldrums at around 50¢(HK) and they had grown tired of waiting for the turnaround. Since those first few months after the reverse takeover, the stock had rarely risen above HK$2 and frequent efforts to create more interest in SPP had had little or no effect. It continued trading at well below its break-up value. Birchall conducted a survey of SPP's shareholders to find out why they weren't bidding the price up. The results were a shock. Hong Kong investors weren't too keen on anything overseas and they regarded Australia, in particular, as a graveyard for investments; the Egyptian project, they felt, was a wild goose chase; and they were also unenthusiastic about anything in the accommodation industry. Munk and his partners knew that it didn't matter what they did — the price of SPP was never going to move on the Hong Kong exchange.

Munk's seventeenth golden rule:
If the market discounts your shares, you can't use the market to raise capital — so buy back your shares.

So they decided to privatize SPP. At that point, Munk, Gilmour, and Birchall owned 9% of SPP. Khashoggi owned 29%, P&O owned 24%, Trust Houses Forte, J. G. Boswell, and the other directors owned 6% between them. The general public owned 32%. The only partner who was interested in putting more money into the company was Adnan Khashoggi, so he and Munk negotiated an agreement to buy out all the other shareholders. In a complicated series of intercompany transactions, the SPP shares owned by Khashoggi, Munk, Gilmour, and Birchall (totaling 38%) were transformed into shares in Barrick Investments, their new holding company, and the 62% of the SPP shares owned by the rest of the shareholders were bought with loans from Wardley's Bank ($10.75 million) and Khashoggi's holding company, Triad ($6 million).

Barrick Investments then owned all the shares of SPP. It, in turn, was 50% owned by Khashoggi and 50% by Monex, a holding company incorporated in Liechtenstein. Monex was owned by Khashoggi (with 74%) and Munk, Gilmour, and Birchall (who owned 26% between them). The three now effectively owned 13% of SPP through Barrick, compared to 9% before the takeover. There was one critical proviso, however. The agreement between the four parties specified that Monex had the right to manage Barrick, free from interference and that there would be five directors of Monex — Munk, Gilmour, two nominees from Khashoggi's Triad, and a fifth independent director to be chosen by Munk. In other words, Munk had clear management control. Khashoggi also agreed to increase Munk's group's ownership of Monex if certain profit targets were met.

In all his dealings with Khashoggi, Munk was always prepared to walk away from any deal if he did not get management control. "I learned that lesson in Nova Scotia," he says. "We insisted on control. [Khashoggi] put in $12 million but we had to have control. And when we went private, he could have had many more shares, but we insisted that I was the permanent chairman with the casting vote. I would not do it otherwise. I wouldn't do it today even if we were poor." Munk knew that the King of Saudi Arabia could lean on Khashoggi any time he wanted to. "All he had to do was say, 'My dear Khashoggi, you control a big company. If you want to get the next oil contract, you've got to do me a favor and put up three new hotels in the desert in Jeddah.' He could not say no. But if Khashoggi says Peter Munk is controlling this company and there's no way anyone can convince him, he remains rich. Khashoggi understood that."

> ***Munk's eighteenth golden rule:***
> *A successful partnership always has someone*
> *who ultimately can make a decision and*
> *take the responsibility.*

The offer to buy out all the other shareholders was priced at 80¢ in Hong Kong currency. This represented a moderate premium on the share price, which had been hovering around 50¢ for most of the first half of 1978. However, as in the privatization of Travelodge, the offered price was well below the asset value per share, which had been shown as HK$1.77 at the end of 1977. The independent report on the fairness of the offer was prepared by BT (Asia), an affiliate of Hoare's Ord-BT. The report included a pro forma balance sheet that was updated from the year-end accounts in 1977 to reflect changes in circumstances[2] since the year-end — and arrived at an estimated asset value per share of HK$1.25. The report suggested, however, that the company's assets were worth — at most — 92¢ to

---

[2] Principally a significant downward revaluation of the Fiji properties by Jones, Lang, Wootton.

94¢ in a situation where the assets were being sold.[3]

The report then estimated earnings for 1978 at HK$5.7 million or $3\frac{1}{2}$¢(HK) a share, which meant that the offer for 80¢ a share represented 21 times estimated earnings — a generous ratio in most circumstances.

As it had in the Travelodge takeover two years previously, this valuation of shares was based on an extremely pessimistic perspective. In fact, Munk and Gilmour displayed a very different perspective when they filed a pro forma balance sheet with their successful application for a bridging loan from Wardley's Bank. In that statement, they used an asset value per share of HK$1.75, which was adjusted only slightly from the valuation that Coopers & Lybrand had given the company at the end of 1977. This statement informed Wardley's that they expected to sell half the Travelodge shares for $24 million in 1980, valuing the company at $48 million, compared to $25 million used in the pro forma in the BT report.

There was, however, one sentence in the report that really made everything else irrelevant. It noted that P&O, Trust Houses Forte, and J. G. Boswell had all agreed to sell their shares at 80¢. As board members for a full decade, they were perceived as better qualified than anyone to judge the value of the shares. If they thought it was fair, what chance did anyone else have of expecting more?

The offer closed in September without incident. The company that had been worth $28 million when it was floated in 1972,

---

[3] He suggested that selling all the Travelodge hotels would depress the market, pushing prices well below the values shown in the accounts. Also, there were ongoing obligations in the Fiji resort that would not be covered by future income — and the final cost of the settlement of the Egyptian project was so unpredictable that some extra allowance had to be made for it.

and into which Khashoggi had pumped $12 million, was now being bought back at a price that valued the company at $25 million. It was a fabulous deal for Munk, Gilmour, Birchall, and Khashoggi. Their equity, which the transaction valued at almost $10 million, was sold for $130 million three years later, not counting the significant sum of money they had already withdrawn from the company.

The timing for taking SPP private was exquisite for Munk and his partners. When the machinations were first beginning, Travelodge had been whipped into better shape, but it was still not breaking any world records. At the end of 1977, George Haines had resigned and Kirby had been named managing director some months later. The chain had been rationalized. From a total of 72 hotels in 1975 (28 of them joint ventures), Travelodge was halfway to shrinking to 36 hotels by 1980 (7 of them joint ventures). Munk had slashed costs and got the debt under control. The managers were better motivated and upgrading their skills. The chain was better run and its profits were creeping up. But it was still, in the eyes of Munk, Gilmour, and Birchall, a third-rate chain of hotels. As the prospects for Egypt dimmed, the three partners realized they had to apply the full force of their energies into making Travelodge a chain they could be proud of.

That decision was to have profound ramifications.

Gilmour was particularly underwhelmed with the Travelodge hotels, so he got involved with adding a bit of class to the operation, but it was, as always, Munk who led, adding his own special twist to the upgrades. He zeroed in on some selected managers, trying to pinpoint where the upgrading dollars could be spent most effectively.

"He could take the smallest detail and put it into the context of the big picture," Birchall says. "What does it mean to give them this lovely Pierre Cardin perfumed soap? What does that really mean, [what are] its financial ramifications? He was trying to find how we were getting that customer into the room, and how much that customer would pay. He was not looking at it in a costing sense, but more in the revenue sense. He would not try to second-guess a manager in terms of pricing a product, but he would question some of the guy's philosophy in the components of the pricing of the product. In other words, if there are fourteen factors to take into account in pricing, Peter will pick unerringly the two or three most relevant ones, and discuss them in depth. Depending on the logic of that discussion, he will take on trust that the other 11 or 12 are going to be correctly handled."

This became an important tool for Munk's long-distance leadership. "He did not try to run the business," says Kirby, "but just to confuse us, he would get involved in some small, arcane detail of the business — in the process usually embarrassing an executive who had not pulled his weight in some area."

It's a practice he has continued ever since. He can zero in quite unexpectedly on a detail like a laser gun, picking it apart as if he were preparing for a PhD on the subject. But always in the context of the big picture. He would use the detail analysis to question many of the managers' most basic assumptions as to how they run their business — and then leave them to figure out how to apply their new insights. He would also ask for regular reports from Kirby on aspects of the operation affected by that test-tube issue, so that he could follow up his initiative.

At about the same time as the upgrading, Munk hit on another, even greater, opportunity/problem with Travelodge. One night in 1978, he and Melanie went to a movie. Munk had A$40 in his pocket and it was all gone by the time he had paid for the two movie tickets, parking, and a coffee. That was a bit more than the average rate for a night in a Travelodge room and the realization stopped him in his tracks. It didn't seem right. The next morning, he asked an analyst at the office to do some research on major cities around the world — places such as Hong Kong, Toronto, New York, London — to find out what the ratio was between the price of an average hotel room for one night and an evening at a downtown movie theater for two, including parking and a coffee. The answer came back at three to one.

"We went bust or became rich on those damn hotel rates," he said later. "OK, we removed the overheads, we removed the art department, we stopped building hotels, that's obvious. But we still had 50 hotels. And everything was the room rates. You lived and breathed or you suffocated and died depending on your room rates. Your occupancy was somewhat beyond your control. But it sure wasn't beyond your control what you were going to ask people to pay if they're going to stay in your goddamn hotel. And was I going to let them stay there for the price of two movie tickets, one parking, and a cup of coffee? No way."

A day or two later, he asked Kirby to come round and see him at his home on Point Piper. Kirby knew there was something big in the pipeline and after some chitchat over sandwiches and a bottle of chardonnay, Munk delivered his message. He told Kirby that the tariffs charged by Australian hotels were so low that it was suffocating the industry. They did not produce enough cash flow to pay for expansions and refurbishing, let alone building entirely new hotels. In half an hour, he had convinced Kirby that unless he doubled his tariffs in a year, there was no future in the industry.

It was a tall order. Inflation was running at about 10% and

Travelodge had been edging its rates up at about 12%, sneaking ahead of inflation. Historically, head office followed the suggestions of the individual managers, who made their recommendations for the amount of their tariff increases after talking with a few key contacts in their communities.

"We thought we were being quite aggressive," Kirby says, "but in Munk's context, they were puny increases. I went back to the office and talked it over with Bill Allen [joint managing director with Kirby at that time and head of operations]. He accepted the logic but found the practicalities hard to swallow."

Allen was perhaps being polite. Most of the people running the hotels thought Munk had lost his marbles. Some of the senior people threatened to quit. They resented this man coming over from England, knowing nothing about hotels, and telling them how to run their business. Munk didn't mind. "I'll take full responsibility for that," he told them, "because I'm absolutely certain I'm right." Doug Stewart, the marketing director, commented later that "only Munk could do that. An operations guy could never have done it, because you are really putting your balls on the line." Munk was happy to do that. "Industry insiders become inward looking and lose their common sense. As an outsider, I can understand an industry better because I am not in it."

Despite his iron-willed conviction, Munk was very careful to propose the "great tariff hike" in a way that it would be accepted by the people who had to implement it.

"Of course, the fact the suggestion came from the chairman does hold some weight, but he never put it as an instruction," Kirby remembers. "He told us, 'This is not an order, but if you accept the logic, I want you to think very carefully and if you want to do it, you go ahead and do it.' I went back and said we'd go ahead. We went in gung ho."

Toward the end of 1978, Kirby, who was by then the sole managing director, raised tariffs by 35% across the board. He had not refurbished the hotels — all he did to compensate for the higher rates was add a basket of fruit, a plate of cookies, and two free newspapers every morning. It cost A$2 out of the extra A$10 they were getting. He also upgraded the toiletries in the bathroom. It wasn't much. The employees all knew it was a bold price increase for very little value added, and they were uncomfortable with it. "The people who ran the chain, including me, had no world experience," Kirby says, "so it was very hard for Munk trying to persuade what he saw as a bunch of hicks to think in his terms about what a hotel should be. The tariff hike was very big — the biggest thing he did to the industry."

As the price leader in the Australian industry, Travelodge alone had the power to raise the whole level of hotel tariffs — and the rest of the industry appreciated the gesture, because it took some of the pressure off their own operations. But would they use the tariff hike to gain market share from Travelodge? Munk had taken care to prepare them for it. He characteristically took the bull by the horns and went to visit his four main competitors.

"I said, 'You know, guys, we have got two alternatives here. We stay put in our industry and commit hara-kiri, because that's what we're doing here — we can't replace our beds or carpets, so eventually less and less people will come to our hotels and we'll be a flophouse and we'll kill the industry. Or we can do what people all over the world do and charge a higher rate so we can create a healthy industry and secure the employment of our people and have enough cash to give the guests good beds and nice carpets and nice lobbies. If all of us charge higher rates, then it won't hurt the volume. If your grandmother dies in

Adelaide, then, of course, you've got to go. And if you've got a business deal in Melbourne, you're not going to worry if the hotel is $40 or $48 — you gotta go because you gotta go. We are the dominant player in the industry and I may as well tell you that as of next month, I will instruct my people to raise the rates. If you do it, that's fine. If you don't do it, then you may force us to lower our rates and then we have a fight.' And everyone said, 'Mr. Munk, if you do this, we'll do it.' So we all did it."

It wasn't quite that straightforward. The competitors didn't raise their tariffs as much as Travelodge, so they gained a competitive advantage. Travelodge's average occupancy in Australia dropped by five percentage points, from 75% to 70%, after the 35% hike. However, the financial impact of the drop was swamped by the increase of almost 30% in the average room tariff (after discounts).

Despite Munk's conviction, it was still a tense period for the company. "We lost a fair chunk of business," says Kirby, "and Munk started getting a little irritable. Most of our competitors were running pretty full, so we were at the bottom of the queue — once they were full, we'd get the customers. After a while, they realized that they were daft, so [the rates] started to creep up and the differential got smaller. So we hit 'em again. Munk used to go spare sometimes. He'd say to me, 'Christ, this is terrible, you're too aggressive.' But it worked. It pushed tariffs up right across the board in Australasia. It also opened the doors to the big boys — the tariffs were getting within cooey[4] of their affordability rates. So they came in. They diluted the market right down and it really hurt."

Meanwhile, Munk and Gilmour had received a visit in

---

[4] Australian for "within shouting distance."

London from a man named Marty O'Toole, who picked up their feelings about the quality of the Travelodge hotels (which wasn't hard to do) and who wrote a report suggesting all the things they wanted to hear about the need for Travelodge to be completely refurbished. They sent him off to Australia and told Kirby to do absolutely everything O'Toole told him to do. Kirby managed to persuade him that that didn't mean he was the new managing director, and O'Toole set to work upgrading the whole chain. Kirby told the press it was an A$8 million program and Munk insisted it be accompanied by Travelodge's first advertising "image" campaign. He wanted Australians to know that Travelodge had changed its name to Southern Pacific Hotel Corp. and that it was in the big leagues. The ads blared: "We've got 5,000 rooms, we welcomed 2.1 million guests this year, and we have more than 4,200 employees to take care of your needs."

These changes helped give a sense that there was extra value behind the extra tariffs, but it was still a slow process. In 1980, Kirby pushed the tariffs up again, raising the average room rate by $17\frac{1}{2}$% to A$45 from A$38.30. To their great relief, the occupancy rate held at just below 70%. By then, however, the benefits of the great tariff hike were obvious to everyone — although Munk still had an occasional anxiety attack. The bankers had not always been pleased with the financial impact of the early stages of the price increase and Munk and Birchall had to sweet-talk them more than once.

The great tariff hike was central to the turnaround but the development that really helped Travelodge was the improvement in the economy after 1978. Tourism rebounded and Travelodge soared into two years of fabulous success. By the end of 1979, Travelodge had doubled its gross profit margin despite having halved the number of hotels it managed and owned.

This was the year when the hard work and angst of a whole decade finally paid off for Munk, Gilmour, and Birchall.

The program to sell off the marginal motels accelerated in 1979. The initial spurt of sales after Munk took control had slowed down in 1977 when only A$4 million of properties was sold at prices so low that they fetched about the same amount as Travelodge had paid for them. In the two and a half years from July 1977 to December 1979, however, the prices received for the properties improved considerably, contributing an extraordinary profit of A$5.7 million. The program was completed in 1980, when Roger Kirby announced that Travelodge had sold 30 unprofitable motels for a total of A$20 million in three years.

With a slimmed-down chain of larger, profitable hotels for which tariffs had been increased by 70% in three years, Travelodge began to spin off cash flow beyond their wildest dreams. All of a sudden, Munk was scrambling to protect his profits from excessive taxation. He paid $6 million to Barrick Investments under a curious Australian regulation that allows companies to take money out of the company tax free if they reduce their shareholders' capital. Travelodge also paid healthy management fees to Southern Pacific Hotel Services, which didn't pay Australian taxes. And dividends were resumed in 1978, for the first time since 1972, with a massive payout of A$6.4 million. In the following two years, another A$3.3 million were paid out in dividends. It was payoff time. After 20 years of reaching for the stars, Munk was beginning to touch them.

Earlier in 1979, Birchall had been given an even bigger surprise. He called Wardley's Bank to ask them to provide a valuation of Travelodge to support the collateral for his loans. Wardley's came back with the answer — A$45 million. He was astonished. "We didn't realize how it had appreciated," he says.

"Australia had suddenly become the investment of choice for Hong Kong investors. There were people all over the region who were taking an interest in the accommodation industry in Australia."

Munk wasted no time capitalizing on the increased values. He put Jones Lang Wootton to work. They estimated that the assets could be revalued upward by A$41.2 million at the end of 1979. Then they followed that with another revaluation of about the same amount in 1980, bringing the total revaluation to A$82.1 million over the two years. The net tangible assets of A$24 million had appreciated to more than A$100 million.

Also in 1979, Travelodge purchased Pacific Harbour from its own parent, SPP, for A$13 million, burying the ongoing pain of the flagging Fiji development. It lost more than A$2 million for Travelodge in 1980.

"The industry was on the verge of being successful," says Pat Samuel. "It helped to change the name to Southern Pacific Hotel Corp., instead of Travelodge, which had a demeaning market connotation. But the other things — the upgrading, the refurbishments, the different logos, the different hotel names all had some effect. Most of all, however, there is no doubt that the tide was rising and our boat rose on it with all the others."

On top of the huge increase in asset value, it soon became obvious that continuing to grow Southern Pacific Hotel Corp. had become a much riskier proposition. Kirby was being offered properties to own and to manage that were going to cost A$100,000 a room to build. The expected room revenues of these new hotels were A$75 a night.

"Our existing properties," says Birchall, "had cost us historically A$7,000 or A$8,000 a room and we were getting A$65 a day. That caused us to pause, and ask ourselves whether or not we really had a true commitment to expanding in the hotel business. It was obviously getting riskier — the only way to expand was to buy or build a room at 12 times what it had cost us, in return for 15% or 20% more revenue."

It was time to sell. By the middle of 1981, they found Tan Sri Khoo Teck Puat, a wealthy Chinese businessman from Malaysia, who paid A$105 million for the chain. With the final adjustments and profit sharing kicker in the sales agreement, the all-inclusive price worked out to $130 million.

It turned out Tan Sri Khoo wasn't as wealthy as he said he was. He owned a minority interest in the Bank of Brunei, which was controlled by the Sultan of Brunei, the richest person in the world. Tan Sri Khoo's son was managing director of the bank and it turned out he had "borrowed" the money to help his father pay for Southern Pacific Hotel Corp. without telling the Sultan. This upset the Sultan somewhat, so he threw the son in jail and tried to extradite Tan Sri Khoo, who had to flee to Korea (which doesn't have an extradition treaty with Brunei). Seven years later, Tan Sri Khoo resold the company to a Hong Kong entrepreneur for $540 million, so he was able to repay the Sultan and they became friends again.

By the time he sold Travelodge, Munk had already been back in Toronto almost two years, seeking to restore the reputation he had lost so traumatically when Clairtone had collapsed almost fifteen years earlier. He now had more than $100 million in his back pocket after giving the shareholders of Barrick Investments a handsome dividend, and he was ready to dive into oil and gas.

7

BLACK GOLD, YELLOW GOLD

eter Munk had been eyeing the oil and gas business all through the second half of the 1970s. How could he avoid it? His Arab partners were luxuriating in their lakes of easy money, siphoned off from the oceans of cash gushing from their oil wells. The incredible wealth generated by oil in the 1970s must have seemed so much more attractive than his own arduous route to riches — and he couldn't wait to get into the game himself.

He had, in fact, bought a few oil properties in Australia with Adnan Khashoggi, but they didn't amount to much. He was getting his feet wet, readying himself for the next diversification. He was also building his network of potential partners in preparation for the time when he could start into the industry in earnest. That time came when he and his partners sold SPP.

As he surveyed the scene in 1981, with $130 million burning a hole in his pocket, Munk believed he had landed in the right spot at the right time. He was now a seasoned, successful business leader, and the oil industry appeared to have a future of limitless potential. With the price of oil hovering around $28 a barrel, the Canadian government had just imposed a confiscatory tax regime on its oil and gas industry based on the assumption that the price of oil would rise to $60. Swiss bankers were forecasting that the price would go to $100. The dollar signs were ringing in Munk's head. In 1981, he told one reporter, with his characteristic enthusiasm, that the oil and gas business represented "an unparalleled opportunity in our lifetime for the formation of large pools of capital."

Munk's nineteenth golden rule:
Be prepared for trouble when bankers are optimistic about your industry — especially when the bankers are Swiss.

Munk approached the industry methodically. First he brought in a couple of experienced investors in Canada — Norman Short, who ran Guardian Capital mutual funds, and Joe Rotman, who had been in the oil business since the early 1960s (first in home heating, then in the international oil trade, and finally in the exploration business). He talked to a lot of experts, found out how the industry worked, and gradually put together an impeccable strategy. Like so many of his strategies, it was in two parts. On the one hand, he wanted a solid, small, North American oil company with a good cash flow from its producing properties. On the other hand, he wanted to gamble on high-risk/high-reward exploration plays, looking for promising, unexplored geological formations that had the potential to be an "elephant" — a giant oil field that would make him and his partners rich beyond their wildest dreams. The second track gave him huge upside potential; the first protected his downside: If the gamble on the putative elephants failed, he would still have the producing company, which would grow steadily, if less spectacularly, through North American exploration.

His approach to the elephant hunt was a classic oil play. He assembled large blocks of land and then farmed them out to exploration companies. He allied himself with experienced partners and let them do the technical work. He didn't want to try to compete with the Canadian oil companies — they had many years of experience in the oil-bearing strata in Canada and he would be doomed to picking at the leftovers. So he decided to go global, buying land wherever he could find it.

Greg Wilkins, the president of Trizec, was a junior accountant with Munk at the time: "The oil and gas episode was perfect for an MBA study. We had the assets and the talent and we tied it all together perfectly. You couldn't fault the strategy. But it didn't work."

In July 1981, however, Munk, Birchall, and Khashoggi (Gilmour had faded from the scene by then) were brimming with enthusiasm. Munk was determined not to dawdle in reinvesting the $130 million. He was concerned that as the warm glow of the big profits from Travelodge faded, his shareholders would start withdrawing their share of the profits and leave him with a dwindling pool of capital to build on. So he gave the shareholders something to keep them happy — he paid out a dividend of one-quarter of the cash. Then he took the $100 million that was left and dove into his new strategy. First he had to buy a small, producing company that would give him a solid, defensive base. He had three criteria. He wanted the company to have producing wells; have good management with the necessary expertise and track record; and be short of cash.

In the course of the next several months, he and his team looked at dozens of proposals. As soon as they were interested in a company, the owners would sell it before Munk's team had completed their due diligence. The industry was white-hot, at the peak of investor frenzy that invariably precedes a dramatic collapse, and Munk's financial caution was out of synch. "I'm not a genius," he said a decade later, "but I'm not an idiot either. I study a company very carefully before I buy it. I ask a lot of questions. If I'm convinced, I put my money up — then I can get other people to invest with me." Most were not so cautious and it was getting tougher and tougher to nail down a deal.

They eventually found their target in Oklahoma. Barrick Resources, a new subsidiary of Barrick Investments, paid $60 million to buy 55% of Viking Petroleum. The company hired D. O. "Swede" Nelson as chief executive. A former top gun from Chevron, Nelson had contacts all over the world and was plugged in to the U.S. industry.

Soon afterwards, Barrick formed a new subsidiary, Barrick Explorations (in which Rotman and Short owned shares) to launch a global search for elephants. Over the next two years it bought shares in exploration plays in New Zealand, Australia, Turkey (with the Turkish government and Munk's Arab partners from South Pacific days), and Tunisia (with Elf Aquitaine, the huge French oil company). Barrick also bought into six plays in the United States (in Wyoming, Montana, Arkansas/ Mississippi, Texas, and Oregon). All told, Barrick Explorations sank $30 million into a wild fling with fate. They all came up dry.

Viking didn't turn out any better. Nelson, it turned out, was Mr. Big Bucks in Big Oil — he just didn't understand the capital constraints of a small company. By the time his controlling shareholders had figured out what he was doing, he had blown all the cash the company had. By the end of 1982, Viking was in a workout with the banks, who were trying to salvage what they could of their loans. The shareholders got nothing. Munk tried everything. He approached numerous potential buyers, including Spain's national oil company, but no one would take the company off his hands. "In a boom, there is always another fool to take you out," Munk said much later. "You can make mistakes without suffering. In a bust, the fools stay there."

How could the strategy have gone so drastically wrong? Bill Birchall, with the dry detachment of an accountant who has seen it all, cuts to the core: "We are very tough on due diligence when we have a concept that we want to implement. When you buy something, on the other hand — whether it be a public company or a private company — you have got to recognize, frankly, that you have to take quite a lot on face value. You don't have the luxury of time, which you do when you are developing your own concept, or the luxury of being able to construct the building blocks of logic to support the concept. So there we were, looking at this business. Insurance companies from Kansas have invested in it, reputable banks have lent money to it. Wall Street institutions have funded the company. We hire a petroleum engineer to do an evaluation of its assets and he finds that the price of the shares is at a 30% or 40% discount from the underlying value of the assets. The cash flow projections are there and all the rest of it. We are not exactly experts when it comes to talking about drilling wells and the rest of it. If other people have done their due diligence, then we're prepared to take it on face value."

They bought at the peak of the oil boom, a matter of months before everything turned down and the industry went into a deep recession.

Munk's twentieth golden rule:
Never buy high, hoping it will go higher.
Buy low and hope it will go higher.

"Quite frankly," Birchall adds. "It was a load of puffery. Three years later the banks fired all their petroleum engineers for being totally incompetent or overoptimistic. We really didn't know the risks. And that means you're gambling. When we really looked inward into our souls, we realized that we had been gambling. We may have been gambling with banks, with Wall Street and other good people, but we'd been gambling nonetheless."

Rotman, the most experienced of the company's directors in the oil business, was a little less hard on the venture, in retrospect. "It didn't work because (a) the scale of the exploration was too big for the size of our company and (b) we made a couple of bad deals. The biggest mistake was Viking, and that was picking the wrong guy."

It was a devastating blow for Munk. In the summer of 1983, he went to the luxurious New York apartment of Adnan Khashoggi, the partner who owned half of the equity in their company. (An incentive plan had increased the share of Munk, Gilmour, and Birchall to one-half from one-quarter). Khashoggi had his own problems. His recent estrangement from his wife of many years had cost him £500 million plus some property, which the *Guinness Book of Records* rated as the biggest divorce settlement in history. He would not have been in a mood to hear about the evaporation of one of the few really successful investments he had made. It was not an easy thing for Munk to do, but he insisted on doing it in person, taking the consequences of his massive miscue on the chin, in person.

"Adnan, I am terribly sorry, but we have lost all that money," Munk told him. "I don't know what to say to you."

Khashoggi, ever the optimistic salesman, didn't rant and rave. Instead he seemed more concerned about Munk himself. "Peter," he said, "I am much more worried about you. You must not be depressed, because that will stop you from being able to bounce back and make it again. Don't worry about the money."

Easier said than done. For the third (and last) time in his life, Peter Munk was staring abject failure in the face. It had been bad enough with Clairtone. It was touch and go in the doldrums of 1974/75, when Pacific Harbour and Travelodge were sliding into oblivion. But this time, he had not even glimpsed the stars before the slide set in. The money just slipped away, without ever looking — even faintly — like a potential blockbuster.

Munk's twenty-first golden rule:
When you're young or when you're old,
failure should not be an impediment
to trying again.

"It was a very stark situation," Bill Birchall remembers. "It was a bad time for us. We really felt we'd lost our way, that every principle we'd ever enunciated had just been thrown out the window in a sort of a wild . . . It was stark."

Not all the shareholders were as accommodating as Khashoggi. However, everyone had had the opportunity to contribute to the formulation of the strategy, so they could all sympathize with Munk and take some share of the blame.

Munk, however, was prepared to admit more than his share.

"He not only accepted personal responsibility, but financial accountability beyond what any partner could have expected," says Rotman. At Munk's insistence, Barrick Investments (the holding company for Khashoggi, Munk, Gilmour, and Birchall) picked up some expenses in the debacle that should rightfully have been paid for by Rotman, Short, and the other oil and gas partners. "We argued with him, but he would not change his mind," Rotman states. "It's a prime example of what he's all about. He is not triggered by greed or the moment. He saw things in a long-term perspective. He has a sense of fairness and equity that is beyond belief."

The unmitigated disaster of the foray into oil and gas did have a positive side. The loss was so complete that there was no point in trying to salvage anything. They could move on to the next strategy with a clean (if wealth-challenged) slate. "If we had been moderately successful," Birchall says, "Barrick Gold would never have happened. We'd have put more and more of our money into it, chased the banks, borrowed more money, and we would have been mired down like every other immoderate oil and gas producer in North America."

Long before the oil misadventure, Munk had started looking at gold. In making his rounds of institutional investors in Europe, he had chanced upon a major problem they were grappling with. They all liked to have some gold stocks in their portfolios as a hedge against the erosion of European currencies, and for many years that had meant shares in the big mining houses based in South Africa, which accounted for well over half the free world's annual gold production at that time. The political situation in southern Africa, however, was beginning to look extremely dangerous. Ian Smith had unilaterally declared independence from Britain and the world had heeded Britain's call for the total isolation of Rhodesia (now Zimbabwe). Could South Africa be far behind? Already, the pressure was mounting for "disinvestment" of South African stocks. These institutional investors knew it was only a matter of time before they would be forced to liquidate their South African gold stocks and they had very little to replace them with. The pension funds for the Dutch Post Office and the French railroads did not want to hold junior gold stocks that were promoting traces of gold in their drilling samples in the fond hope that they would transmute into a major orebody. Funds like these needed solid, producing mines in a country that was politically stable.

Munk and his partners looked at the available stocks in which the funds could invest and they found out that companies like Campbell Red Lake and Homestake Mining were trading at 50 or 60 times earnings. That meant investors were prepared, just for the privilege of having a stake in gold, to buy gold stocks with an annual yield of less than 2% a year. It might have been more than the yield on owning gold bullion, which yielded nothing at all, but it was very low compared to any other type of investment. To put it another way, for every dollar of profit that Munk could generate in a gold mine, investors would be prepared to give him up to $60 of capital.

But could he sell his idea to his board of directors?

Munk's twenty-second golden rule:
Don't stop dreaming — and don't stop dreaming big
if you want to succeed.

"They needed it like they needed a hole in the head," Munk said later. "They've just lost $100 million. They're going to take one more idea from Peter Munk?" Indeed, the board scoffed at the idea at first, but Munk characteristically put together an unassailable argument for the leap into gold. It was vintage Munk — and a far cry from the putative tycoon with $100 million in his back pocket, racing for his first billion. Once again, he had to create a new business with no assets and he rose to the challenge.

The timing was perfect. The price of gold had gone berserk at the end of the 1970s, climbing a perpendicular graph past $800 in the space of a few months, then, not much less dramatically, slipping gracefully, but steeply down. By the end of 1980, prices had breached $500 on their way down. They continued down steadily, breaking under the $300 level by the middle of 1982. If anyone wanted to buy a gold mine, the summer of 1982 was the perfect time to start looking, because everyone had given up on gold. The corollary to the dismal price performance was that a lot of gold mines were up for sale. During the 1970s, the big oil companies had demonstrated their own inability to resist the herd instinct and bought into every kind of mining venture they could find in a mad rush to diversify their soaring profits into different industries. By 1983, they were suffering from a severe hangover and started dumping their properties — including some interesting gold prospects — on a market that was already fragile. Gold, as Munk later said, was on its ass.

Unlike the "mature" oil cycle, the gold cycle gave Munk a prevailing wind in his sails and he persuaded his board to accept his vision. In the spring of 1983, Barrick Resources started its limping transformation into its new persona, American Barrick, while its board of directors crossed their fingers, praying that the real Peter Munk was the man who built the hotel chain in the South Pacific, not the man who chased hydrocarbon elephants around the world.

His strategy was crystal clear from the outset and never wavered. Barrick Resources aimed to become a leading producer, operating strictly in North America; grow through the acquisition and development of existing mines; follow conservative financial policies; and eliminate the risk of short-term fluctuations in the gold price with an effective hedging program.

As had happened with the oil companies, there was no shortage of promoters willing to sell him their fabulous geological prospects at a very large discount from their putative real value. They found Munk a hard man to deceive, but he was in a weak position because he knew nothing about gold mining (just as he had known nothing about drilling for oil). He had to find a partner who knew the business. He was looking as much for the right operator as he was for the right mine.

His initial forays into gold were less than stellar. Later, Bob Smith, the canny mining engineer who became the partner he was seeking, looked at the properties his new boss had bought in his first year in the business and pronounced them "dogs." They were imaginative though. Munk went into partnership with the City of Juneau, Alaska, and Alaska Electric Light and Power who jointly owned a cluster of properties, including the Treadwell mine and the Alaska Juneau — two mines that had been the biggest in North America in their day. They had closed down in 1914 and 1944, respectively, but Munk figured there were at least a million ounces of gold the old-timers had missed. There was some gold, he discovered, but not a million ounces. There was also the 23% interest in Valdez Creek in Alaska, which actually produced some gold in 1984. As a newcomer to the industry, however, Munk could not buy into really hot properties; both these initial investments were turfed out of the Barrick portfolio soon after Smith took the operating reins.

The third mine that Munk bought into on his own was Renabie, near Wawa in northern Ontario. Renabie never did much for Barrick, but it was a producing mine with 30,000 ounces a year. More important, it got Munk into the game. It gave him the credibility to take the next step in hooking bigger fish. The real innovation in Renabie, however, was the financing that Munk and his financial lieutenant, Stephen Dattels, put together in an industry previously devoid of financial imagination.

His challenge was that he had no cash, so Step One was to buy the mine for no cash. Barrick paid C$40.45 million for the mine and immediately sold off half of it to Cullaton Lake Gold Mines, which also agreed to operate the mine for the partnership. Cullaton paid for its C$20.2 million share with common shares and cash. To pay for his share of the cost, Munk issued C$11.6 million worth of common and preferred shares in Barrick Resources, then he scrounged up C$8.6 million from the cash he received from Cullaton plus the proceeds from liquidating all of Renabie's superfluous assets and cash.

Step Two was to raise enough money to develop the mine. He used a technique that was to become Munk's hallmark. The Barrick–Cullaton Gold Trust raised C$15 million, net of issuing expenses of C$2 million, at an interest rate of one-quarter the prime rate at that time. The Trust committed to pay, in lieu of interest, a variable royalty on the gold produced by the Renabie mine every year. The mine was then producing about 30,000 ounces of gold a year and Barrick expected to double that to 60,000 ounces through improvements paid for with the money being raised. The royalty was set at 3% of the mine's production if the price of gold was less than $400, 4% if the price was in the 400s, 5% if the price was in the 500s, and so on up to 10% if the price went over $1,000. The gold price at the time of the issue in early 1984 was between $370 and $400, so, if the price didn't change and production stayed the same, the investors stood to earn a return of 2.5% on their money. To earn prime rate, which was then 11%, production would have had to double and the price would have had to rise to $500.

It was a formula that had never been tried, anywhere in the world. If the price of gold had gone back up into the stratosphere it had pierced four years earlier, the investors would have received a handsome yield on their money while Barrick would have made huge profits on the net revenues. Peter Munk was prepared to share the upside with his investors, in return for a break on the downside. In the event, the final cost of the interest on the Barrick–Cullaton Trust worked out to 3.7%. Renabie never did raise its production much above 30,000 ounces a year, although it did reduce its operating costs from a level *The Northern Miner* described as "outrageous," to become a small, but efficient, mine by the end of the decade.

The Renabie mine may not have been too impressive, but it did get Munk to first base. Its biggest drawback was that Munk didn't have anyone on his payroll who could operate it — he had to let a competitor run the mine. Nevertheless, he now had an operating mine that was throwing off a positive cash flow and, thanks to the Barrick–Cullaton Trust, was backed by a presentable balance sheet. This was all he needed as a platform to go after his next target, Camflo Mines, the employer of Bob Smith. Munk knew he could revolutionize the financing of gold mining, but without an effective mine operator who knew the industry, Munk could never hope to build a great gold mining company. Smith was the solution to his problem. He was the yin to his yang. Apart, they were both good in the gold mining industry, but not great. Together, they made like epoxy glue; they assembled the most profitable gold mining company in the world.

Camflo was then owned by Bob Fasken, who comes from an old, distinguished Ontario family. He bought the Camflo mine in about 1974, and rode the wave of its best years, when it delivered 50,000 ounces of gold a year at a cost of only $140 per ounce — among the lowest recovery costs on the continent. It was a little jewel of a gold mine.

But Fasken wanted more. When oil took off and energy prices skyrocketed in the 1970s, he decided to use his stake in gold to make a fortune in energy — including coal, oil and gas, and geothermal. Unfortunately for him, he also borrowed extensively from the Royal Bank to make his own dollars stretch a little further. By the early 1980s, the energy bubble had burst, slashing the prices for oil and coal and making alternative energy sources like geothermal uneconomic. Worse still, punishing interest rates that peaked at more than 20% in the summer of 1981 had devastated every Canadian balance sheet with a heavy debt load. By the spring of 1984, Camflo and its holding company, Bob-Clare Investments, were weighed down with C$100 million in debt and the Royal Bank put its loan to Fasken in its workout department.

"We went through a period of 18 months when the bank was overseeing every check that was written," Smith remembers. Embarrassing for Fasken, and very frustrating for Smith and his technical team — Brian Meikle, Alan Hill, and Dit Holt. Together, they had got the Camflo mine to the point where it was a very well-run operation, but they could do nothing with it, because they had no money. They had all dreamed they might get rich on the price of gold as it took off in 1979/80. They didn't have a lot of shares, but they had a bonus plan and they had a great little mine. "Four or five years earlier, we were sitting on top of the world and now we were on the bottom of the world. We'd seen both sides and where we were looking from wasn't very attractive."

With his slow, halting delivery, Bob Smith is not your glib, smooth-tongued executive. He is about as down-to-earth as you can get, in a suit that looks off-the-rack no matter how hard his tailor tries. His hair is cut to within a frightened half-inch of his scalp. His deeply tanned face looks like it is chipped out of granite, his expression permanently deadpan. When he's with people with whom he is not comfortable (non-miners all), he looks wooden. It's not that he's ill at ease — in fact, he's very sure of himself — but he conceals his emotions to the point of annihilation. When he's with the mining people he so enjoys, however, he lifts up a corner of the deadpan and his light blue eyes light up and sparkle, dancing in the to-and-fro of a miner's banter. The language can get pretty blue, although never offensive. It's a kind of jargon, a required expression of solidarity that brings everyone down to the same level. And the emotion comes pouring out, in the particular idiom of a macho miner — unarticulated and rough, but straight up.

It would be difficult to find someone less like Peter Munk. The elegant, passionate, volatile European with a brilliant financial mind and a casual worldliness — next to the blunt, reserved, rough-hewn, and self-deprecating miner with a mind like a steel trap. The one supremely comfortable in the corridors of power, Old Masters, and fine wine. The other walking on tacks in the elegant bank towers, wishing he could get out to the mines, away from the paper trap, most relaxed with a gin and stogie at the cottage by the lake. He once confided to Munk: "Christ, Peter, I'm the world's worst salesman. I couldn't give a goddamn refrigerator to an Eskimo." But he sells himself short. When he has something to sell that he truly believes in, his integrity and his conviction make him a powerful motivator of people.

Despite all their differences, they didn't clash when they met for the first time in the midst of negotiations. Says Smith: "I had one brief meeting with Peter. I had never met him before and I took an immediate liking to him. But, Jesus, I didn't understand him. He talks so damn fast and he has that European accent, that I only caught every second or third word." He didn't know it at the time, but Munk was not at all sure about him. Bob Fasken had told Munk that one of the people who reported to Smith would be a better choice to run the mine.

Munk didn't know what to do. He was still trying to get the feel of the people in his new industry. "They all speak so badly. This mining fraternity hates glib promoters and they associate quick talk with glib promoters. So, subconsciously, they become bad speakers. They all speak the same. They're halting. Anything over three syllables, they can't pronounce it right. It's an amazing similarity between these miners. And they are quality people. You can trust your kids with them. But they are not smooth, polished international individuals who are prone to new thinking."

In the end, Munk decided to see how Bob Smith worked out before he made any decisions. Smith, meanwhile, had had another offer to work for a mining company in New York City. It was about the last place in the world where he would have liked to live, but it was a genuine offer. At least he had a choice. He talked it over with his three key executives and they decided to stay with Camflo and try Munk for six months. They figured he would find them some money to do some serious mining. Typically, Smith didn't make the decision on his own. Had Munk let him go, he would have lost the whole team of Meikle, Hill, and Holt as well.

The respect that Smith enjoys from his team is remarkable. It's most obvious when an outsider is attacking him or even questioning his judgment. Their hackles rise, and everyone focuses intently on the conversation. It's a two-way sentiment, built on many years of staying close to his employees. "None of this 'Mister' shit," he says gruffly. "I think the same way as them. We try to get it across to our managers, supervisors, foremen that the guys in the pit are the guys who get the job done. If you treat people as human beings, 90% of the time they'll work their arse off. And sometimes they have logical beefs!"

Smith joined Camflo in the year it built its mill, 1964, near Val d'Or in northern Quebec, 300 miles due north of Toronto. He nursed it through its teething years, honing it into one of the best-managed mines on the continent. Every year at Christmas, he would get up and give his French-speaking miners his annual message in their own language. He is not kind to the English language, and he inflicts terminal damage on French, but his miners respected him for trying. On one occasion, one of the underground miners, a giant weighing at least 250 pounds, who couldn't speak a word of English, decided he didn't need words to express how he felt. He walked up to Smith and gave him a big hug. It broke one of Smith's ribs. To this day, Smith is inordinately proud of that moment.

"His" people have become his family. It's a metaphor he uses constantly. "Part of why we've been so successful, as I look back, is all of us have become very close, like a family. There's no one individual, it was a collection of tremendous human beings that all pulled together at the same time and we all benefited. It's almost like a family coming from the wrong side of the tracks, and they make it. We did a hell of a lot of things that most other people wouldn't have bothered to do. We took the extra step, maybe two extra steps. We tried harder."

Of course, the aw-shucks-down-at-the-pit routine is, like the language, a form of jargon. Smith and his team were (and are) as technically brilliant a group as any in North America. Over the next few years, they would find value in mines where dozens of the best and richest mining companies in the world had looked hard and found nothing. In concert with Peter Munk, they would lift the entire gold mining industry onto a new plane, as they embarked on developments that were bigger than anyone had ever done before — and completed them within budget, faster than anyone would have guessed possible.

Before this team could start to shake the tree, however, Munk had to complete the purchase of Camflo from Bob Fasken. The company was essentially bankrupt and Munk's board of directors was not impressed. They saw no benefit at all in adding C$100 million to their debt load in return for another 50,000 ounces a year and they argued strenuously against their chairman. However, Munk outlined his plan for financing the deal in such a way that the debt could be paid off in a year and the balance sheet strengthened significantly. To their subsequent great joy, they saw the light and signed on. Munk then approached the Royal Bank with a proposal to merge Camflo and Bob-Clare Investments with Barrick Resources.

The immediate reaction of the bank was to question the financial acuity of the man who had led Clairtone into failure. Joe Rotman flew up to Montreal to meet Brian Gregson, the man in charge of the workout department and told him of

Munk's great success after Clairtone. The bank was skeptical, but it was contemplating a major write-off anyway, so it agreed to sell the company for its debt, provided Munk could raise C$30 million in equity. The deal was concluded for the Royal Bank by John Clarke, Gregson's deputy, because Gregson was a close personal friend of Fasken's and had a conflict of interest. "They knew they were paying too much," Clarke remembers now, "but I could see he wanted that mine so badly, he would pay what I asked for. They tried to back out but we wouldn't lower the price, although we changed it around a bit."

Raising the C$30 million, however, was not an easy task. Munk's biggest problem was that he had sold shares of Barrick to Prince Nawaf and the Kuwaiti Investment Office the previous year for almost C$2 and the share was then trading at about C$1.90. If he sold the shares at market price, his Arab partners would feel they had been given a bad deal, so Munk and Birchall quickly decided to set the price for the issue at C$2.10.

"It was the hardest thing I ever did," Munk said later. Barrick's stock drifted from C$1.90 to C$1.75 on the Toronto Stock Exchange. He pulled out every last IOU, he poured out the last ounce of enthusiasm and salesmanship he could muster. "It was a combination of credibility, contacts, and my success in the hotel business. It was also the fact that I'd put my own money into it. I was very serious, but it was still very, very tough. If I hadn't had some good friends at the end . . ."

How do you get someone to pay C$2.10 for something they can buy for C$1.75 somewhere else? Munk argued:

1. The pro forma company is worth more than the market and I am not going to sell shares below their worth — it's C$2.10 or nothing.

2. The share float is too small, so if any investors try to buy shares on the market, the price will shoot up over C$2.10 anyway.

3. I am putting my own money in (C$2 million borrowed from the Midland Bank), so obviously I really believe they are worth C$2.10 or I would have bought on the open market.

4. In three years' time, the value of these shares will have increased so much, they will be the best buy you have ever made, so why quibble over 35¢?

Munk's twenty-third golden rule:
It's management's job to do what's right, not what's easy or convenient.

With the equity issue in the bank, the Royal rescheduled Camflo's loans, giving Munk one year to pay off the remaining C$70 million. He collected C$32 million by selling the oil and gas interests that Fasken had bought for more than C$42 million and then raised C$53 million with his second gold issue, the Gold Company of America, another brilliantly conceived financing. This time the interest was paid in gold, at a rate that varied with the price of gold. If the gold price was $365, the interest rate was 8%, which represented cheap money for Barrick at a time when the prime rate had been 11% to 13% over the previous three months. If the price rose, the interest rate rose with it. If gold went up to $1,500 an ounce, the Gold Company of America was set to earn 40% a year. Once again, he hung out an outrageous bait, counting on investors' cupidity when it came to gold. People lined up to buy the issue. Gold never returned to the highs of 1980, of course, and Barrick once again had raised very cheap money.

The gold-backed issue deprived Camflo of more than 20% of its annual output of 35,000 to 40,000 ounces a year, but the combined company had a balance sheet with no debt and was moving toward a respectable level of annual production. With Camflo, he had satisfied his first three criteria — annual production in North America was in sight of 100,000 ounces a year and his balance sheet was squeaky clean and conservative. The only trouble was that it wasn't making any money. In its early days Camflo had yielded its gold at a cost of $140 an ounce, but the declining grades of the orebody were pushing the recovery costs higher and, by 1984, they had passed $200 an ounce. With gold trading at $300 to $350 for the first two years that Barrick owned the mine, that didn't leave a lot of room for profit: after depositing the 20% of production as interest to the Gold Company of America, the effective revenues worked out to $240 to $280 an ounce. They had no cash flow and the banks would not lend them a penny.

Munk monitored cash flow on a daily basis. He collapsed the pension plan and took the surplus of C$1.7 million into general funds. He froze salaries and gave everyone stock options instead. For Smith and his dedicated team, it was a distressingly familiar routine, but Munk worked his magic. He exuded confidence that he could raise the money they needed. All it would take, he told them, was for Bob Smith, Brian Meikle, Alan Hill, and Dit Holt to find a few mines that would generate some serious profits. He would find the money to buy them.

The test was not long in coming. One year and two weeks after he closed the Camflo deal, Munk closed the purchase of the Mercur mine from Texaco. In between, Smith had looked at a lot of companies. None panned out until they heard about Mercur. All the top gold mining companies had looked at it and no one wanted to touch it. Its recovery costs were $270 to $290 while the price of gold in the first half of 1985 averaged about $300, hitting a low of $282 and never going higher than $339. Texaco was in a bind, however, because Wall Street was beginning to harass the oil companies for their ill-fated diversification into other mining industries and Texaco was extremely anxious to get Mercur off its balance sheet. But not that anxious. The minuscule Canadian company didn't register very high on the Richter scale when they approached the man in charge of disposing of Texaco's surplus assets, Peter Bijur, a tough but fair-minded executive used to dealing in billions rather than millions. Munk got him to listen, however.

Bijur then met with Smith and assured himself that Barrick would look after the employees, that their pension plan would not be touched, and that any layoffs would be done properly. He also knew that Smith had a first-class reputation in the industry, thanks to the squeaky-clean operation he had run at Camflo for 20 years. His biggest concern, however, was that Texaco be paid. He wanted it all in cash.

Munk and Smith knew they had to have this mine, but at what price? Munk could raise the financing if the price was low enough to make it a profitable deal, but Bijur was known to be a very tough bargainer. They had to find out if there were ways they could change the management of the mine to squeeze more profit out of it than Texaco could — and Bijur allowed them to spend two days at the mine to find out. Two days is not a lot of time to assess an entire mining operation, especially when the managers and miners were thoroughly disillusioned by the string of distracted owners they had already endured. Morale was low and the prospect of another unstable owner, this time a really small company with negligible resources, made it sag even further. In those two days, however, Smith and his team saw things that the entire industry had missed.

"They didn't dissect it enough," Smith says. "We went in there with the attitude not that we were going to walk in and buy a Cadillac, that the engines would be all tuned and away we'd go. We went in there realizing that we were buying a bit of a wreck. How could we fix up that wreck as fast as we could and make it run?"

It turned out that the mine was a first-class facility. It had the best equipment and a good workforce, but it was hopelessly badly managed. Smith put together a swat team, consisting of his three technical men, two key people from Kilborn Engineering, the premier consulting firm in the business, and him. Alan Hill looked into the quality of the ore reserves, Kilborn's Roger Mendick looked at how they might increase the throughput in the mill, Dit Holt was responsible for assessing the overall geology of the region, and Brian Meikle crunched the numbers on costs. For two days, they combed the property looking for clues in their area of responsibility, while Smith and Kilborn's president, Jack Mitchell, pulled all the pieces together and figured out how they could make it work. When their time was up, the six of them retired to the Little America Hotel in Salt Lake City. Each one of them shared their observations and debated the implications and they slowly developed a consensus. By 4 a.m., they had a cash flow forecast they felt comfortable with and a commitment that they could lower the recovery costs to $230.

On the basis of that cash flow, Munk figured he couldn't raise more than about $30 million — not a king's ransom considering Getty Oil, the previous owner, had spent $100 million bringing the mine into production. He put in his bid, but Exxon offered $60 million, which was way out of his reach. However, in doing its due diligence, Exxon began to get cold feet. A former partner whom Getty Oil had bought out was suing the mine for $650 million because he was unhappy with the deal he'd made. Also, the price of gold was continuing its steady decline toward $300. Exxon withdrew its bid.

Bijur could still have continued the search for another buyer at $60 million or thereabouts, but Munk clinched the deal in a late-night session, arguing that every other buyer would take months to decide while they picked over the same old issues, whereas he could make an instant decision and take Mercur off his hands in a clean deal. He also convinced Bijur that he could raise the money to finance the $30 million price tag. That wasn't enough for Bijur, who would not take anything less than $40 million to his board. Munk played his last card. He would pay $31 million in cash, plus a kicker. If the price of gold went above $385 (it was then trading at $325), Texaco would receive half of the revenues from the excess over $385, up to a maximum of $9 million. It worked. Bijur could say he had sold Mercur for $40 million and Munk had to raise only $31 million. If the gold price earned the extra $9 million for Texaco, Munk could raise the extra cash out of cash flow.

When he got home the following night, he opened a bottle of champagne. Melanie was a little puzzled. Her husband drank very little and it was quite out of character to sip champagne late at night. But he was elated, as she soon found out. He knew he had made the breakthrough that would lift him into the second tier of North American gold mines. For the third time in his life, he had entered an industry about which he knew absolutely nothing and had put down strong roots. He had created an operating business with a cash flow that would enable him to grow and he had married it to an effective management team. As it turned out, Texaco got its $40 million — and there wasn't a happier man than Munk when he paid up.

With the new mine in his pocket, Smith wasted no time. He tore into it like a whirlwind. He let the general manager go and within six weeks, he had turned around the morale problem. The Mercur workers didn't know what to expect from the Canadians. Smith soon let them know. He persuaded Frank Wicks, one of Texaco's mining executives, to leave his desk in Salt Lake City and come to Mercur, 35 miles to the southwest. The workers all trusted Wicks and Smith's team soon got Wicks so excited that he caught the Barrick enthusiasm and passed it on to the workers. Smith almost lived at the mine for the first eight months. He was in the machine shop, riding the trucks, at the pit face, everywhere, talking to people, showing an interest in them. This was a new experience for the miners. In the board-room of the administration building, he put up a big board that recorded how many ounces they recovered every day. "It was a sort of a contest," he says. "Can we do better?"

Within three months, Smith had ratcheted recovery costs down to $190 an ounce, and increased production from 79,000 ounces in 1984 to 93,000 ounces in 1985 and 111,000 ounces in 1986. They increased the value of the mine to five times the purchase price. "The previous management were more concerned with making budget than with making money," Smith comments. "They had a big-oil mentality. They were not stupid or lazy, just misguided."

Although Smith made all the decisions regarding mining matters, Munk's leadership was a critical ingredient in the recipe. "Part of it was Peter's desire to succeed," Smith says. "I told Peter that I thought we could make a go of this and I god-damn well wasn't going to let him down. I think the operating guys wanted to show Peter that indeed we could get the job done. We got caught up in the challenge. Every decent mining company had looked at this thing and turned it down. So here we come along. In those days, most people would have said, 'Jeez, those guys aren't for real, they don't know what they're doing and they haven't got the staying power.' We were out to prove that everybody else was wrong. There was just that desire to succeed. We'd travel at night to work all day . . . I mean, we didn't give a shit."

Smith had never had a boss like this before. Munk gave him the ball and let him run. "He never, never questions my decisions concerning operations," he has said many times. "In certain areas where he doesn't think I have the same expertise, he'll question, which is super. I would never second-guess his financial decisions. I wouldn't think of it."

This trust is what makes the Munk–Smith partnership special. Each knows his own skills and respects those of the other. Of course, this extraordinary level of trust is not unconditional. If Munk is satisfied that someone is doing a job, he leaves them alone. The minute he senses something isn't working well, however, he gets deeply involved, and quickly. He will do whatever has to be done, whether it involves the lowliest employee or a member of his board who turns out to be incompatible: "You tell them to step down if they don't fit. I have conviction for my views and I have no problem doing whatever they dictate." More than one of his board members has quietly disappeared from view, and he doesn't spare a second in recriminations. It was his mistake inviting the person to join the board and if it didn't work out, there's no percentage in agonizing over it. Just fix it.

"To anybody, to my best friend, if you have got to communicate, you have got to communicate the bad news. It's a very

Anglo-Saxon thing to talk of the good things only. You gotta tell people. That's what relationships are for. Life is not a cocktail party where you only say meaningless pleasantries."

Munk's twenty-fourth golden rule:
Trust is the foundation. You cannot substitute for trust.
Trust means you say the truth.

It's an integral part of the whole package, consistent with the man's relentless focus on what's best for the company. If he had spent time second-guessing Bob Smith's views on the Mercur turnaround, neither would have been as effective. That focus is what keeps everything in line. Everyone understands what's expected of them and they deliver. Mercur was the first test of that approach for Munk and Smith, and it worked beautifully.

In the summer of 1986, Munk was breathing easily for the first time in several years. After Bob Smith had worked his magic on the production costs of the Mercur mine, Barrick was finally in a position where it had some cash flow that gave it room to maneuver. It actually made an operating profit for the first time in 1985 — and that was the year Munk chose to write off past losses of $20 million, wiping the slate clean from Barrick Exploration's disastrous foray into oil and gas. Now, in 1986, after-tax profits were running at $12 million and Barrick was throwing off a cash flow of $25 million a year. Annual production was running at 185,000 ounces, making Barrick a solid, second-tier player in the gold industry. Munk was respectable, even if he was still some way behind the biggest producer in North America at the time, Placer Dome, which had an annual production of 836,000 ounces.

Munk had set himself a target of 300,000 ounces a year by 1988 and he now began an energetic search to build up his production. As before, he intended to achieve his expansion through judicious acquisitions. His engineers at Mercur told him of two jewels of gold mines that were owned by Consolidated Goldfields PLC (ConsGold) of London — Mesquite in California and Chimney Creek in Nevada. Between them, these two produced 430,000 ounces of gold a year at an impressive average cost per ounce of $106. With combined reserves of 5.2 million ounces (and still counting), they would have been perfect to take Barrick to the next stage in its ambitious growth.

James Capel, a London firm of stockbrokers, had recently prepared a report suggesting that ConsGold was an excellent target for a takeover. Its shares were then trading at £4 to £4.50, while its underlying assets were worth between £7 and £10 a share. Munk got a copy of the report and decided to try to do a deal with ConsGold. His primary objective was to buy the Mesquite and Chimney Creek mines, so he developed a proposal to offer ConsGold a significant stake in Barrick in return for the two mines, on condition that ConsGold leave management control with Munk. If that didn't work, Plan B was to buy all of ConsGold and sell off the assets he didn't want. He figured that he could sell the unwanted assets for about the same amount it would cost him to buy the whole company, so he would, in effect, get the two mines he was after for nothing.

It was a cheeky plan, to put it mildly. The value of all Barrick's shares on the stock market was then slightly more than $200 million. The market capitalization of ConsGold was more than $1.5 billion, or almost eight times larger, even at its undervalued price. ConsGold's annual pre-tax income of $340 million was 25 times more than Barrick's $13.4 million. Its mines, not all wholly owned, produced among them 5.3 million ounces a year, or more than 28 times Barrick's annual production. ConsGold was founded by Cecil Rhodes in 1887. Barrick Gold had a history stretching all the way back to 1983.

When Rudolph Agnew, ConsGold's chairman, was told in November 1986 that Barrick wanted to talk some serious turkey, he was not amused. It was derisory that such a minnow would have the temerity even to ask for an appointment with such a captain of industry, let alone threaten him with a takeover. ConsGold was an international giant, with properties on four continents. It owned 38% of Gold Fields of South Africa, which owned Kloof and Driefontein, the richest gold mines in the country. Its properties included 26% of Newmont Mining, the largest gold mining company in the United States, and a slew of mining companies in Britain and Australia.

Munk, however, had prepared himself well. In the early stages of his planning, the price of gold had come alive. Gold shares took note and went along for the ride. The price of Barrick shares doubled in six months. This was a situation tailor-made for Peter Munk's first principle — raise money when the market is hot. In that fall, he went to the market twice to raise $81 million through equity and bond issues.

At the same time that his fall financings were approaching completion, Munk instructed his London brokers to start buying ConsGold. In the six weeks to the middle of October, he accumulated a 4.5% stake in ConsGold at a cost of $84 million. The strong market for gold shares was working on ConsGold too, of course, and by the time he had completed his purchases, it was trading at £6.69, up from £5.02 when he had started six weeks earlier. While he was buying his ConsGold shares, he was also busy negotiating a line of credit for £900 million with Midland

Bank and the Hong Kong and Shanghai Bank, giving him a war chest of $1.75 billion for ConsGold. This was more than enough money to buy half of ConsGold. He would have been content with only half, because 30% was already owned by Minorco, the Luxembourg subsidiary of the South African gold mining giant, Anglo American — and Munk was banking on working cooperatively with the Oppenheimer family, who controlled Anglo.

He decided he would offer Agnew Plan A, and if he didn't like that, Munk was ready with Plan B, which could be implemented at a moment's notice. Agnew liked neither. He was outraged. He accused Munk of greenmail. He refused to negotiate "under threats." He told Munk that he would destroy his reputation. "Even if you get ConsGold, I'll make sure your name is mud and your children will be embarrassed to have a father like that." He hired Kroll, Britain's foremost accounting firm in the esoteric field of dirty tricks in fighting takeovers. Kroll set to work to dig up as much dirt as it could on the "Hungarian émigré," while Agnew calmed down and promised to think about Munk's proposal. It was a ploy to buy time, of course, but Munk decided he'd bitten off more than he could chew. He had not wanted to pay much more than £7 a share for ConsGold and the share price looked like it was going well above that. He decided to sell off his 9.7 million shares in the first two months of 1987 at a sizable profit. He had other fish to fry.

At about the same time that he was looking at ConsGold, another opportunity was working its way through Barrick. In the course of 1986, Joe Rotman, who had joined Munk's board for his foray into oil and gas, but had stayed on as a director after Barrick shifted into gold, found himself wrestling with a gold property he had inadvertently bought as part of PanCana Resources, an oil and gas company he had purchased from the

233

Royal Bank in 1979. He turned, naturally, to Munk and Smith for advice.

Rotman is indisputably one of the heavyweights on the Barrick board. His principal business now is Clairvest, a merchant bank that seeks turnaround situations where it can supply cash and management expertise. He doesn't like operating companies himself — he sees himself as an investor who backs entrepreneurs. He had originally intended to become an academic, obtaining his Master's degree in Commerce from the University of Toronto, then studying for his PhD in business at Columbia University in New York. But he never got his doctorate — the pull of business was too strong, and he quit academe to take over the family business. His father, Manny, an illiterate immigrant from Poland, had built a coal business that was easing into oil when the son took over in 1963. Rotman built it some more, then moved on to become an oil trader, buying and selling whole tankers of raw crude in an arbitrage business that rationalized international discrepancies between demand and supply. In 1973, he decided he'd had enough — there was more action in oil exploration. So he sold everything and went out west to learn the business.

Rotman's understated, impeccably tailored suits are a perfect mask for his entrepreneurial flair — although he might be less than enthusiastic about being called entrepreneurial. He is more comfortable with words that conjure up images of strategy, sound business sense, and logic. That is how his fellow directors see him. His counsel is respected by all of them and closely heeded by Peter Munk, who rates him "very good." Although their styles are quite different, he and Munk are twins in methodology. Extremely cautious, Rotman researches his business concepts with the rigorous detachment of an academic; he cuts through the "noise" of misinformation and confusion with the cool focus that separates the creators of super wealth from so-so achievers. Like Munk, he doesn't move until he has nailed down every conceivable angle; unlike Munk, he rarely jumps into the fray himself, preferring a serene detachment to the passionate involvement that defines Peter Munk.

Rotman moves just like he speaks — with grace and deliberation, never hasty, always in complete control. He has a suave charm, which can stretch to gallantry, but behind the charm is a mind that never stops calculating. Self-contained, emotionally distant, he watches, waits, and ponders his next move. He can turn his charm on and off with a seamless display of diplomatic savoir faire, camouflaging a ruthless determination that will brook no opposition once in pursuit of a goal he has set for himself. He is a tough man when a business deal goes awry. He himself acknowledges that he has burned a few too many bridges with his harsh reaction to the flawed business acumen of some of his former associates.

He became a public persona in Toronto when he negotiated the loan of the Barnes collection to the Art Gallery of Ontario, where he was serving a two-year stint as president. The extraordinary collection of Impressionist paintings assembled by Dr. Albert Barnes in Merion, Pennsylvania, had never traveled before 1992 because Dr. Albert Barnes had willed it so. But when the museum building needed more repair than the entrance fees could ever hope to pay for, a judge agreed to allow the trustees to break the will temporarily and lend the collection to five galleries around the world. The winners, from the dozens of cities that competed for the right, were Washington, Paris, Tokyo, Fort Worth, and Toronto. Actually, Toronto was initially turned down in favor of Los Angeles, but Rotman got the trustees to change their minds. It was a quite extraordinary effort of salesmanship, cajoling, charm, and influence peddling, pursued with relentless determination by a man who simply refused to take "no" for an answer.

Not long after his triumph at the AGO, he donated C$3 million (with more still to come) to the Faculty of Management at the University of Toronto. The donation enabled the faculty to build new facilities, the Joseph L. Rotman building. He finally got his doctorate, an honorary LLB, three months before the building opened.

When Rotman had first bought PanCana in 1979, he had tried to unload his small gold mine, called Goldstrike, but no one would buy it. It was a dog. It may have been in the Carlin Trend, the richest gold-bearing belt in North America, but it was losing money and the staff were demoralized. Even Newmont Gold, the huge gold company that owned a lot of the land in the Carlin Trend and was Goldstrike's next-door neighbor, turned him down flat. Rotman decided to keep it and hired some mining executives to try to build it into something. But he did not hold high hopes — he carried the mine in his books at $1.

His partner in Goldstrike was Western States Minerals Corp., which was the operator of the mine. Western States was owned by S. J. Groves, a construction company in Minneapolis, which was in trouble, and it was offloading some of its equipment on Goldstrike, where it just lay around rusting. Because it was strapped for cash, S. J. Groves refused to spend any money on the property. "They were not miners," Rotman says. "They were earth movers and they took the earth-moving principle and applied it to strip mining because they had the equipment and the people for that kind of operation."

Rotman leaned on Western States to drill at least one

exploratory hole to see what reserves might be on the property at greater depth. They finally agreed to do so and came up with a very promising drilling sample — 391 feet of high-grade ore, indicating significant reserves. However, the reserves were all refractory ore, which is extremely difficult to extract. Western States declined to drill any more holes, hoping that the promise of big reserves from its single hole would be enough to tickle the fancy of potential buyers. It didn't work. Newmont, which knew the orebody better than anyone else, said the metallurgy did not exist to extract the gold from the refractory ore at a profit. Meanwhile, the financial situation was deteriorating for S. J. Groves, which was then forced to sell an asset. The owner had to choose between selling his horse farm in southern Kentucky or the Goldstrike mine. He chose the mine.

In 1986, Rotman introduced Western States to an investment house in Toronto, Burns, Fry, which started hawking the property. Rotman was hoping he would acquire a partner who would be easier to work with and he tried to introduce Munk to Western States and Burns, Fry. However, Western States insisted on a full bidding process and Burns, Fry refused to see Munk, because they felt Barrick was too small to be considered as a feasible purchaser. Rotman finally took matters into his own hands. He took Smith aside after a Barrick board meeting and asked him to take a look at the operation and advise him. "I think they're screwing me," he said. He was right.

Smith and his team went down to Elko, Nevada, to take a look at the property. As had happened with Mercur, they found that the operators were not exploiting the orebody to maximum advantage. The mine had official reserves of 625,000 ounces of gold and was producing about 30,000 ounces a year. It was losing money and the capital base of the mine was too small to engage in sophisticated recovery techniques. Smith and his team were confident that by spending a little money and using a variety of recovery methods, they could increase the recoverable reserves to 1.2 million ounces. He was interested in buying it.

Meanwhile, Burns, Fry had still had no luck with Western States's position. Newmont was sitting on 250,000 acres in eastern Nevada, much of it with promising gold deposits. It had enough on its plate to keep it busy for many years to come, so Goldstrike's 6,900 acres were not going to make much difference. It offered a derisory price for Goldstrike. Burns, Fry finally had to talk with Munk and Smith. However, they were not interested in part ownership, so before Munk bid for the Western States shares, he called Rotman and asked if PanCana would sell its share of Goldstrike to Barrick. Rotman agreed, and Western States accepted his offer. The deal closed on December 31, 1986.

When Smith and co. were checking out Goldstrike, Brian Meikle had stood at the lip of the open pit one day and said to his colleagues. "You know, we've got Genesis a few miles to the south [3 million to 4 million ounces of reserves owned by Newmont], we've got Bootstrap and Dee a few more miles to the north-west — that's another 2 million ounces — and there's all these little small pits, scattered all over the place. I wonder if all these pits represent a leakage from something major, at depth." No one took it any further, but they all knew it was a possibility.

Meanwhile, Smith had crunched his numbers and figured that even if they didn't find another ounce beyond the 1.2 million they knew they could deliver, Barrick could pay $62 million for the mine and still break even. Munk never questioned his estimate. He never even visited the mine. He offered $62 million and all the shareholders accepted. Groves had wanted

$35 million for its 50%, so a price of $31 million was not a lot lower than what it had asked for — but it was still a ridiculously high price according to virtually every single analyst on the Toronto and New York stock exchanges.

The analysts soon had to eat their words. A couple of months later, Smith was vacationing in Florida when he got a call from Brian Meikle, telling him the core from their first exploratory drill hole was showing 0.36 ounces of gold per ton for a depth of 330 feet. That was five times the gold content at Barrick's best mine. Smith's immediate reaction was, "Some son-of-a-bitch has salted the core. That's too good to be true. Drill another hole ten feet away." He didn't even tell Munk. Meikle obliged and gave Smith even better assay results. Smith started ordering other holes further and further away and gradually it dawned on them that the orebody was just what Meikle had speculated it might be — a massive gold-bearing deposit deep underground that spread its tentacles all around the area. They knew they had hit the jackpot.

8

GOLDSTRIKE

The Goldstrike mine is one big hole. From the air, it looks like an amphitheater, its walls pitched steeply at a 35° angle and its serried benches carved out by the access roads that spiral round the pit. A small army of machines claws incessantly at the pit face, pushing it steadily back and deeper, as they haul out more than 400,000 tons of earth a day. That's 150 million tons a year. The trucks roll gently down the benches, descending at a 7° grade, in an endless procession from the rim, until they reach one of the 42-cubic-yard "shovels," which are creating new access roads from what's left of the old ones they have chewed away. The trucks back into one of the slots reserved for them on either side of the giant shovel. Within seconds, the first mouthful of rock and sand crashes into the truck's box,

240

followed by two more in the next half minute, by which time the box is full. Within seconds, the operators roll their trucks away to make way for the next truck, which is already backing into the spot. They retrace their path, trundling up the access road again, at the same inexorable speed, until they crest the rim again and roll easily on to the mill.

The peerless organization is pervasive. The shovels (all nine of them) never stop. The 75 trucks barely wait as they arrive and leave in ordered sequence. For 24 hours a day, seven days a week, in rain or shine or snow, these workhorses claw away at the amphitheater, pushing it back 50 feet, moving a mountain every few months. From the air, the scene does not appear extraordinary. The trucks appear "normal," the shovels quite ordinary, their proportions in perfect synch with the pit. Inside the pit, however, the sheer enormity of the project is awesome. The pit is one and a half miles long and one mile wide. In late 1995, it was already 330 yards deep, with another 200 yards to go before it is finished. Each truck carries a 190-ton load — each mouthful of the shovel dumps 65 to 70 tons into its box. One shovel-load would fill an average living room up to its ceiling. The trucks are as big as an average two-storey house, standing 24 feet high.

It looks so easy. The engines of the trucks aren't straining, there's no sense of rush. But it's deceptive. The workload exhausts these $1.3 million steel monsters after only 15 months of full-time operation. Their wheels are 12 feet high — the tires cost $16,500 each and last for about five months. If they go too fast, they burn up, so they stick to 8 mph when they're fully loaded and going up a normal grade. Even then, they consume 113 gallons (U.S.) of diesel fuel an hour. To ease the strain on the trucks and cut back on diesel fuel, Barrick spent $26 million installing an electric trolley assist system. The electrical power comes on pylons that thread their way along the main access roads, carrying 7,000 volts to the pit face. When the trucks go up the ramp fully loaded, they raise their pentograph (a bar above the cab) and connect up to the overhead wires that power them up while the engine idles. The system more than pays for itself, because it cuts fuel consumption to about eight gallons an hour.

The elaborate mesh of intricate maneuvers is orchestrated from the dispatch tower perched on the edge of the rim. The "lords of the pit" keep a watchful eye on their computers, which track every shovel and every truck, tracing their progress on a graphic diagram that instantly shows logjams or gaps. Spaced at strategic points along the roads are signal points, electronic sensors that pick up the ID of every passing truck and send it to the lords of the pit, who can see instantly if a driver is taking his load to the wrong destination. These sensors will soon be replaced by electronic devices that bounce a message off a satellite and back to the tower.

Every load has a specific destination — one of 11 possible piles. Before each new section of the pit is exposed to a shovel's bite, several holes are drilled to assess the gold content of that section. This enables the mining engineers to estimate the gold content of each mouthful of the shovel so they can calibrate the mixture of ores that is sent on to the mill. The different piles of sand and rock at the door of the mill vary from "sub-ore" (less than 0.065 ounces per ton) through nine grades of ore that start with the low concentrations of 0.065 to 0.15 ounces per ton and reach to the highest concentrations of 0.65 ounces per ton and up. The last pile is waste, which is dumped elsewhere.

The lowest grades of less than 0.065 ounces per ton cannot be economically processed and would normally be discarded or treated with a very cheap process that recovers a small part of the gold. This mine, however, is so big that there is a sizable fortune locked in the sub-ore. Barrick is doing its best to wrestle even this low-grade material into gold bars. One of many ideas it is currently investigating is the possibility of using bacteria to "eat" the gold, then extracting the bacteria and adding it to the higher grade ores. Bob Smith is skeptical of this idea, favoring instead a technique that douses the sand with a mixture which attaches the gold-bearing ore to bubbles; these bubbles float the ore up to the surface where it can be skimmed off. Either way, Barrick will leave very few specks of gold in the tailings when it finally abandons the open pit at Goldstrike.

The mill itself is something of a marvel. It can process 17,500 tons of ore a day, which it smashes, mashes, remashes, and grinds into a dust the consistency of baby powder. This, one quickly understands, is not panning for gold nuggets. The gold in this orebody is measured in microns and submicrons — less than one thousandth of a millimeter — that are locked into a larger "host" from which they must be chemically separated. This is by far the most common form in which gold appears all over the world. There is actually a great deal of gold in the earth's crust, but very rarely in concentrations that are economic to recover. The oceans are estimated to contain billions of tons of it — but, at six parts of gold per trillion parts of sea water, it's impossible to make any money "mining" it.

The most common method of recovery today is cyanidation, which was first discovered by the South Africans in 1890. The gold is dissolved out of its host when the crushed ore is sprayed with sodium cyanide, mixed with lime (which prevents the solution from becoming acidic, at which point it would give off lethal cyanide gas). The cyanide solution is then subjected to activated carbon, which acts as a magnet for the gold in solution. The "pregnant carbon" is then stripped and the gold in solution is electro-plated onto steel wool. Finally, the steel wool and gold are melted and a powder (flux) is added to absorb the iron and other impurities. The flux separates from the residual gold (now 93% pure) and is chipped off the bullion when it has cooled.

Cyanidation isn't the answer to all orebodies, however. It works well with oxide ores, where the hosts to the gold have been oxidized by years of very high pressure in the presence of oxygen. These are most commonly quartz and clay, which are porous, enabling the cyanide to reach into every cranny of the host and dissolve the flecks of gold locked into the structure. Most of the reserves at Goldstrike and at Mercur, however, are refractory (non-amenable) ores, locked into sulphides like pyrite and marcasite. Sulphide ores are not porous and the cyanide can recover only 20% to 30% of the gold locked into them.

Up until the mid-1980s, most gold mines put the refractory ores through a heap leaching process, which sprays the ore with sodium cyanide, collects the pregnant solution, and adds carbon. It is feasible only because the ore does not go through the mill and is therefore not as expensive to process — but it is a terrible waste of gold because the recovery rates are so low. Before Barrick bought it, Mercur was milling a mixture of sulphide and oxide ores, which was one of the main reasons recovery costs were so expensive — the milling of sulphide ores doesn't help recover much extra gold, so the expense of milling it is a waste. The first thing Smith did was to separate the sulphide ore and stockpile it until he found a better way to get at that gold, thereby dramatically improving the recovery rate from the pure oxide ore going into the mill.

Smith already had some idea of how he might get at the gold

in the sulphide ores, but the technology was still unproven and widely regarded in the industry as inapplicable to gold ore-bodies. Autoclaving had been used in many base minerals for years, starting with aluminum in the early part of this century, but the first people to use it on gold were, once again, the South Africans. Only one mine in North America was using an auto-clave — a few years previously, Homestake Mining had commissioned one at its Californian gold mine. So, when Barrick commissioned an autoclave unit for Mercur within two years of buying the mine, it was taking a huge risk on an unproven technology that was being used by only three gold mines in the whole world.

An autoclave is a giant pressure cooker. It takes in a slurry of heated ore and raises the temperature to 425°F under pressure of 420 pounds per square inch. In 55 minutes, it does what nature needs millions of years to do — it oxidizes the sulphides, so that the transformed slurry can go through the usual process for oxide ores, yielding more than 90% of its gold content.

This little loop in the production process is not quite as simple as that, of course. The success of the process depends on the nature of the orebody. If it is carbonaceous, the autoclave doesn't work well, because the carbon acts as a "pregnant rob-ber," which attracts the gold dissolved in the cyanide. Fortunately for Barrick, however, the sulphides at both Mercur and Goldstrike are suitable for autoclaving. The process is also very sensitive to the gold content in the slurry. The slurry spon-taneously generates heat during the process and it boils over if the gold concentration gets too high; on the other hand, if the gold content is too low for the design of the autoclave, steam has to be added to achieve the required temperatures (and that costs money). This is why the ore has to be dumped in nine piles at the entrance of the mill — so that the ore can be mixed and matched to keep the gold content steady.

The success of the autoclaves also depends on the overall gold concentration in the orebody. Each autoclave costs about $30 million to build and $13 per ton of ore to operate. If the gold content is below about 0.065 ounces per ton, increasing the recovery rate by 60% still doesn't yield enough extra gold to pay for the processing cost of the autoclave. So there must be solid assurance that a mine will deliver more than 0.065 ounces per ton over the life of the autoclave.

With all these problems and unknowns, putting an autoclave unit into Mercur was a massive leap of faith. The board of directors was nervous, but Munk trusted completely Smith's opinion that it would work. The first unit, designed to handle 750 tons a day, was commissioned in early 1988, and recovery rates on the sulphide ores quadrupled to 81%. Encouraged, Barrick started planning to install autoclaves at Goldstrike.

Smith knew the technology was still problem prone, but he also knew that the sulphide reserves at Goldstrike were very rich, with concentrations consistently above 0.3 ounces per ton. That meant there would be a huge payoff from increasing the recovery rate from 30% to 90%-plus. With the dawning realization that the sulphide reserves at Goldstrike were massive as well as rich, the stakes had become very high indeed and Munk could see no virtue in hesitating. Still, the projected cost was $180 million — a massive bet on autoclaving before anyone really knew if it would deliver the estimated economic benefits. The board wrestled with the autoclave issue for years, gingerly giving the go-ahead in clumps of one or two, testing them extensively and monitoring them carefully. But they gave Smith the green light in the summer of 1988, and he started the process of installing the first 1,500-ton unit. Ultimately, six autoclaves were built at Goldstrike with a capacity to process 17,500 tons of ore a day.

It proved to be a brilliant decision. The autoclaves have been very successful, particularly at Goldstrike, where the grades are averaging 0.35 ounces per ton and there is little carbonaceous ore, enabling Barrick to recover 93% of the gold content. At Mercur, the results were less impressive, mainly because the gold content in the ore declined rapidly in the 1990s, falling to only 0.05 ounces per ton by 1995. At that level, the returns from autoclaving are minimal and Mercur's recovery cost rose to more than $300 per ounce.

Without the autoclaves, Goldstrike would still have been a heap leach operation producing 30,000 to 40,000 ounces of gold a year. With the autoclaves, it is the biggest commercial gold deposit on the continent, pumping out 40,000 ounces of gold a week in 1995.

As soon as Barrick took possession of Goldstrike, Smith started a comprehensive drilling program to find out just how big the reserves were. By the end of their first year, they had identified 1.4 million ounces in the oxide orebody on the surface, surpassing Smith's guess of 1.2 million ounces when he, Meikle, and Hill first saw the property in 1986. More important, however, they had identified 7.3 million ounces in the deep sulphide orebody that they named Betze-Post. It would take several years before the full size of Betze-Post was confirmed (by the end of 1995, the property they bought from Western States and Pan-Cana for $62 million had yielded almost 38 million ounces in reserves and production, with more discoveries still expected to come), but Munk knew enough by mid-1987 to give the green light to the most ambitious development plan ever attempted in the industry.

It took Bob Smith and his team a little over two years to complete the development plan for Goldstrike. It is a masterful display of engineering, stretching out 17 years from 1989 to 2006 and covering every base imaginable — the environment, the local community, wildlife, autoclaving, the continuing exploration to delineate the orebody, and a host of technical challenges. The plan also promised very fast results, projecting gold production of almost a million ounces a year within three years of starting the development.

Originally, Smith had assumed he would have to use his 20 years of underground experience at Camflo to bring in Betze-Post. However, as the realization dawned that the orebody was bigger than they had dreamed — and that what they had thought were two separate orebodies, the Betze and the Post, were, in fact, joined — it became feasible to use an open pit instead of underground shafts. The only trouble with an open pit is that all the overburden of waste has to be removed to get at the ore. This can be expensive. Even after removing the overburden, only 15% of the earth removed from the pit is sent to the mill. The sheer size of the deposit, however, made an open pit feasible and Goldstrike became the biggest earth-moving project in the United States, handling 400 million tons of earth in four years.

In 1986, total capital spending by Barrick had been $17 million. The next year, it rose to $100 million. For the next six years, capital spending averaged more than $200 million a year, of which more than 90% was spent on Goldstrike. In those six years, Barrick spent $1.1 billion on capital spending and development drilling on the Goldstrike property.

The drilling program did more than delineate the Betze-Post orebody — Smith's people found another large deposit one mile

north of Betze-Post at what is now called the Meikle Mine (estimated reserves 6.6 million ounces) and they were still engaged
in proving out additional deposits at several other locations
within the original land position. Furthermore, Barrick bought
a 40% interest in the nearby orebody in the High Desert Area.

Production from Goldstrike soared from 40,000 ounces in
1987 to 119,000 the next year and 207,000 the year after.
The 1-million-ounce mark was passed in 1992, the 2-million
mark in 1995, with the Meikle Mine coming into production
in 1996 at a rate of 400,000 ounces per year. The Betze-Post
development plan was completed ahead of schedule and within
budget (adjusted for some subsequent expansions).

The Goldstrike acquisition may well produce 50 million
ounces for Barrick once all the development drilling has been
completed. Needless to say, the impact on the company has been
overwhelming. At the end of 1993, with its development program largely complete, Goldstrike *was* Barrick. The company
had four producing mines by then — Goldstrike, Mercur, Holt-
McDermott (an orebody that came with Camflo and that
Barrick had developed from nothing) and Pinson (20%
owned). Camflo had been closed down the year before and the
original acquisitions had all been sold. That year, Goldstrike
accounted for 95% of Barrick's total reserves and 88% of its
production. The operating cost per ounce at Goldstrike was
$158, compared to $258 at the other three — which means
Goldstrike accounted for about 93% of Barrick's profits.

The transformed Barrick stunned the stock market. After
adjusting for stock splits,[1] Barrick's shares rose from $1.90 at the
end of 1986 to $5.20 a year later, then $10.87 three years later,

---

[1] Barrick split its stock 2-for-1 three times — in 1987, 1989, and 1992.

and $15.50 two years after that, in December 1992. Then, in 1993, it almost doubled to $28.50. Over the full seven years, Barrick shares rose 57% per annum on average. At the end of 1986, when Barrick was still ranked as a second-tier gold miner (almost), its market capitalization had been $335 million. Seven years later, its market capitalization was $8.2 billion. It was bigger than most of Canada's banks and the biggest of all the gold companies in North America. Someone who got in early and bought $1,000 of Barrick shares at the end of 1984 could have sold them for $158,000 at the end of 1993, not counting dividends.

Barrick's annual production had drawn equal to Newmont's and was about to overtake the two largest, Homestake and Placer Dome. Barrick was the most profitable gold mining company in the continent and accounted for 35% of the profits of the ten largest gold producers[2] in North America. It had the fifth highest profit margin of all the companies in the Fortune 500 industrials. Its operating cost per ounce was 20% lower than that of the other nine major gold companies.

The market, evidently, liked what Munk had done. In 1986, the first year that Barrick made a profit, the market valued the company at 29 times net income. In 1993, it valued the company at 38 times earnings. Not only did the market recognize Barrick's growth in profitability, but it awarded it a significant premium, reflecting its expectation that the company would continue to show extraordinary growth.

It didn't last, of course. The market had to catch its breath and, in 1994, as Munk contemplated life after Goldstrike, the market took away the premium it had awarded Barrick. The stock

---

[2] Among them, the ten largest producers accounted for two-thirds of total production in North America.

started sliding, despite its superior performance compared to other gold companies. The analysts were looking for an encore.

This astounding growth would never have occurred if money had not been available to finance the capital investment. Munk's ability to mobilize the stock market to meet his financial needs may have been less widely recognized than the tangible creation of a mine, but it was as important a contributor to Barrick's success as any other factor. In the three years 1987–89, he raised $858 million — or almost three times his total market capitalization at the beginning of the period. It was a performance that Smith (and every other leader in the industry) would never have dreamed possible in early 1987.

When Smith was in the early stages of putting together his development plan for Goldstrike, he and Munk were discussing the broad outlines of how they would tackle the mining operation. Smith was thinking conservatively, talking of chewing up the orebody in manageable bites. Munk listened for a while, then interrupted him to ask:

"How much capital do you think you need?"

Smith, caught off guard, replied half-jokingly, "Oh, about half a billion."

"I think I can do that," Munk shot right back.

Smith almost fell off his chair. He had been thinking in terms of producing half a million ounces a year from Goldstrike, which would have put Barrick into the major leagues in North America. With half a billion dollars, he could produce a million ounces a year. "Jesus," he thought to himself, "that's too big for us." But it didn't take him long to get over the shock and start getting excited. The board of practically every other mining company would have shared Smith's initial reaction. They would have been impressed with a plan to produce half a million ounces a year. Barrick finally settled on a capital cost of $365 million (later rising to $450 million after adding a few improvements).

Smith may not have known it, but Munk moved onto a whole different plane in 1986 and it would be several years before the rest of the mining world caught up with him. After three years of struggling against the odds to raise money for Camflo and Mercur, the pressure had finally eased enough for him to start applying his own first golden rule: Never raise money when you need it. Raise it when financial markets are buoyant. In late summer of 1986, the price of gold began to move up sharply. After a stagnant year and a half during which it inched up from $300 to $350, the price began suddenly to surge in August, rising quickly to $443, pausing for a couple of months, then steaming ahead over the next two years when it averaged more than $440, before sliding back toward $350 for the following five or six years.

Munk jumped on the opportunity, going to the market twice in the fall of 1986. First he raised $30 million by issuing 2 million common shares at C$18.50 each, throwing in a little sweetener to remind everyone they were dealing with a gold company — each share carried two warrants giving the shareholder the right to buy 0.02 ounces of gold for $9.20. That's equivalent to $460 an ounce, just above the level where gold was trading at the time — not a big risk for the company, but sexy. Then he raised $50 million in a gold-backed, five-year Eurobond carrying an effective interest rate of $7\frac{1}{4}$%. Typically, he had a gold angle, offering bondholders the right to convert their bonds into gold at $560 an ounce. This offered them the prospect of a healthy bonus if gold rose above $560, which clearly appealed to them in a strong gold market. Certainly, it was attractive enough for them to accept a below-market interest rate on their bonds.

As it turned out, of course, the gold price never came close to $560, but the interest rate stayed where it started. Munk even tilted it a little further toward Barrick's advantage: he set the coupon rate at $5\frac{1}{4}$%, and gave the bondholders a premium of $11\frac{1}{2}$% at maturity, in effect delaying one-quarter of the annual interest charge until the bonds matured. The net effect was to keep the carrying costs of Barrick's loans four percentage points below the prevailing prime rate of $9\frac{3}{4}$%, while its chairman built its financial muscle.

The Eurobond demonstrated once again how Munk plays the financial markets like a violin, realizing the delicate balance between hard-nosed financial returns and the volatile psychology of prospective gains and losses. Despite centuries of evidence to the contrary, gold retains its grip on the imagination of investors everywhere as the ultimate, secure store of wealth in a perfidious world. Everyone remembers the sharp increases in the price of gold in times of dire uncertainty, just as most forget the languid performance that characterizes gold most of the time. Munk understands the perennial cupidity of investors who dream about those dramatic leaps in the price of gold, and he knows how to tease them with their own hopes, always judging perfectly just how far away to dangle his upside offerings to convince them it is worth their while to concede a lower interest rate.

In 1986, Munk raised almost $90 million, compared to $144 million in the two previous years combined. That $144 million, however, was all compulsory financing needed to pay for the Camflo and Mercur acquisitions, and at the end of 1985, Barrick had only $3 million in the bank and a deficit of almost $3 million in current assets and liabilities. At the end of 1986, Munk could afford some pride in his balance sheet, which showed cash and near-cash of $130 million. Shareholders' equity had almost doubled to $141 million. In short, 1986 was the year that Munk finally raised money when he didn't need it.

The next year, gold prices were still firm in the mid-400s, so he just kept right on going to the market, raising $389 million. He issued another two major gold-backed debentures. In February, an issue of notes for $50 million was the first gold issue he didn't call perfectly. (One might have argued, however, that he needed to let the investors win once at least!) He made the notes convertible at a rate that turned out to be quite advantageous to the bondholders, more than half of whom had redeemed their notes by the end of the following year. It was good while it lasted, however — interest was at only 2%.

The second issue was a remarkably innovative financing, which Munk had pioneered two years earlier. Up to that time, banks earned no interest on the large amounts of gold that sat in their vaults. However, they did, from time to time, lend out the gold temporarily at a very low interest rate, called the gold base rate. In 1987, the gold base rate was $\frac{3}{4}$%. Munk persuaded the Toronto-Dominion Bank to lend Barrick 260,000 ounces of gold at 1% over the gold base rate, repayable in monthly installments over six years. Barrick was able to sell the gold immediately at $482 an ounce and pay back the loan out of its production. In effect, it locked in the selling price of that gold at $482, which turned out to be only $20 short of the peak for the entire period from 1982 to 1995. And the interest rate on that loan was a paltry 1.75%.

Important as these two debt issues were, Munk was much more aggressive in pursuing equity capital in 1987. The reason, in tune with his first golden rule, was that the stock price of Barrick was very strong in 1986/87 and investors were ready to lap up whatever he offered them. At the time, his approach was radical thinking in Canada, where it was more common to avoid issuing shares if possible, because they were seen as diluting the ownership of a company and therefore diminishing the control exercised by the managers and/or owners.

Munk's twenty-fifth golden rule:
Always deal from a strong equity base. Dilute every time you can get equity for more than book value.

In 1987, he raised $187 million in cash in three separate share issues. He also issued $29 million worth of shares to pay for the half interest in Goldstrike that Joe Rotman sold to Barrick. The public couldn't get enough of his shares — in the year up to March 1987, Barrick's shares had increased four and a half times, from a little over $3 to a high of $17. Six months later, Barrick shares had broken through $30. It was the perfect time to invite people to invest in the company. But he had to act fast, because the window of opportunity lasted only six months — in the last couple of months of 1987, the shares started a downward drift that lasted more than a year, in the course of which, interest in Barrick shares receded. In 1989, the drift ended as Barrick shares launched the second Great Leap Forward, which hoisted the market capitalization of Barrick from $1 billion to $8 billion in five spectacular years.

Munk returned to the market for equity financing in 1989 and afterwards, but he never again had to go to the market for cash on the scale that he did in 1987. The financings he rammed through that year enabled him to break out of the financial limitations that had bound him throughout his career, with the exception of a brief interlude when Travelodge had turned around. He had $130 million cash in his bank and a business that was throwing off cash at a rate of more than $50 million a year. Plus he knew that he had barely scratched the surface of Goldstrike's potential. All this only four years after he limped into the gold business in the wake of blowing $100 million on oil and gas. The Barrick story after 1987 is the one the investors know, but the story up to 1987 is both the foundation and the heart of Barrick's achievement.

So, when Munk asked Bob Smith how much money he would need to develop the Betze-Post orebody at Goldstrike, Munk already knew what kind of financing he had in mind. If Smith had asked for much less, Munk would have raised exactly the same amount and invested it somewhere else. Later, at the beginning of 1989, Bob Smith, Alan Hill, and Jerry Garbutt, the chief financial officer, made their presentation to the financial world, announcing the Goldstrike development at a cost of $365 million. The analysts listened politely until they could finally ask the one question they all wanted to ask: "How are you going to finance this?" Garbutt stunned the room when he said it was already fully financed. That may have been a slight exaggeration, because the last leg of the financing would close only two months later, but the outcome was not in any doubt.

That last financing was a blockbuster — the fifth of a series of bullion loans that Munk initiated in December 1985, when he borrowed 77,000 ounces. In all, he raised $637 million by borrowing more than 1.5 million ounces of gold, at an average rate of interest of only 2.6% p.a.

The fifth loan was more than enough to finance Goldstrike all on its own. By this time, the market had begun to copy Munk's innovation, so the gold base rate was not quite as cheap as it used to be, but he still managed to borrow 1 million ounces of gold at an interest rate of 2.9%. The price of gold had slipped below $400 an ounce by then, but it would not return to that price for another four years, so he was effectively selling his future production at a good price. Best of all, however, he was borrowing at less than 3%. The month that the final gold bullion loan was issued, the prime rate went to $13\frac{1}{2}$%.

Apart from these bullion loans, Munk also floated several gold-backed debentures, under which the principal was repaid in gold taken from Barrick's production. The effect of these transactions was to remove the financial risk of declines in the price of gold. It also removed some of the debt from the balance sheet, into an off-balance-sheet category. The net effect was a balance sheet almost devoid of debt despite a massive financing program. No one in the industry had ever been able to achieve that degree of financial caution, even with growth rates much slower than Barrick's.

Munk's twenty-sixth golden rule:
*Be very aggressive operationally
and very conservative financially.*

With his imaginative financing instruments, he was paying interest on his loans at about one-quarter the going rate. In 1988 and 1989, the peak years for investment in Goldstrike, Barrick's net profit was $30 million to $35 million. If Munk had had to pay prime rate on his loans, there would not have been much profit left.

Few people watched the development of the Goldstrike mine more closely than the executives who ran Newmont Gold. Not only had they turned their noses up at the Goldstrike deposit, but part of the Betze-Post orebody was in their own land. They woke up every morning to see the one that got away staring them in the face. Understandably, their feelings toward Barrick turned prickly.

The stormy relationship between Newmont and its neighbor actually predated Barrick's arrival. There are veiled reports of a confrontation between Western States and Newmont at the borderline between the properties, when the two companies flirted with a shoot-out at the Goldstrike corral, assembling platoons of their giant earth-moving equipment in a menacing face-off. It sometimes gets tense with Barrick, too. The Newmont executives aren't rushing to have the top Barrick people around for dinner. The people at Barrick vehemently denied for many years any suggestions that there was anything but peace and harmony between the two companies, but it strained the credulity of anyone who knew them both. There were, nonetheless, powerful arguments for keeping at least a civil relationship. They shared a gigantic deposit of gold in the Carlin Trend; they *had* to cooperate — even if every agreement between the two companies was signed grudgingly on Newmont's side.

Inevitably, everything Barrick did soon became the standard against which Newmont's performance was measured. Although they were the biggest gold mining company in the United States, they looked almost sleepy next to Barrick's dynamic strategy. It wasn't long before the fallout started. In the middle of 1987, Newmont became the target for the most famous corporate raider of them all: Texan T. Boone Pickens. He had become a legend, buying companies in order to dismember them at great profit.

Newmont reacted violently. Its board declared a special dividend of $33 for its shareholders. Since its shares were then trading at $36, it amounted to a scorched-earth policy — the dividend cost $2.2 billion and Newmont had to borrow $1.75 billion to pay for it. It didn't do much for Newmont, but Pickens got the message. Just to make sure he didn't change his mind, Newmont persuaded its largest shareholder, ConsGold, to ride in on its white charger and increase its holding in Newmont to 49% from 26%.

Munk watched the battle from the sidelines, having already experienced what it was like to play with ConsGold. He thought Pickens had made a strategic error in going for Newmont instead of ConsGold, so he started accumulating ConsGold shares again in the fall of 1987. His kitty was getting to be quite large by now, thanks to his string of visits to the capital markets; despite the exploding development costs of Barrick's mines, he had accumulated almost $170 million in spare change at the end of the year. He was shopping again, looking for opportunities. Apart from his 1.4% of ConsGold, he also bought a significant stake in Lac Minerals, which he was to revisit seven years later. He still had a year or two before the massive capital demands of Goldstrike began to gobble up all his cash.

That's where it rested for about a year. Then Minorco took a run at ConsGold. Minorco is the main conduit through which the Anglo American group is developing its non-South African holdings. With assets of $2.4 billion and net earnings of $775 million in 1988, it was a significant financial powerhouse. It had one serious problem, however — all its investments were minority holdings, so its cash flow was made up solely of dividends. It had no operational cash flow to pursue an aggressive investment strategy. The Minorco board therefore decided to shed its passive holdings and concentrate on investments where it ran the show. That was the context for its decision to make a bid for ConsGold. It had broached the idea of a merger with ConsGold in October 1986, but been turned down. When Munk first began sniffing around ConsGold, Minorco moved into action again, proposing to acquire ConsGold provided the ConsGold board supported the bid. Rudolph Agnew, ConsGold's chairman, turned them down again. Minorco stewed over Agnew's stubbornness for a little more than a year, then decided on a hostile bid, which it launched in September 1988.

The principal shareholders of Minorco were all companies in the Anglo American group — Anglo itself (39%), its diamond-monopoly subsidiary De Beers (21%), the Oppenheimer family (7%), and other subsidiaries of Anglo (4%). Together, they owned 71% of Minorco. The Anglo American group is one of the three giant conglomerates that dominate the South African economy. It is impossible to know its real size, but it is clearly a huge, sprawling empire. Its vast holdings are shrouded in an intricate web of thousands of companies that have invested in virtually every industry in the country. And in 1988, it had equally huge holdings throughout the world. Its wealth was built on gold and diamonds, and it is still the dominant global force in these two commodities. For the moment, anyway.

Agnew threw every missile he could muster at Minorco. He accused the company of numerous crimes against securities and monopoly regulations. He accused them of scandalous stock trading practices. He lost every battle. He then persuaded his subsidiaries in the United States and Australia to launch law-suits against Minorco, too. He failed in every effort there as well, except for one. Newmont's president, Gordon Parker, grateful for the way ConsGold had bailed him out in the battle with Boone Pickens, went to battle for his major shareholder. He sought an injunction against the bid on the grounds that if Minorco bought ConsGold, it would also control Newmont, which would "unduly concentrate ownership of gold production." It was a desperate nuisance suit of dubious validity, but it worked, probably because the American courts had long wanted to get their hands on De Beers for its monopoly practices in the diamond marketing industry.

As a brief aside, in the middle of this vicious fight, Minorco had said it would dispose of Newmont, if it succeeded in its bid for ConsGold, so Munk teamed up with Placer Dome to see if they could buy it together. Their valuation of Newmont, however, was so far below the price at which the shares were trading that Minorco dismissed their offer out of hand.

The Newmont suit killed the bid from Minorco, which capitulated in May 1988. One month later, Hanson PLC, the asset-stripping king of Britain, led by David Gilmour's two friends, offered £14.30 a share for ConsGold, then quickly raised the offer to the equivalent of £15.30. The ConsGold board recommended acceptance and Hanson took control in August. The Minorco bid had initially been for £14, but they had raised it in two stages to £15.50. The resistance of ConsGold's CEO, Rudolph Agnew, had been totally futile. The vast expense of his legal battles had resulted in his shareholders getting 20 pence less per share. Worse, for him, Minorco had offered to keep him as chief executive officer and expand the company. Hanson disbanded the whole company, selling off its components piece by piece. Agnew lost his job.

The South African and Australian assets of ConsGold were gone by March 1990 and soon, only Newmont remained. It went in October. Lord Hanson struck a deal to swap his 49% of

Newmont with Sir Jimmy Goldsmith, another high-profile British deal-maker. In return, Goldsmith[3] gave him Cavenham Forest Industries, the sixth largest timber operation in the United States. Neither of them wanted Newmont. Hanson considered it to be a serious underperformer and Goldsmith's primary interest was getting out of Cavenham tax free — so Newmont, with its non-taxable listed shares, was only the first step in that process. Because of the tangled U.S. tax regulations, it is a lot easier for a foreigner to sell publicly quoted stocks than a timber forest.

Goldsmith was no Agnew. The former chairman had left Newmont's board to its own devices, but Goldsmith quickly established his dominance over them, then decided he didn't want to keep the company. So he approached Munk in May 1991, suggesting the two companies merge. Munk took Greg Wilkins and Bob Smith down to New York to meet with Goldsmith. It left a deep impression on Smith. Goldsmith is a supreme deal-maker with subsidiaries on every continent, totally at ease in Paris and London, friends with the rich and the famous around the world, a man whose ambition knows no boundaries, for whom nothing is unthinkable. Bob Smith confided to Munk after the meeting: "I learned one thing at this meeting, Peter. I now understand why [Goldsmith] was married to or bred most of the beauties of this world, because after 20 minutes, he had my underwear down below my knees." In a later reminiscence of that meeting, he commented, "He was the smoothest, most convincing talker. There was an aura about Jimmy . . . He could almost mesmerize you. There are few men

---

[3] Goldsmith had a partner in this transaction, St. James Place Capital PLC, a company controlled by Lord Rothchild, which shared proportionately in the swap.

in the world like that. Peter's much like that. There's something about him — it's the mystique, the mystery, how convincing he can be."

Goldsmith's proposal was tempting. Munk would run the combined show. "Peter," he told him, "you will run the biggest gold producer in the world." The two companies had radically different cultures, but the prospect of dominating the whole Carlin Trend was too alluring and Munk worked hard to bring them together. By then, however, Barrick had become a power-house in its own right, with annual gold production scheduled to reach 2 million ounces within three years. Besides, Goldstrike was just getting better and better and the price being offered to Newmont shareholders in the form of Barrick stock quickly began to look too high. To the enormous relief of most Barrick people, Munk turned down the offer in July. The Newmont culture was bureaucratic; Barrick was super-entrepreneurial. It would have been frustrating for both sides.

A few months later, when gold markets were strong and gold shares stronger, Goldsmith floated his Newmont holdings in a secondary distribution, neatly extricating himself from the North American industry.

In 1995, Newmont and Barrick entered the ring once again to spar together. Newmont launched an injunction against Barrick, charging that it had not respected their joint agreement on the disposal of water from the Goldstrike mine. Dewatering is one of the most difficult technical problems at Goldstrike. The water table lies only just below the surface at ground level on the site. That means the water has to be pumped out to mine the pit. The development plan envisaged pumping 40,000 gallons of water per minute. That's a lot of water to pump and there were initially some problems with the system — until Bob

Smith put his foot down. On one of his visits, he went down to the wading pool at the bottom of the pit in his galoshes, and turned to his engineers. "The next time I come here, I want to be able to walk here in my slippers." On his next visit, he got what he wanted — plus a new pair of slippers.

By 1995, Barrick was pumping almost 70,000 gallons a minute. That's equivalent to emptying a full-size Olympic swimming pool every three or four minutes. Twenty-four hours a day. Some of the water is being pumped into an adjacent aquifer, some is going to a ranch where it is used for irrigation, and some is going into a containing dam owned by Newmont. The two companies had signed cooperation agreements to share the work of mining and milling the orebody they share, and part of this was the agreement on water disposal into the reservoir owned by Newmont. This dam became the focus of the injunction, with Newmont claiming that Barrick was taking too much of the holding capacity for its own mining operations. Without the disposal capacity, there can be no mining under Nevada's environmental regulations. The two biggest gold mining companies in the United States were now pitted against each other.

Like everyone else who has become embroiled in a lawsuit with Peter Munk, Newmont will find him a determined opponent. Munk's most celebrated U.S. opponent (unsuccessful, of course) was Secretary of the Interior Bruce Babbitt. Early in the Clinton administration, Babbitt stopped granting all patents (title) to mining companies in the United States while he tried to reform an 1872 law that set the patent fee at $5 an acre for hard-rock minerals. He had no right to stop granting patents, but he did. At that point Barrick was halfway through the process of obtaining its patent, and Babbitt picked on the "foreign-owned company" as an example of "the biggest gold heist since the days of Butch Cassidy." Barrick sued him to stop his de facto moratorium. In his defense, the Secretary told the judge the delay in Barrick's case was caused by consultations between the Bureau of Land Management and the Wildlife Service over the impact that the Goldstrike development would have on the Lahontan cutthroat trout. The judge didn't buy the argument and ordered him to grant the patent. Babbitt still didn't go quietly. His staff estimated that the value of Barrick's gold in the ground was $10 billion (almost certainly a gross underestimation) and at his press conference to deliver the patent to Barrick, he had a six-and-a-half-foot poster made up showing a check made out to Barrick from the American people for $10 billion.

It was an effective campaign, if grossly disingenuous. Had the Senate's proposed amendment gone through, setting a royalty rate of 3% on gross revenues from gold, it would have cost Barrick about $20 million a year, which would have yielded hundreds of millions of dollars to the federal government over the life of the mine. A lot of money, even if it wasn't $10 billion. The *Washington Post* dubbed Goldstrike "the mine that got away."

The threat of losing $20 million a year off the bottom line was a severe shock to Munk and he threw himself into the task of stopping Babbitt dead in his tracks. For much of 1993, he spent a lot of time in the District of Columbia, getting his feet wet in the convoluted world of hard-ball Washington lobbying. At that stage, Brian Mulroney, Canada's former prime minister, had just joined the Barrick board and he immediately went down to Washington to establish contact with the key senators, using his close relationship with George Bush to good advantage.

He set up meetings for Munk with the key senators when the issue was being debated in the Senate and Munk was able to give them his side of the debate.

The crisis had passed for Barrick, but it left an indelible impression on Munk, who swore he would never again allow himself to be sideswiped by political surprises.

While the incredible wealth generated for Barrick by the Goldstrike development attracted its fair share of jealous attention from other people who wanted a piece of the action, it had a quite different effect on the mining industry. He turned the gold mining industry on its ear. Apart from the innovative financing and the speed of the development, perhaps the greatest change Munk wrought on the industry was his now-famous hedging program.

He initiated the program in early 1986, shortly before he was able to put into action his first principle of raising money only in buoyant markets. The basic idea of hedging is very simple. At that time, gold was trading just above $280, which was as low as it got in the 1980s. Munk decided to stop selling at spot prices as the gold was produced and instead to sell into the futures market. In the market for gold, future prices are always at a premium over current prices, because future prices are determined simply as the spot price of gold plus interest.[4] This premium is called a "contango," which may sound like an exotic Latin American dance, but is really just a mathematical formula. The advantage of selling into the futures market was twofold: It guaranteed a higher price, and it meant

---

[4] The interest rate is actually the difference between current interest rates and the gold base rate, or the cost of borrowing gold bullion from the banks.

he didn't have to worry about what price he would get when Smith did his calculations about monthly production quotas.

The miners didn't like the idea one bit. Getting involved with contangos is not something that sits well with the average mining executive. Miners are tough people, simple people. They deal in tangible realities, often personal danger, and they don't have much respect for fancy tricks that depart from the hard reality of their world. Smith voiced his team's discomfort at something they felt was almost sacrilegious. Hedging felt to him and his team like a lack of commitment. It was making their product disappear as it left the mill and vanish into an ethereal financial world they didn't understand.

Smith's expression of discomfort with this financial manipulation failed singularly to impress his chairman. Munk does not often have any patience with people who express opinions in areas where they do not have expertise and he gave Smith's comments short shrift. "I don't give a damn what miners do," he told him. "It's my money. I don't want to lose it if gold goes down when I buy a new mine. If the investors don't like it, they can go and buy someone else's shares. If it's good for me, I can't see why it isn't good for Mr. Corn or Mr. Smith."

Smith didn't argue any further. Barrick hedged — and Smith soon saw the light. Not right away, however. In the first year of the program, the hedging program lost money for Barrick, because gold prices jumped up sharply. The higher price of gold was, of course, what sent Munk off on his financing frenzy, but it didn't do anything for his hedging program. Barrick would have got more for its gold if it had sold later at spot prices. He sold his gold output at an average price of $364 (which was about $30 more than the spot price at the time of the sales) and delivered the gold to those contracts when the spot price was averaging $447. The hedging program lost $8 million that year.

The process obviously needed a bit of refining. The solution was puts and calls. This is an ingenious way of locking in a base price without losing the potential to get higher prices if the spot price goes up. First of all, Barrick bought put options that gave it the right to sell gold at a fixed price, which was significantly higher than the spot price, for example, $400. That meant that Barrick's gold would never be sold for less than $400. To help pay for the cost of buying those put options, Barrick sold call options — which gave the buyers the right to buy gold from Barrick at a fixed price, which was significantly higher than the floor price already established, for example, $500. Barrick sold call options on about half its gold production and the income received from selling the call options was about the same as the cost of buying the put options. So the program cost the company very little. Its effect was dramatic, however. When the time came to deliver on the contracts, if the spot price was below $400, then all the production was sold at $400. If the price was between $400 and $500, then the put option contracts were allowed to lapse and all the production was sold at the spot price. The buyers of the call option let their contracts lapse because they were not going to buy at $500 when the spot price was less. If the spot price was above $500, then Barrick sold half its production at $500 and half at the (higher) spot price.

After a couple of years, the financial markets started to catch on, although it took the gold industry a lot longer. The market became volatile, and it was very difficult to make the program work. So Munk dreamt up a new scheme with Greg Wilkins — they started pestering the investment bankers to issue "spot deferreds," which are forward sales at a fixed price with a one-year life. The seller (Barrick) of a spot deferred normally has the right to defer the maturity date for a period after the end of the year, but at first the investment bankers would offer extensions of only six months or so, and Munk refused to buy any contracts.

If he sold spot deferreds under these terms, he would be locking in his price — and if prices rose suddenly, he would be caught just as he was in his first year of the hedging program. That's gambling. Having a six-month extension helped, but only marginally. To solve that problem, he had to be able to extend the maturity date indefinitely. Then, if spot prices rose suddenly, he could defer the spot deferreds and sell his production at the (higher) spot price. If the prices stayed up, he would defer again. Each time he deferred, the price in the spot deferred contract would rise by the contango and he would then keep deferring his spot deferreds until the spot price dropped below the price of the spot deferreds — and then he would exercise his contract. Without an extension, spot deferreds are a gamble. With the extension, Barrick gets the best of all worlds.

Munk's twenty-seventh golden rule:
Don't ever confuse gambling with business. You take your chances but you hedge your bets.

Finally, after badgering the investment houses for months, one offered a two-year extension. Munk turned them down. Then J. P. Morgan & Co. came out with ten-year extension terms and the game was on — the other dealers started doing them at five to ten years. Once again, Barrick had driven the market, creating a new financial instrument.

By the end of 1995, the spot deferreds started becoming unattractive. During that year, the South Africans came into the market and sold 20 million ounces of spot deferreds. It was very impressive that the market could absorb this amount of gold, but it did, without the price collapsing. However, the gold base rate soared to 8%, which flattened the forward market.[5] The rate has since come back down to 2.5%, but that is still a little high to make the forward market attractive. Once again, Munk changed tack, and cut back the hedging program by a third.

Hedging is perhaps one of the greatest contributions Peter Munk has made to the gold industry. All the gold companies do it to some degree now. But it has paid off most for Barrick, because it has always been able to lead in the adjustments required to keep pace with an ever-changing market. The hedging program increased Barrick's revenues by $344 million between 1988 and 1995 at a cost of $75 million, thereby increasing profits by $270 million. That constitutes about a quarter of the total profits of $1.1 billion over that period.

It is tempting to attribute Barrick's success with Goldstrike to luck, especially when Munk and Smith do nothing to discourage the idea. But luck is sometimes a function of skill and being prepared. More important still, however, luck provides only the opportunity. It rarely secures results. Many, many people in the gold mining industry could have been in Peter Munk's position with Goldstrike and still not made even half as much of it as he did. Above all, Munk is a matchless implementer. He turned a great orebody into a money machine with a series of bold decisions — financial and operational — that were sometimes risky,

---

[5] The forward price is the spot price plus the contango, which is the difference between the current prime rate of interest and the gold base rate. If the gold base rate rises to 8%, the contango disappears and the forward price is the same as the spot price, thereby eliminating the advantage of selling forward.

always innovative, and stretched the potential of everything and everyone involved to their outer limits.

He developed the mine in half the time anyone else would have. He pushed for the autoclave, which was still a pioneering technology but which ultimately made Goldstrike one of the lowest cost producers in the continent. He raised a huge amount of debt at interest rates so low that he was able to finance his expansion at a fraction of the cost borne by the rest of the industry. He was never afraid to raise equity — it may have diluted ownership, but it never diluted shareholder value and it gave him a balance sheet so strong that he could invest $2 billion without batting an eyelid.

Of the total profits earned by Barrick in the period between 1988 and 1995, close to one-half can be attributed to the hedging program and the low interest rates on the Barrick debt. The accelerated development of Goldstrike has also meant much higher profits in the short term than if the mine had been developed at a more conventional pace. Barrick was indeed lucky when Goldstrike turned out to have up to 50 million ounces of reserves instead of 625,000, but the benefits that have flowed from the mine are mostly the result of the way the mine was managed and developed. That was not luck.

9

THE LAC TAKEOVER

W hen he returned to Toronto from Klosters in the spring of 1994, Peter Munk had his eye fixed firmly on South America. The triumph of the previous year, when the stock market had finally given his stock the respect it deserved, was already beginning to fade as the market began to whittle away at the handsome premium it had awarded Barrick. He knew he had to broaden his horizons from its strictly North American base — and South America was his answer. After years of chronic political instability, Latin America was getting its act together and mining was once again becoming feasible for foreigners. Barrick had already dipped its toe in Peru, but the most exciting country was Chile, which had gone from a reviled dictatorship to a functioning democracy. Its economy was growing rapidly and its government had indicated it was prepared to put out the welcome mat to foreign investors.

Smith immediately set to work drawing up a series of possible blueprints for expansion. Munk would have preferred an acquisition, but they weren't counting on one. Admittedly, it would be convenient, because a takeover offered the prospect of dramatic growth in very little time, but it was hard to find good value in the generally overpriced gold market. So they were busy building a strategy to grow from the ground up with small acquisitions and grassroots exploration. The board had been summoned to an unusual summer meeting to approve the plans and Munk was gearing up for a growth spurt.

On July 7, the whole gold mining industry was stunned when Peggy Witte announced a C$13.59[1] bid for the shares of Lac Minerals, which were then trading at C$11.375. It was a classic case of the minnow trying to swallow the whale. Lac was one of the pillars of the industry and it dwarfed Witte's upstart company, Royal Oak Mines, in every department of the gold business. Lac's annual production of gold was 4 times bigger than Royal Oak's, its cash flow was 6.7 times bigger, and its proven and probable reserves were a bit more than 3 times bigger. Three-year-old Royal Oak had taken aim at a company roughly 4 times bigger than it was, on the strength of financial resources that could best be described as puny compared to those at the disposal of its target.

Witte's justification for such chutzpah had to be good — and it was. She told Lac shareholders their assets had been mismanaged: $1 invested in Lac in 1991 was worth $1.16 in July 1994;

---

[1] Royal Oak bid C$3.75 plus 1.75 Royal Oak shares for each Lac share. The day before the bid, Royal Oak shares had been trading at C$5.625, so that made the bid worth $13.59. Alternatively, Lac shareholders could take 2.416 Royal Oak shares for each Lac share.

over the identical period, $1 invested in Royal Oak had grown to $6.25. Lac shareholders would, she said, be collectively better off if they pooled their assets with hers and assumed three-quarters ownership of the combined enterprise. Provided she ran it.

Like everyone else, Munk was surprised but he was neither impressed nor interested. Smith's team spent a couple of days crunching the Lac numbers and Smith reported back that "her bid doesn't make sense on the basis of those reserves." C$2 billion-plus was too much money to pay for a lackluster company with reserves of 8.6 million ounces, even if annual production was more than a million ounces. Barrick put away its spreadsheets and went back to its plans for smaller companies with great potential. The rest of the industry agreed with his assessment. There were many other companies that could have claimed they could manage Lac's assets more effectively but they all stayed away from the party. For the moment, at least, Peggy Witte had the field to herself.

Lac did not appreciate Witte's brazen gall, gruffly dismissing it as a reverse takeover that was intended to rob Lac shareholders of their assets, partly with the help of $435 million in cash that Lac had stashed away in its kitty. But the bid wasn't quite as quixotic as it first appeared. Lac was, in fact, wounded and bleeding. It had lost $63 million the previous year. Indeed, over the four years to 1993, it had lost a total of $100 million. Nevertheless, there were other more encouraging developments that should have counteracted the impact of the losses, serious as they were. In the four years from 1989 to 1992, Lac more than tripled the annual production from its high-quality properties, which included the Chilean mines it had bought in 1989 from Australia's tottering magnate, Alan Bond. And it had become much more efficient in its mining operations, having reduced its operating costs to $199 per ounce in 1993 from $278 in 1989.

The market, however, was underwhelmed by Lac's good news. The price it was prepared to pay for a Lac share stagnated throughout the period of its most dynamic growth. At the end of 1993 — a spectacular year, when the price of gold stocks doubled — Lac was still trading below the price it had enjoyed four years earlier. The market capitalization[2] of Lac was only $1.2 billion, or three times Royal Oak's $388 million.

Analysts like to compare companies by measuring their market capitalization per ounce of reserves[3] — the value the market puts on each ounce of reserves in the ground. It represents the market's assessment of how profitably and efficiently a company can be expected to extract its reserves and sell the gold. When Witte made her bid for Lac in the summer of 1994, Lac's "market cap" per ounce was $149 compared to Royal Oak's $144. That might be taken to mean that the market viewed the companies as being quite similar in quality, but nothing could be further from the truth. It was costing Royal Oak $315 an ounce to extract the gold from its low-grade mines, while Lac had to spend only $199 on its premium properties. As gold was selling in a range of $370 to $395 in 1994, that meant Royal Oak had only about $70 per ounce — or $19 million — to pay for running the company, exploring for more gold, paying interest on its debt, allowing for depreciation of its equipment, *and* putting something aside for the shareholders' profit. Lac had $185-plus per ounce to do the same thing — or more than $200 million. Normally, the market would have valued Lac's

---

[2] The multiple of the share price and the total number of shares outstanding; the market capitalization represents the market's estimate of the total value of a company.
[3] Total market capitalization (number of shares outstanding multiplied by the share price) divided by the total proven and probable reserves of the company.

reserves much more highly, because it could afford to spend more on exploration to find new reserves and should have been making much more money. But it didn't. The market valued the two companies almost exactly the same.

The low price assigned to the shares of Lac Minerals was an indication that the market did not like the way Lac was being run. Peter Allen had run Lac Minerals for 20 years by the time Peggy Witte went for his throat. He had inherited a controlling interest in the company from his father in 1974, at the age of 34, after spending nine years as a partner in his father's firm of stockbrokers. Perhaps because he had been deprived of the opportunity of having to struggle for his place in the sun, Allen was seen as patrician and aloof. There was also a perception in the investment community that Lac management had not maximized shareholder value in some difficult situations in which the company had found itself.

One of the principal roots of this perception was Allen's expensive — and ultimately unsuccessful — fight to retain control of the $3 billion Page-Williams mine in the Hemlo belt in northern Ontario. After eight years of nasty court battles, the Supreme Court of Canada ruled against Lac in August 1989, awarding the mine to International Corona Corp. Many felt that the two companies could have achieved an out-of-court settlement that would have awarded the mine to Lac on a basis that was equitable for both companies and avoid an all-or-nothing result. In the end, Allen got less than nothing after paying several million dollars in legal fees, but the court did at least require Corona to repay the $180 million that Lac had spent drilling the property and developing the mine. Allen turned around and used the settlement to buy 65% of Bond International — but the price was generally seen (incorrectly, as it turned out) as too high, because it caused Lac's earnings to dive as a result of the high goodwill costs of the acquisition.

Through all his vicissitudes, Allen made no attempt to explain himself, believing (shades of Alan Greenway) that his company's performance in the long run would vindicate him. Unfortunately for him, there is no long run in the stock market, where everything is for sale today. Investors did not want to be told that Allen would keep them posted when he felt the time was ripe. Peggy Witte, like everyone else in the industry, was aware of this situation, but gave it little thought until her manager of investor relations, Graham Eacott, returned from a tour of Europe earlier that year. Eacott told his boss that European institutional investors despised Allen's leadership. That got Witte thinking and she decided to take a closer look at the company. She quickly saw that the company was significantly undervalued relative to its assets. She figured that under her leadership she could persuade the market to revalue the Lac assets and make a very large sum of money.

Allen had, in fact, assembled an impressive collection of gold mines — as Barrick was soon to find out, to its great joy. But he did not have Barrick's ability to put a shine on his assets, so he paid a high price in lost profits and an even higher price in lost credibility.

Taking on the establishment was not a novel idea for Peggy Witte. Being a woman in the mining industry had given her no alternative but to become a loner. She looks more like the music teacher her father wanted her to become than the CEO she is, comfortable rather than hard-edged, but looks are deceiving. She has her fair share of scar tissue from the rough and tumble of mining deals, not all of which worked out. In the process, she developed the toughness she needed to survive in an industry where the stakes are high and the rules are loose.

The miners at Royal Oak's Giant gold mine in Yellowknife have seen her steel. They turned down the contract she offered them in 1991 and went on strike. She brought in replacement workers ("scabs," as the union calls them), which prompted a member of the angry union to sabotage the mine, accidentally killing nine of the replacement miners. Witte said she was "haunted" by the experience, but she never shrank from doing what she thought she had to do.

Her success can be attributed to other things than toughness, however. She is a gifted salesperson and paid her way through college by selling fur coats in Reno, Nevada — in the middle of summer, in the middle of the desert — to the wives of gamblers who had enjoyed a bit of luck at the casino across the road. She left university with a master's degree in metallurgy and, after a few years in a mine, got a job as a metallurgist with the Ontario Research Foundation in Toronto. It didn't last long, however, and two years later, at age 27, she quit to start her own metallurgy business, Witteck Developments. The security blanket for the leap into self-employment was a contract with Lac Minerals.

Her business prospered and five years later, she had 40 employees and a long list of happy clients. She was beginning to notice, however, that her clients were flush with cash as they were lavishing an inordinate amount of money on their consultants. Maybe it was time, she thought, to tap into that cash by owning a few mines herself, especially since a new tax wrinkle was pulling millions of new dollars into the industry. She didn't have any money herself, however (when she made her bid for Lac, she owned only 2% of Royal Oak's shares), so she decided the best way to break into the business was to buy marginal gold mines that had been abandoned or were losing money. At least they would be extremely cheap to buy. Then she could turn them around and make some money. As a metallurgist, her major contribution to the profession had been to develop a new technique for recovering gold from low-grade ore, so she had the expertise to grind down operating costs to make her marginal mines profitable. Five years later, she had assembled five mines that she combined to form Royal Oak.

In its short life, Royal Oak had performed creditably, buying a series of closed or unprofitable mines and reorganizing them. She had quickly built her production to 276,000 ounces of gold in 1993, making a profit every year and paying off all her debt. Her company had identified 2.7 million ounces in reserves plus another 5 million ounces of resources.[4] And the stock market gave the company a price much higher relative to its accomplishments than any major gold company in Canada.

The biggest problem was that her five mines still had very high expenses even after she had worked on their operating costs. With operating costs per ounce of $315, Royal Oak was extremely vulnerable to a fall in the price of gold. Even if she had made money so far, no one felt confident she would continue to do so. The bid for Lac Minerals was, in fact, a brilliant strategy that held out the hope of rescuing her from her marginal operations, just as Camflo and Mercur had rescued Barrick from its marginal starter mines ten years earlier. However, the disparity in size between Lac and Royal Oak and her own tenuous financial situation made it unlikely from the beginning that her bid would succeed. She did the industry a favor by putting Lac into play, but the whole market knew that Lac was being discounted because of the general

---

[4] Resources are mineral deposits that have been positively identified, but are not yet sufficiently well explored to be certain that they represent a feasible mining project. Reserves are mineral deposits that are known to be economically feasible. Economic feasibility depends partly on the price of gold and partly on the cost of extraction of the minerals.

dissatisfaction with the way it was being run, so any bid was bound to attract other, more powerful bidders. She was prepared for this, too, and had bought some judicious insurance — 2.6% of Lac at about $11 a share — that would generate enough capital gains to pay her legal costs in the event she lost the bid.

On July 18, 1994, 11 days after Witte announced her bid, the Lac board issued a statement saying that the company had been working for several months on a new business plan arising out of a radical reassessment of its reserves. Lac now had, they said, three times as much gold in its properties as it had previously estimated — 13.5 million ounces of proven, probable, and possible reserves and 13.5 million ounces of resources. The board had approved a plan to spend $600 million over the following three years to expand annual production to 1.6 million ounces — with most of the expansion coming from the Chilean mines.

That caught Munk's attention. Lac's Chilean assets, which Lac had now more than doubled, were a perfect fit for Barrick's strategy. If necessary, he could sell Lac's Canadian mines to reduce the cost of the South American assets or find a partner.

Munk's twenty-eighth golden rule:
Do deals only if they help you achieve your strategic objectives.

Smith's team brought their spreadsheets back onto their computer screens and quickly decided that the numbers based on the new reserve estimates were promising. Two days after the release of the new reserve estimates, Peter Allen approached Munk to suggest he make a bid for Lac. He confirmed the new estimate for the reserves was based on solid geological data and could be trusted.

For the next couple of days, Smith's team combed the public Lac data, building models for each mine to guess how they would handle them and what kind of operating improvements they were likely to achieve. These models were passed on to David Macdonald, the managing director of investment bankers, Bunting Warburg Inc., who had earlier recommended against proceeding with a bid to challenge Witte. The number crunchers at Bunting Warburg then turned Smith's projections into financial models. By the end of the week, the numbers were beginning to justify making a bid. Munk decided to put together a team that would assess the prospects for a takeover bid for Lac, develop the strategy, and manage the bid. He set its first meeting for that weekend of July 23 and 24. In fact, Munk had already made up his mind. He wanted Lac. But he was not going to buy it regardless of the cost. He was going to buy the company on the most advantageous terms possible.

The day before the meeting, the strategy that was emerging from these discussions was turned on its head. When Peter Allen approached Barrick on Wednesday, July 20, it looked like the takeover would be friendly — Munk was being cast as the white knight to Peggy Witte's black knight. Two days later, after the stock market closed for the weekend, Allen resigned and Jim Pitblado, the deputy chairman of the board and retired chairman of Dominion Securities, took over as chairman and CEO.

When Witte's bid was first launched on July 7, the Lac board had decided that all issues relating to the company would be handled by Allen and all issues relating to the bid by Pitblado. They knew about the negative attitude toward Allen and expected to defuse the issue by asking Pitblado to deal with the shareholders. During the week following her bid, Pitblado made a tour of institutional investors and analysts and was surprised at the depth of feeling against Allen. He knew then that the first line of defense against Witte's argument that Lac's assets had been badly managed would have to be Allen's departure.

Pitblado adopted a strategy radically different from Allen's. No cuddly, friendly takeover for this battle-hardened veteran of the stock market. He immediately made it clear he was not going to roll over and die. He signaled that Lac was a jewel its shareholders should keep for themselves. He fully intended to embark on the company's exciting development plans alone. It was a ploy, of course. He knew that Lac would succumb to someone, but he was going to play hardball to leverage the price as high as he could get it. He was going to run a hard-nosed auction.

When he assembled his takeover team for its first meeting on Saturday, Munk was quite frank with them. He told them he had never done a hostile bid for a public company before, so he would be relying heavily on the people around Barrick's huge round table that weekend. It was an impressive roster. It included all the key people in Barrick and Horsham — Bob Smith, Alan Hill (mining development), Greg Wilkins and Randall Oliphant (finance), Pat Garver (legal), David Wynne-Morgan and Vince Borg (public relations), and Belle Mulligan (investor relations). He also had two of his most trusted lieutenants — Bill Birchall and Howard Beck. Plus he had his professional advisers. From one of Toronto's top three legal firms, Tory, Tory, DesLauriers and Binnington, there were Jim Baillie, a former chairman of the Ontario Securities Commission, and Dick Balfour. There was also David Macdonald and a colleague from Bunting Warburg; two senior partners in Coopers & Lybrand, who were Barrick's auditors; and Rocco Mazzuca and Joe Lash from Kidder Peabody, a U.S.-based investment banker (now defunct) that Munk wanted to include because it was owned by General Electric, whose chairman, the legendary Jack Welch, had done him a favor some years before.

That weekend meeting was the first of many. Munk decided to accept a suggestion from David Wynne-Morgan that the team should meet every morning for the duration of the bid — a practice that was almost unheard of in Canada, although it was quite common in the vicious takeover battles in Britain that Wynne-Morgan had experienced. These meetings were to prove a vital element in the venture's success.

Munk went into the first meeting thinking he should mount the bid with a partner and should aim at announcing Barrick's bid sometime later during the following week. As the views around the table came tumbling out, he changed his mind. By the time the meeting was over, he had abandoned the idea of a partner. Barrick would do it on its own, selling off Lac's Canadian assets if necessary. Equally important, he decided to announce the bid the next morning at 9 o'clock, before the markets opened. They all went home at 11 p.m. on Sunday, having developed an overall strategy, complete with all the corresponding tax, legal, economic, political, and competitive ramifications. The tight intensity of the discussions over the five days, culminating in the weekend meeting, had achieved what would take most companies several weeks.

The decision to announce the bid on Monday morning was a strategic coup. Munk was convinced that Allen's resignation would prompt a surge in the price of Lac's shares and his advisers felt that if they announced their bid the next morning, it would put a cap on the price. The offer they made — C$13.92[5]

---

[5] Barrick's bid was C$4 plus 0.31 Barrick shares. The day before the bid, Barrick had been trading at C$32.375, making the bid worth C$13.92. Alternatively, Lac shareholders could take 0.43 Barrick shares for each Lac share.

— was only a fraction higher than Royal Oak's and it sent a strong message to the market that they should not expect the bidding to get out of control.

It worked. The price rose less than C$1 on the Monday, ending up only slightly above C$14.

The combination of Allen's resignation and Barrick's entry into the fray took the wind out of Witte's sails. When she made her bid on July 7, Lac was trading at C$11.375 and her bid was worth C$13.59. In normal circumstances, a bid from a company like Royal Oak would have been virtually ignored by Lac, but Witte had done a superb job of selling herself against Allen in the stock market. "She has," says one of the Barrick team, who wishes to remain nameless, for obvious reasons, "the balls of a racehorse." The investors and analysts liked her style and determination. They had a lot of money tied up in a stock that wasn't moving and they were angry. They asked themselves why not take a punt on her? Two weeks later, just before Allen resigned, she claimed that 40% of Lac shares had already been tendered or promised — but the Lac shares were still trading below the value of Royal Oak's bid. That meant the market was doubtful if Royal Oak would succeed. And with Allen out of the picture, her position was even weaker, because her prospective added-value for Lac had been undercut.

During the following two weeks, there were no substantive developments. All three players in the game, plus a few others who were thinking of jumping into the fray, elbowed and jockeyed each other in efforts to maneuver themselves into the best position for the moment when they entered the final stretch. It was a battle for the minds and hearts of the big institutional investors, who held most of the Lac shares and the arbitrageurs (the "arbs") — speculators who buy shares during takeovers in the hope of making lots of money in three to four weeks by out-guessing the market.

Witte, as the underdog, had to set the pace. As soon as Munk announced his bid, the balance of opinion on the street tipped in Barrick's favor. His management team had more experience, a better track record, and they had just completed — without a hitch — their masterful development of the Goldstrike mine. Given the choice of holding Barrick shares or Royal Oak shares, most of the major Lac investors preferred Barrick's solid reputation.

Witte adopted the classic entrepreneurial strategy of turning her biggest weakness into her biggest strength. She argued right back that Lac investors would miss out on a major opportunity for long-term capital gain by doing that. She explained that Barrick's shares had a high value relative to their assets because their past performance was so impressive. Royal Oak, on the other hand, with its less seasoned performance, was valued much lower relative to its assets and therefore offered an opportunity for greater appreciation in the value of its shares. At that time, the market had assigned a value of about $1,000 per ounce of production to both Lac and Royal Oak, compared to $4,000 an ounce for Barrick. Obviously, she argued, Barrick shares did not have much upside potential — and adding Lac's reserves to their own wouldn't change that equation much. This argument sounded really good, but didn't last long, because the market assigns values on the basis of expectations for the future, not past history — and production is history.

Her follow-up argument was that the market assessed Lac's value at about $150 per ounce of reserves, compared to $192 for the other major gold producers. She said that her leadership would quickly lead to Lac's being assigned a value in tune with its peers, so the upside potential was a minimum of 25% if investors chose Royal Oak. If they chose Barrick, she suggested, there would be very little upside potential because Barrick shares were already fully valued. Why, she hinted, would the future be any different from the past? She had taken Royal Oak from a total market capitalization of C$700,000 in 1990 to C$550 million in 1994. Who knows what it might be in another five years . . .

Munk and his team responded that the Barrick offer was close to a cash offer, whereas Lac shareholders who accepted the Royal Oak paper would be locked in for years. Royal Oak would increase the total number of its outstanding shares by 250% to 350% if it succeeded, while Barrick would increase its share float by 16%. The investors could cash in their Barrick shares without disturbing the market, but any attempt to liquidate their holdings in Royal Oak would collapse the market.

To emphasize her point about the growth rate of Royal Oak, Witte released her half-year results at the end of July. Profit for the period was C$18 million, a 435% increase over the same period the year before. It was to be the peak profit performance for Royal Oak for some time. In response to the widely believed argument that her reserves were marginal and low-grade, she pointed out that it cost Royal Oak $334 per ounce to deliver each ounce of gold to the bank — including operating expenses, refining, exploration, interest on debt, and head office overheads. It cost Lac $376. In other words, her operating costs might be high, but she ran such a tight ship that her total costs were lower.

Her pitch was effective. Bill Martin of Benham Capital Management in California spoke for many when he said: "I feel comfortable with her heading up Royal Oak and I would feel comfortable with her heading up Lac Minerals. I'm just not quite so comfortable with having to wreck Lac's balance sheet to get to the position of having her there . . . The fact is she gets the job done. She's just effective."

Pitblado,[6] meanwhile, was doing everything he could to ignore Witte — or at least to marginalize her bid. Lac had already made it clear to Munk, through Peter Allen, that they did not want Royal Oak to win and they would be comfortable with Munk. Pitblado's immediate priority, however, was to persuade everyone that he was comfortable with *no one* and that the bids on the table were far too low. The only way he could do that was to demonstrate that Lac was worth a lot more than C$14 a share. First of all, he talked up the improving financial picture by announcing Lac's half-year results, which showed the company back in the black with a $9.3 million profit, compared to a loss of $164,000 a year earlier. He also told the market and the media as often as he could that he was talking to two or three other potential bidders who could be expected to place a higher value on Lac's shares. "I feel like they are picking my pocket," he told the *Globe & Mail*.

In a surprising move to demonstrate his "commitment" to pursue an aggressive independent expansion program without any help from anyone else, Pitblado hired Peter Steen to be the new CEO. Steen's most recent job had been chief operating officer of Homestake Mines, which had taken over his former employer, International Corona Corp. When he was running Corona, Steen had led the bitter battle with Lac for control of the Page-Williams mine. The thought of him sitting at the same boardroom table with Peter Allen (who had resigned only as CEO, not as a director) had more than a few minds in the industry

---

[6] Pitblado declined to be interviewed for this book. Observations of his actions and motives are drawn from people who witnessed his actions and/or were in touch with other people close to the Lac team.

boggling. It was a triumph of sorts for Pitblado to persuade such a respected man to jump to Lac at that point in its history (his employment contract was never revealed), but his plan didn't work. The 63-year-old Steen was clearly an interim CEO, and the market shrugged off his appointment as irrelevant.

Pitblado's biggest weapon, however, was Lac's "poison pill." Like many companies that had seen the takeover carnage of the 1980s, Lac had a "Shareholder Protection Plan," which gave the board of directors the power to sabotage an unwelcome bid for control. If the plan was triggered, the shareholders had the right to buy two shares of Lac for the price of one, which would double the price to a successful bidder. In practice, the Ontario Securities Commission had the power to force a company to rescind its poison pill, but it would do so only if the bidder or bidders could demonstrate that there were no other potential bidders and that the "auction" of the target company was being conducted fairly. In other words, management cannot use a poison pill to entrench themselves, but they can use it to buy time until they have flushed out all the potential bidders.

By hinting at other bidders, Pitblado was sending a signal that he would not withdraw Lac's poison pill. As the expiry date (August 9) for Royal Oak's bid drew closer, it was obvious that Witte was not going to win on the first round of bidding, but it was still not clear if there really were any other realistic bids waiting in the wings. There had been two attempts at friendly mergers by much smaller companies. TVX Gold and Kinross Gold had announced to the press on July 28 that they had submitted a proposal to Lac to exchange their shares for Lac's assets, with Kinross taking all the Canadian mines and TVX taking the U.S. and South American mines. Lac did not even bother to respond as it was not a proper bid and it was not interested in being "saved" by another two minnows. Eight days later, on August 5, Amax Gold announced it had also been sniffing around seeking a friendly bid, but it got nowhere either.

The major problem for any company seeking to buy Lac was an accounting conundrum — how to handle "goodwill." When one company buys another, the price it pays is often higher than the value of the assets shown in the books of the target company, because those assets are shown as being worth whatever it cost to buy them originally, which is usually much lower than their current value. Any increase in the value of these assets is not normally reflected in the books, unless the assets are revalued. When the two companies are combined, the acquired assets are carried in the combined company's books at the same value as they were in the original books and the excess of the cost of the acquisition over the "book value" of the assets is called goodwill, which is shorthand for the earning power in the assets that is not reflected in the book value. Goodwill is normally written off as a charge against profits over the life of the assets that have been purchased. It is not a real expense, because no cash is taken from the bank to pay for it — it is purely a paper entry by the accountants — but it depresses the published earnings of a company, so most companies try to avoid it. Munk had announced, for example, that Barrick was prepared to absorb an annual charge of $55 million for 15 years to write off the good-will it would incur from buying Lac. There are only three gold companies in North America that could still be reasonably sure of making a profit after such a charge against earnings: Barrick, Placer Dome, and Newmont Gold.

The goodwill problem is particularly severe for gold companies because of the extraordinary quirkiness of gold bugs. There's something about gold that transcends common sense.

Perhaps it is the gut conviction that it is the only true repository of lasting value. Perhaps it is the timeless expectation that the price of gold will always go up more than any other commodity. Perhaps it is the unquenchable optimism that further discoveries of fabulous wealth lie just around the next geological fault line. Whatever it is, the stock market puts a value on gold shares that is significantly higher than their identifiable economic value. Call it the "blue-sky factor." For any other stock, the basis for valuing a share is its DCF — Discounted Cash Flow from future operations. In simple words, the DCF is an amount of money, invested today at current interest rates, that will be exactly repaid (with interest) by the expected future cash flow from the company's operations. The DCF is the "economic valve" of a stock, and, in most industries, stock prices average out at the industry's economic value. In the summer of 1994, the average price of gold shares was 1.7 times their DCF. In other words, the price of gold shares had a blue-sky factor of more than 40%. The blue-sky factor for Lac was about a third. For Barrick, it was 60% — the investors really believed in Munk's wisdom. For Royal Oak, the blue-sky factor was 73%: for each $1 invested in Royal Oak, shareholders were getting only 27¢ of economic value or discounted cash flow.

The consequences of this blue-sky factor are sweet music to investors who buy their shares before the company discovers gold — it multiplies their profit. For investors buying mature assets, the blue-sky factor means they can lose their shirts unless they dramatically improve the performance of the company. Accordingly, no one ever takes over a mature gold company with cash — the only realistic way to buy gold assets is by issuing shares of other gold companies in exchange, because both pieces of paper are overvalued by the same blue-sky factor. Both

Barrick and Royal Oak, however, had to absorb the blue-sky factor in respect of the cash portion of their bids — about 28% for both of them. Witte raised a few eyebrows when she proposed to write off her goodwill over 25 years, although her assets had a life expectancy of only seven years. Munk had 15 years to play with in his write-off program and he knew he could absorb the goodwill charge without having to show a loss. He also had an ace up his sleeve. He knew that he could reduce the goodwill because he was an unparalleled master in the art of revaluing his balance sheet by putting a higher value on his assets, having served his apprenticeship in the weird and wonderful world of real estate in the South Pacific.

As the Barrick team surveyed the strategies of Pitblado and Witte, they saw two major risks. The first was a third bidder. The second was that the Lac shareholders might, as a result of some technicality or misjudgment, choose Royal Oak's paper even though Barrick's paper was much more respected.

Munk knew that the only other companies that could raise the necessary cash and handle the goodwill problem were Placer Dome and Newmont. Bunting Warburg's David Macdonald had combed the data on these companies and concluded that Placer Dome was unlikely to bid because it already had too much on its plate and had recently been bruised by an unsuccessful takeover attempt. Newmont, he felt, was a possibility, but there were a lot of problems in a cross-border takeover. They didn't rate the chances of a third bidder very high, but they could never be certain.[7]

As for their fears that the Witte bid might slip through, all the

---

[7] In fact, there very nearly was a third bidder. Pitblado wasn't bluffing. Newmont had been talking seriously with him, but they could not strike a satisfactory deal.

market indicators pointed to a lack of interest in her paper, but again, they could never be certain. The arbs had moved in on the Lac shares after Barrick announced its bid — and neither they nor the institutional investors were about to give Barrick any comfort. They told the Barrick people how much they admired Witte's entrepreneurial approach and they fully intended to tender to Royal Oak. It is a game. They all wanted the best price for their Lac shares, so they hyped up the competition in the hope they could push the two parties into an extravagant bidding war. But Barrick stayed calm.

The big concern was whether the Lac shareholders would behave rationally or let their emotions get in the way. Macdonald's colleagues at Bunting Warburg had been bombarding Lac shareholders to find out who still owned the stock. They found that the arbs held 25% of the shares outstanding and that 127 of the 141 institutional investors they had identified in the first week of the bid still owned their Lac shares. That meant that most of the shares were controlled by professionals. There would be no technical mistakes or misjudgments. They could be confident that the market's signals were driven by pure self-interest. And the market's message was clear — they were not going to buy Witte's offer because they didn't like her paper. Macdonald could safely tell the daily meeting that Barrick did not have to compete on price with Witte.

Meanwhile, Bob Smith had set to work trying to put a realistic value on Lac's reserves. He did some smart detective work. Some of his information came from one of his employees who used to work at Lac. More information came from another Barrick executive who took a trip down to Chile to speak to some people he knew in the local mining industry. "We made a conscious decision," Smith says, "that there was an excellent chance we could convert 50% of the resources into reserves. We had enough confidence in the quality of the assets that we knew we were right." In other words, Barrick was buying 20 million ounces of gold, not the 13.5 million that Pitblado thought Lac had. If they had to, they were prepared to raise their bid a lot higher than C$14.

Despite this "comfort margin," Munk still could not afford to pay too much for Lac. In all his previous takeovers, the market felt he had paid too much for his acquisitions — Travelodge, Camflo, and Goldstrike to name just three — and if this reputation was confirmed in the Lac acquisition, Barrick would become the target of every promoter looking for a sucker. Now that he could, for the first time, truly afford to pay too much, it was doubly important that he not do so. There was never even any discussion about the maximum price Barrick could afford. Everyone focused on the lowest price with which they could win. The whole strategy then revolved around the best tactics to maneuver Pitblado into accepting a "good" price — good from Barrick's point of view, that is.

Throughout the two weeks following the announcement of the Barrick bid, Munk steered his team through his daily meetings. The first weekend, he was acutely aware of his lack of experience in this kind of situation. "He was genuinely more dependent on his advisers than would normally be the case," says Jim Baillie. "As the deal went down the road, he took an increasingly active role and the chemistry changed. His confidence ascended through the process and hence his dominance of the process ascended. He would direct it, he would decide how much of a shaft to sink in a particular issue. And sometimes he came in with an agenda of his own. When he did, it was hard to get airtime for other things."

The daily meetings followed a pattern. "We would start with a review of what had happened in the market, the press, what key people were saying," says David Macdonald. "We'd talk through the key tasks — the draft, the circular, preparing for the OSC hearings. We would talk through a combination of overall campaign strategies and we'd block out time for when we were going to do what, right down to micro-tactics. Like chess players, you think through all the different permutations. Peter did what a general should do. He got all the intelligence he could get from every quarter. He'd get market intelligence from us and pass it to Belle Mulligan. He had other sources. He'd then get the best analysis from the lawyers, the bankers, and his own people and do different scenarios. Every day, decisions had to be made and he would make them.

"Sometimes it was easy to forge a consensus, sometimes it was more difficult. Clearly there were times when he came into the meeting with a view and he'd listen to everybody and he still thought his view was best at the end. But there were other times when he came in with a view and listened to everyone and changed his view. Peter was unique in being willing, as the founder/leader, to have his ideas fully challenged. His ego's strong enough that he said, 'I want to get the right outcome and I'm willing to listen to good ideas and good analysis from whatever quarter they come.' But he was also able to say, 'OK, here's the decision.'

"Throughout all these sessions — and some of them were three or four hours — the most important thing to him was getting all the relevant information on the table and analyzing it rigorously. If someone had a new dimension, he wanted to hear it and he would suspend judgment until we had talked things through. He wants to be challenged, he wants to adopt the best course. He likes the challenge."

Munk's twenty-ninth golden rule:
Listen to smart people.

Munk's team make their share of mistakes, of course, but, for the five weeks that Barrick dropped everything to concentrate on Lac, they were very few. It operated at an extraordinarily high pitch. And it was a once-in-a-lifetime "high" for everyone who participated.

Having decided that Witte was not a serious competitor, the Barrick team knew that the game would end with a one-on-one meeting at which Munk and Pitblado would negotiate the final price and terms. Munk's instinct, of course, was to pick up the phone a day or two after the bid and arrange that meeting with Pitblado. That's how he liked to cut deals. His advisers knew, however, if he did that, Pitblado would trumpet the meeting to the media and everyone would assume that Barrick was going to bid higher. At one point, Munk was on his way to the phone and Jim Baillie physically stopped him by standing in his way and saying, "Peter, you can't do that." Munk eventually went along with the unanimous advice but he warned them, "Don't deny me the chance to meet with Pitblado and negotiate."

The Barrick team had a similar problem with the "road show" to explain the Barrick bid to all the major investors in Lac shares. Munk went with Smith, Randall Oliphant (chief financial officer) and Belle Mulligan (investor relations), and his enthusiasm was soaring. He could taste the benefits from the merger of the two companies. The members of his daily meeting were getting concerned. "He wanted to go into it high, wide, and handsome," Baillie says. "He wanted to just go in there and sell, sell, sell — and tell them what wonderful things would emerge from the merger of these two companies. His investment advisers were telling him 'If you say it's such a wonderful company, they won't tender their shares. Don't oversell.' I was saying, 'Every word is grist for later lawsuits — they'll ask why you were misleading the market, touting your shares.'" Munk listened and took their advice. "It was a triumph," says Baillie. "He managed to do the selling while still staying within the grounds we laid down."

The Barrick strategy worked like a charm. Munk consolidated Barrick's advantage over Witte's paper. He was firm in saying that he did not anticipate raising the price of his bid. As August 9 approached, Witte knew that she was not going to win the battle even though her offer was nominally 50¢ higher than Barrick's. Pitblado knew that she would not win, so he did not withdraw his poison pill and Witte could not proceed with her bid. On August 8, she raised her bid to the equivalent of C$16.50.[8] It cost her dearly. She had to promise her bankers to float an equity issue for C$120 million within a year. She also had to increase her bridge loan to C$475 million from C$425 million. Her strategy was now being dictated to a degree by her bankers.

Because Royal Oak was so much smaller than Lac, the higher bid didn't make a big difference, even if it looked impressive. The Lac shareholders were still buying their own assets. They would get more cash — C$5, instead of C$3.75, but their collective ownership of the combined Lac/Royal Oak assets

---

[8] C$5 in cash plus two Royal Oak shares or 2.87 shares. Royal Oak was trading at C$5.75 on August 8 so that made the bid worth C$16.50.

increased only from 72% to 75% under the new offer — and the 75% would soon be diluted by the promised equity issue of C$120 million. Lac's assets would constitute about 80% of the combined company.

The professionals were not fooled. If the institutional investors had thought Witte was a probable winner, they would have sold their Royal Oak shares and bought Lac, because the Lac shares were trading almost C$2 below the value of Witte's bid and that was therefore the quickest route to profit. But they didn't. In the next two days, the price of Lac shares rose 25¢ and Royal Oak's fell proportionately. Witte's second bid was floundering after only two days.

Barrick's offer had an expiry date of August 26, so it was not in a hurry. Witte set her second expiry date a few days before Barrick's, on August 19 — she hoped that investors would take her higher bid out of concern that Barrick might not raise its bid and they would be left out in the cold. But the Barrick team was confident that the institutional investors and the arbs had decided against her. Munk now tasted victory. He wanted desperately to sit down with Pitblado and cut a deal. But the discipline held. Barrick did not even apply to the Ontario Securities Commission for a hearing to have the Lac poison pill disallowed. Having let Peggy Witte do all the dirty work in attacking Peter Allen's competence, they now let her set the pace against the poison pill.

The hearing was on August 18 and 19 — right on Witte's expiry date. Barrick and Royal Oak wanted closure on the poison pill, but Pitblado stared them down to buy time. He told the Commission that there was another interested party and he was not at liberty to disclose who it was because disclosure would wreck the negotiations. The Commission bowed his way and left the poison pill in place for another ten days, unless one party acquired 65% of the shares. No one had two-thirds acceptance yet, so Royal Oak was forced to extend its offer four days to August 23.

The arbs were now beginning to get worried. Barrick was not budging. Their teasing wasn't working. They went into high gear. "In that kind of process," says Macdonald, "you have a whole succession of events, where if you are not disciplined and if you don't stay cool, you can make the mistake of firing your gun too early. You have Jim Pitblado taking over, you have the arrival of Peter Steen as a credible operator and he asks the shareholders, 'Why should we let the value of these assets go with someone else when you can have the full upside potential by staying with us?' After Peggy's second bid at C$16.50, the arbs were telling us, 'Why should we tender to you when Peggy's bid is so much higher?' The arbs are shameless — they will call your wife, they will call your kids, they'll call you. They'll talk to your barber, they'll talk to your banker, they'll call your lawyer. There's nothing they won't do to glean whatever intelligence they can get. They want to get the *tone*. We had one arb who made 20 phone calls in one day to 10 or 11 people involved in the deal, asking the same question. He was looking for a breach of the data."

Still Barrick didn't budge. Munk and his team sailed through all the turbulence without changing course one degree. By August 23, Witte's extended expiry date, she still had not got enough acceptances to win and it was now clear that Barrick had won. The biggest danger for Pitblado was that Barrick would not raise its bid because it knew Witte was beaten; if two-thirds of the shareholders tendered by the Barrick expiry date of August 26, the poison pill would be automatically withdrawn and Barrick would be in control. Witte extended her bid again, but it was now irrelevant. Pitblado finally cracked. That evening, Tony Fell, the chairman of RBC Dominion Securities, Lac's investment bankers, called Munk to ask if he would see them that evening. Munk finally got to have his meeting and cut his deal.

By waiting for Pitblado to call him, Munk had won all the chips in the bargaining process. He had hung tough and forced Pitblado to come begging. He raised the offer 13% to the equivalent of C$15.10[9] — C$1.40 below Witte's and less than C$2 above his first bid. Pitblado enthusiastically endorsed Munk's second bid and lifted the poison pill voluntarily for him. By September 6, the revised expiry date, Munk had acquired 84% of the shares (Royal Oak withdrew its offer on August 30). He extended one more time to September 19, so he could reach 90%, the point at which he was legally entitled to force all remaining shareholders to sell to him.

No one could accuse him of overpaying, even on the basis of the known assets at that time. Three months later, Munk and Smith knew that the Chilean mines were even better than they had hoped. By then, Smith had taken a closer look at the mine, and he quietly told Munk: "You're lucky I didn't go down before we made the final offer — I would have pushed for a much higher price."

There was an interesting postscript to the Lac takeover: the $942 million of goodwill that Barrick expected it would have to absorb through a charge of $62.8 million a year for 15 years. Once the transaction was completed, however, the accountants reduced the charge significantly. Although Barrick's shares had been trading at about $23 when the final bid was accepted, the

---

[9] C$5 in cash plus 0.325 Barrick shares for each Lac share, or 0.487 Barrick shares. The day before, Barrick had been trading at C$31, which made the offer worth C$15.10.

company's investment advisers estimated that the "fair" value of the 66 million shares issued to Lac shareholders, had they all been issued on the same day for cash, was slightly more than $18 each. There is nothing to stop a company from issuing its shares below market value, of course, but this was the first time this approach had been used to reduce the blue-sky factor in a gold company's books. That took care of $330 million of the goodwill. The balance was eliminated entirely by assigning higher values to Lac assets, for which higher potential had been identified. Barrick had swallowed Lac without even a burp. Net income just kept right on rising.

10

STRATEGIES FOR THE ENCORES

The acquisition of Lac Minerals catapulted Peter Munk into a different league. From a North American–based company with one mine (to all intents and purposes, even though Barrick did own three other mines), he graduated to a ten-mine company operating on two continents. From a plateau where he had gone as far as he could go with his existing properties, he was scaling a mountainside of potential with underexploited mines. He gained control of an international network of offices and working relationships — and his cash flow was headed for half a billion dollars a year. Within a mere five years of announcing his development plan for Goldstrike, he had become a global operator with access to undreamed-of financial resources.

The new Peter Munk began to emerge — now a tycoon who is radically different from the entrepreneur he was for most of his life. The days of scrambling against impossible odds to hit the jackpot are gone. For the first 30 years of his career, he spent most of his time creating visions, selling them to financial partners, and then working impossibly hard to turn the vision into reality before reality dissolved the vision. This aspect of entrepreneurs, almost magical in its power, is widely misunderstood and often deprecated, perhaps because most people do not themselves have the will or the courage to dream visions that defy gravity. All entrepreneurs possess the ability to rearrange conventional perspectives of reality into new, original patterns — and all truly great entrepreneurs combine this unique perspective with the ability to deliver on their promises. Not always on time and not always in the expected form, but sooner or later, they deliver results.

It is never a smooth road. There are times when their unique perspective on reality does not seem real at all. It may always be real to them, and it may become reality, but their vision is invariably perceived as unreal when they first expose it to the scrutiny of others. There have been moments in Munk's life when the exigencies of his immediate purpose have pushed his interpretation of the facts — undisputed facts — to the furthest extreme of possible interpretations, thereby reducing the probability of success to something close to zero. Every great entrepreneur has done this, and inevitably, external events derail their plans, as happened more than once to Munk. But extraordinary achievements never come without great risk — and extraordinary entrepreneurs learn how to minimize their risks.

Munk's thirtieth golden rule:
If you want to dream big, expect big problems.
Big dreams challenge the fates.

This is the essence of entrepreneurship — opening up an impossible gap between the resources they control and those they need to fulfil their dreams. The best entrepreneurs know how to attract the missing resources cheaply or for free. They can paint images of their dreams in such enticing concepts that people step in to close the gap for them. Only an entrepreneur would think of borrowing money at 7% when the prime rate is 12% by offering the lenders a 40% return on their money in the unlikely event that the price of gold would go to $1,500. Only an entrepreneur would persuade professionals to work for shares in his company.

This was the basic equation for most of the first 30 years of Munk's career — he persuaded people to grant him access to resources today by promising them great wealth tomorrow if it all turned out as he expected. The two most important skills he had in those years were: (a) his ability to make powerful presentations, in which he assembled incontrovertible arguments why his particular ideas could never fail (even if no one else could see it); and (b) his ability to implement a plan with relentless determination and flawless precision.

He doesn't need the first skill any more. He's the man with the money now. He can sign a check for half a billion dollars. He can raise a billion dollars with a couple of phone calls. In the early days, he never had to think too hard about the opportunities he pursued, because he didn't have many — he played with the hand he was dealt. Now every week brings hundreds of opportunities across his desk — or across the desk of his senior executives. His problem is different now. His challenge is to avoid buying at full value. If he falls into that trap, Barrick and Horsham will become institutions, growing at a respectable rate of 10% or 15% a year, like good blue-chip stocks, secure in their conservative mediocrity.

The thought of running a bureaucratic, staid corporation, with steady and unspectacular growth, is like the cold hand of death for a man like Peter Munk, who still retains his irrepressible impulse to create beautiful visions for a better company. However, with the great wealth at his disposal now, his dreams would have to be gigantic to qualify as entrepreneurial. That prospect may hold no terror for a man like Rupert Murdoch, who will bet his entire fortune on a single business decision, but it is out of the question for Munk. He will never endanger his wealth when he shoots for the stars. He will embark on no venture that would threaten his survival if it failed. He will choose no objective beyond his means. His challenge, therefore, is how to keep his visions lean, hungry, and starved for resources when he has the power to give them all the resources they need.

In the spring of 1996, in Toronto's cavernous old railway hotel, the Royal York, Peter Munk gave his annual report to the Toronto shareholders of Horsham. The Horsham meetings don't attract the same interest as Barrick's annual meetings — there are fewer people, the mood is more intimate, and the press usually tucks its commentary on the meetings a long way off from the front page to which Barrick has become accustomed. This year was to be different, however. Munk gave them all a jolt that echoed through the press the following day. He apologized.

"We have failed in the most fundamental responsibility that a public company has toward its shareholders," he told them, "and that's really the delivery of value to you. It's not acceptable, we shall not live with it, and we shall do something about it."

He had, of course, been trying to do something about it for some time. His admission of failure to his shareholders was merely a venting of his frustration that he had not yet found a way to solve the problem, which was that Horsham shares were trading at a 30% discount from the value of its assets. At the end of 1995, the asset value of Horsham was $19 ($9.50 of which was its holding of Barrick shares) and its shares were trading at $13.38, where they had stuck like glue for months, while Barrick soared on the excitement of a significant increase in the price of gold. Horsham's share price had increased only 50% in the four years to the end of 1995, while Barrick rose 86% and the value of Clark increased by several multiples. Admittedly, Trizec had been a disappointment, having declined almost 30% from its value in July 1994 — but he knew that Trizec was not a short-term investment, and even then, Horsham's net asset value per share would have been only $1 higher if Trizec had remained at the same value. The problem was deeper than the constituent parts of Horsham — there was something wrong with the way the company itself was structured.

Horsham was more than Munk's vehicle for diversifying out of gold — it was also where a significant portion of his wealth was invested. He held 8.7 million Horsham shares, 7.5 million of which had 50 votes each, giving him 80% of the total votes attributable to the common shares. Whatever his feelings about his personal stake, however, he was clearly stung by the idea of letting down his shareholders.

One of the problems with Horsham was that no one really knew what it was supposed to be doing. The idea was simple enough — to diversify out of gold on the strength of its Barrick

305

holdings — but how? Its annual report said it would apply all the principles that Peter Munk had developed — operationally aggressive, financially conservative, building for long-term growth, and so on — and that its competitive edge was the team of people who built Barrick. But that was more like an operating principle than a strategy. Nobody really knew what its role was, possibly including Munk, perhaps because he had always run it opportunistically, without a strategic vision.

Horsham started on its road to diversification when Munk bought into Clark Refining and Marketing in 1988. It was a good opportunity that fell into his lap and he grabbed it.[1] The next year another opportunity came his way and he grabbed that one, too.

It was November 1989, and the Berlin Wall had just come down with a thud heard around the globe. As most of the developed world sat glued to their television sets, watching in fascination as the Soviet empire crumbled before their eyes, Peter Munk was in Britain, looking at opportunities in real estate. Accompanying him was Andy Sarlos, a director of Horsham and a well-known stock trader in Toronto. Sarlos quietly suggested to Munk that this might be a good time to check out opportunities in Berlin, which was sure to become the entrepôt of eastern Europe now that the Wall was gone. Munk was receptive, so he and Sarlos took off for Berlin.

Sarlos, who was born in Hungary, had a friend who was a friend of the Hungarian ambassador to East Germany. At that time, there were close ties between the East Germans and the Hungarians. Hungary was a favorite vacation destination for Berlin's Communist party bosses and the East German

---

[1] See Chapter 1.

ambassadorial post was the second biggest plum in the Hungarian foreign service. So the Hungarian ambassador was well connected in Budapest, as well as Berlin. He knew all the senior people in the city government of Berlin. He agreed to arrange a meeting with the city officials for Munk, Sarlos, and Peter Sidebottom, a personal friend of Munk's. Sidebottom was a director at that time of Hill, Samuel, a major investment banker in real estate. (Sidebottom first met Munk when Slater Walker sent him to Fiji to assess Pacific Harbour — he wrote a very strong report recommending Slater Walker stay away from it.)

The trio spent a day with their granite-faced Hungarian ambassador, East Berlin's deputy mayor, and a gaggle of his officials, trying to find a way to do a deal. Munk speaks fluent German, so language was not a problem, but the conversation was going round in circles. It became apparent that the city officials wanted something more than what Munk was putting on the table. Toward the end of the day, Sarlos, on a hunch, turned to the city officials and said: "We don't want to do this development on our own. We want to do it with you. You give us the land, we'll put the money in, and we'll do it 50/50." The mood changed. He had found the missing piece of the puzzle and the discussions immediately became serious.

Munk dreamed of a striking development in the "Mitte" district (the Berlin equivalent of New York's midtown or Toronto's Yorkville) that would give the whole city a new focus. He sent off Sidebottom to scout out the best locations. After two days of touring the city, Sidebottom selected the prime sites, which they narrowed down to one block. When they went back to the deputy mayor, his officials told Munk with a big smile that they owned 85% of it. On his return to England, Munk phoned Pat Samuel and asked him to go to Berlin and shepherd the development through the local bureaucratic minefield. Samuel dryly reminded Munk he was perfect for the job except that he didn't speak German and he knew absolutely nothing about the area. That didn't faze Munk, so Samuel went.

Samuel was soon on good terms with the mayor of East Berlin, who liked Samuel's promises of putting his city on the world map with his exciting development plans. The excitement was short-lived, however. It turned out that all property owned by the Communist regime was passed to Treuhandanstalt, the company set up by the German government to redistribute the assets of the East German government. Not long afterwards, East and West Berlin were amalgamated and Horsham's prize contact, the mayor of East Berlin, lost his job. Samuel was back to square one.

The real estate community in Berlin at that time was highly antagonistic toward foreign investors and pressured the Treuhand to award development contracts to Germans. Treuhand decided to auction off to the highest bidder a large number of properties with great potential. On several occasions, Treuhand officials delayed the opening of tenders well beyond the deadline while they waited for "the last couple of bids." Invariably, the winning bid came in late and was a few thousand deutsch-marks above the Horsham bid — a minuscule margin in bids worth many millions of deutsch-marks. The Germans were clearly looking after their own.

Munk poured on the pressure. He recruited to the Horsham board Karl Otto Pöhl, the former chief of the Bundesbank, which is the most respected government institution in Germany. Pöhl opened a lot of doors and smoothed the way. Munk also approached the then Canadian prime minister, Brian Mulroney, to get his officials in Germany to lend a helping hand. Treuhand quickly stopped the cavalier treatment of Horsham, and put together a new committee to select parcels of land and allocate them to bidders for development. The man they appointed to run it was Hanno Klein, who was more even-handed, and he liked what he saw in Horsham's plans. Plans proceeded rapidly for eight or nine months, with Klein offering support and encouragement. Then he was killed with a letter bomb.

The message was beginning to get through. Horsham abandoned downtown Berlin, and Samuel found a 480-acre parcel of land right on the autobahn ring road 13 miles south of downtown. It wasn't as exciting as the downtown prospect, but there were no politics there. Horsham invested 20 million deutschmarks to buy the land. Over the next three years, the property was expanded to 600 acres and Horsham invested a total of $40 million. By 1995, the development had already sold a quarter of the land and was paying its own way with property sales. Its assessed value was $100 million, even if the books still carried it at $40 million. It was a success, but as far as Munk was concerned, it was still only a consolation prize.

Munk didn't pay much attention to Horsham after that, until he raised $600 million with his debenture backed by Barrick shares in late 1993. The ink was barely dry on that issue when he was approached by Tony Fell, the chairman of RBC Dominion Securities, to look at Trizec.

Trizec had been a bright star in Canada's corporate skies for many years, having wowed the country in the 1960s with its first major downtown office building, Montreal's Place Ville Marie. Along with all the other real estate companies that rode the back of Canada's boom years in the 1970s and 1980s, Trizec had blossomed into a giant, only to suffer the humility of a steep decline into deep trouble when the North American property market collapsed in the early 1990s. In 1992 and 1993, Trizec lost a total of C$850 million, which almost wiped out its shareholders' equity. It was in better shape than most of its fellow behemoths, however, and still a very big company. With 41 office properties and 44 shopping malls in many cities in Canada and the United States, Trizec controlled assets valued at $3.5 billion, even after accounting for punishing write-offs to reflect the reduced value of North American real estate.

Trizec's co-chairmen, Kevin Benson and Bill L'Heureux, had worked tirelessly throughout the previous year to come up with an arrangement for the holders of Trizec debt. They sought to convert a significant portion of their debt into equity in order to lower the annual interest charge sufficiently to permit the company to make enough money to repay the outstanding debts. In January 1994, the creditors turned them down. Trizec's debt was then almost eight times its equity, and the company was on the point of bankruptcy. Some of the creditors had applied to a judge in Calgary for the right to seize the company's assets. As a last resort, Trizec retained RBC Dominion Securities to find a new source of equity capital to bail out the company. They had less than two weeks to find someone with half a billion dollars.

"I have always wanted to get into real estate," Munk says now. "Maybe it's my Jewish insecurity! I need something secure and permanent — and real estate provides that."

Trizec started negotiating with Horsham on March 7 and they signed an agreement in principle on March 27, after Trizec obtained an extension to the court-ordered deadline for reaching a settlement with the creditors. A binding agreement was signed two weeks later, a matter of days before Trizec would have succumbed to receivership.

At this point, Munk realized he needed a partner who had a great deal more experience in the industry than he did, and L'Heureux suggested Jerry O'Connor, the chairman of the O'Connor Group, who had also been sniffing around Trizec but had dropped out because he could not meet the deadlines. O'Connor manages several large U.S. portfolios of real estate, mostly funded by institutional investors, and he knows everyone in the business in the United States. He was the perfect partner, so Munk brought him into the deal, through one of O'Connor's funds, the Argo Partnership, with J. P. Morgan as a limited partner. In the end, Horsham bought 48% ownership of Trizec and Argo 27%, in return for $477 million cash from Horsham and $250 million from Argo. Trizec used the cash to negotiate a settlement with the debt holders of the company, who agreed to take common shares in place of $1.1 billion of their long-term debt and $318 million of preferred shares.

Munk immediately took control of Trizec, moving in a new executive team under L'Heureux. By the end of the year, only 3 of the directors (including L'Heureux and Benson) were still on board and only 3 of the 14 officers were still at their posts.

The financial restructuring assured Trizec's survival, but improvements in the bottom line were slow in coming. Almost a year and a quarter later, in April 1996, Trizec shares — for which Munk had paid C$12.56 in 1994 — were languishing under C$10. Munk couldn't wait any longer, so he sent Wilkins into Trizec as CEO to accelerate the turnaround, while L'Heureux stayed on in charge of international diversification.

Trizec turned out to be more complicated than anyone had expected. The timing of the acquisition appeared to be excellent, coming as it did after a precipitous market collapse, when stock prices were at historically low levels. Initially, the

Horsham strategy was to get top dollar by selling off the mature properties with high occupancy rates and a solid cash flow to pension funds that needed security and didn't mind lower yields, so they were prepared to pay high prices for them. Since there wasn't much Trizec could do to improve the asset value of these properties, they reasoned it was better to sell them off and use the cash to invest in underperforming assets, which they could improve to the point where they could sell them off, at great profit, as mature properties.

Unfortunately, the real estate market was in a state of rapid transition and what might have worked a decade before didn't work in the mid-1990s. "You have to come at it unconventionally," Greg Wilkins said shortly after becoming CEO. Macro demographic trends were working against shopping malls, which is where most of Trizec's retail properties are. "Last year was a record year in retail construction — but almost none of it was in malls. It was all in category killers." These huge stores, located in isolation away from retail agglomerations, had the drawing power to pull people away from their traditional shopping locales even if it meant more travel.

It wasn't what Munk had bargained for, but true to form, he and his Horsham team, led by Wilkins, listened to what the market was telling them and then switched strategies, just as he had done with Travelodge. They will sell off unsatisfactory retail malls, and if they find that new opportunities are not that good in North America, they will switch to international real estate.

It's a good illustration of Munk's approach to strategy. He sees an opportunity and then develops a strategic framework to give that opportunity added power and reach. As Rotman puts it: "He's opportunistic with a strategic focus. Clark was opportunistic, but the strategy was the rationalization of the refining industry. It was a good deal because of what was likely to happen as people closed down refineries or upgraded them — with all that capital expenditure, only the strong would survive." The same kind of strategy is emerging in Horsham's real estate business, where Wilkins forecasts a major consolidation in the industry that will restore the best-run companies' ability to leverage their investments.

The strategic framework doesn't mean, however, that Munk has much faith in business cycles and timing, despite his obvious acumen in timing his entry into real estate. "The conventional wisdom of timing is all wrong," he says. "To me, the timing is much less important. My own activities determine the optimum timing for my actions. We made our best money in the worst times, because it doesn't matter to us. We fight our own battles, we create our own problems. We have a great idea, a great concept, and it works. We don't find the waves, we are the boat."

It's not an approach that finds much favor in business schools. Joe Rotman, for example, would speak for many more businesspeople: "When you study business cycles, you get a sense of timing and change. I believe that things are constantly in cycles and you have to find the right time and the right place to get into something." The only trouble with that is it's often very difficult to see the cycles while they are actually happening. Rotman is one of the few who have called some major cycles accurately and he's made a fortune on it. Most people see the cycles only when they are already finished.

Munk doesn't deal in complex macro-economic trends and cycles; he deals in specific opportunities where he can see the potential to make money through specific actions. His genius is that he can see the strategic ramifications of that opportunity and then create an enormous sense of urgency in everyone with whom he is working, which makes it seem like the timing is perfect. And it *is* perfect, but only because he has made it so.

Of the five major investments he has made in the 15 years after selling Travelodge, three have been successful by any measure (Barrick, the Berlin property, and Clark) and two have not done well (the oil and gas venture and Trizec). He may still do well with Trizec, despite its 30% decline in the first two years he owned it. "Strategically it made sense for us to operate a real estate company, to add some value to it," he says, "so long as we could afford the downside. If it dropped 20%, so what? I mean no one can expect to buy everything at the very bottom. But the upside could be very great.

"Every deal I've made I've lost money initially," he says. "It's my work afterwards — the next five years — that makes them more valuable. I've never bought anything cleverly yet. When I bought Goldstrike, the analysts' reports all said, 'Poor Peter Munk overpaid.' When I bought Camflo, I overpaid. When I bought Trizec, the Scotia McLeod analyst said Horsham is a sell — the poor sucker overpaid. You'll see where it'll be three years from now, four years from now. You just wait."

Munk's thirty-first golden rule:
Don't expect to buy at the best price.
Expect to sell at the right price.

Therein lies the heart of Munk's strategy. He is always looking for a home run, as the Horsham executives like to call it. His repertoire does not include a bunt. He wants very few, very big deals. He says 'no' to hundreds of deals, taking a close look only at those with enormous upside potential. He is adamant that Horsham is not like Gerry Schwartz's Onex or Jack Cockwell's

Edper. "Those guys are geniuses. I mean Gerry Schwartz has a comprehension 50% higher than me and Cockwell 75% higher than me — and I've dealt with both. [Christopher] Ondaatje has a comprehension 100% higher than me. Those guys enjoy doing deals because they can always outdo everyone else.

"I hate deals. They outfox me, they outsmart me. I don't like the fact that I don't sleep." He chafes at being at the mercy of someone else's decisions when he's negotiating a deal. "It doesn't matter how much you plan. If the other guy does something that you hadn't counted on, all your plans can be destroyed. I like business where I control, where I maneuver things along the path that I control. That's why I'm hedging gold. I don't like it when the market has control over me. I sleep better and I can focus my mind better — that's important to me. I mean look at Peggy Witte. She could have had the Sultan of Brunei behind her and then what do I do? That's not fun."

His aversion to the uncertainty of deals has never stopped him making them, however. If anything, he is now more open to deals than he ever was. With his fat bank account, he never stops scanning the horizon for another possible home run. And he is not necessarily limiting himself to the industries where he already has a presence. "I like financial services. It's something I understand. I can deal with it. I like real estate. I never thought I would, but I do. It's a bit similar to the hotels. It's very hard to reproduce. Once you get a good location, it's very hard for Bill Gates to get into his garage and come up with something better. I hate businesses where a genius in a garage can knock you out. There are so many garages in America, I don't want sleepless nights. I like to know who's going to fight me."

In fact, however, he will go into almost any industry if the opportunity is right. With a couple of exceptions: "I won't go into high tech. I know that my chances are like throwing darts — I just can't understand it. I will not go into pharmaceuticals, because I know the entry fee is too high. I will never go into the media — there's no money there. It's ego. It's rubbing shoulders with the right people. Dealing with a bunch of prima donnas. There's no real money. Murdoch did it, but he's the only one. The moment you go for trophy properties, you are paying for it. Business is a very narrowly defined activity. It's return on capital. So ego and pride, the desire to cut ribbons, or having your business give you a boost for your inferiority complex which you developed because girls rejected you, those are all bad signs."

It's a consistent philosophy, but it has done nothing for Horsham's stock price. Shareholders may have understood better if he had called the company Home Run Inc. As it was, few people really understood what Horsham was, so they never got interested in it. There was also a fundamental shift in the market opinion on conglomerates. Stock markets everywhere now consistently put a value on the shares of conglomerates that is at a discount from the value of the companies they control. Conglomerates have gone out of style. Stock prices today are set by professional traders — the people who buy and sell for institutional investors — and they no longer want the chief executive of a conglomerate to be deciding on their asset mix. The quantum leap in the amount of information and the speed at which it is made available has enabled the managers of the megafunds, such as the Caisse de Dépôt et Placements or Fidelity Mutual Funds, to do their own product mix and select the industries they want to back. The strategic allocation of assets is all done in-house. They don't want a Peter Munk to do it for them. So they discount the share prices of conglomerates.

"It's endemic in conglomerates," he says, "and it's not healthy.

I'm used to industries where if you perform, you get a premium, so you get your rewards through your paper. I don't like operating at a discount."

Initially, Munk planned to remove Horsham from the conglomerate category by making it an operating company focused on a single line of business, with the sole quirk that it happens to hold an investment of $1½ billion of Barrick shares. He signaled that Clark would be sold as soon as refinery margins recovered and he could get a good price for his shares. That would leave Horsham as a real estate company, which the market could value fully within that category. With a single focus, Munk could make Trizec dominant in its market, like Barrick is dominant in the gold market. Then the market would award him the premium that goes with dominance. If he could remove the 30% discount on Horsham's shares and replace it with a 25% premium, he would almost double the share price. That would please a lot of Horsham shareholders, not least himself.

It was not so easy, however. To become an effective real estate company, he would have had to merge Horsham with Trizec. This would enable cash-rich Horsham to fund cash-starved Trizec and it would have given Horsham the focus it needed. However, Jerry O'Connor would not agree to exchanging his Trizec shares for Horsham shares, because his institutional investors did not want to hold a hybrid stock like Horsham — they wanted pure real estate.

Munk was therefore left without an immediate solution to his problem, which prompted his apology to his shareholders. Three months later, he won O'Connor over to his plan, after some intense negotiations, but the deal fell apart at the last minute. The setback didn't change his unshakable goal of eliminating the conglomerate discount — and it didn't stop the ongoing program to diversify, which will now be implemented in the context of a global network of contacts who were already feeding into Munk a steady stream of opportunities.

It was an evening of gentle banter as George Bush and Brian Mulroney traded affectionate reminiscences of the intersections of their political lives. The appreciative audience — assembled by Peter Munk to celebrate the inaugural meeting of Barrick's International Advisory Board — lapped it up. The elegant intimacy of the Toronto Club, home to the business establishment of Canada, was the perfect setting for the gathering, the kind of gathering that only a handful of Canadians can command. Mulroney was in his element. He was funny, peppering his speech with self-deprecating comments on the joys of being vilified for doing his best. There was no mistaking his feelings, however, for the star member of the advisory board, the former president of the United States, whom Mulroney had personally recruited. His admiration and affection for Bush was reciprocated with warm appreciation for Mulroney's steadfastness as United States's best ally. Bush weaved a string of funny, revealing, and thoughtful anecdotes into his world overview, captivating his audience with his candid observations on current U.S. politicians and the highlights of his own presidency.

It was quite a coup for a Canadian company to entice the 41st president of the United States — now a Barrick shareholder — to lend his name to its advisory board, especially since Bush had made a firm decision not to join any corporate boards. He was there because Mulroney, always the skilled negotiator, had managed to find a convoluted formula for Bush's participation that didn't compromise his wish to focus on helping others rather than helping himself. Bush is, officially, an honorary senior adviser to an advisory board that has no legal authority in Barrick.

Munk certainly has no intention of seeking commercial advantage through the association with Bush, but his presence alone changes the chemistry of the International Advisory Board (IAB). Thanks in no small measure to Bush, the glittering assembly in the Toronto Club that spring day in 1995 represented the cream of the Canadian business establishment. Among the 120 guests were a bevy of ambassadors, the current and former lieutenant governors of Ontario, a former premier of Ontario, the Eaton brothers, Conrad Black, Ted Rogers, Doug Bassett, the editors of the two national newspapers, and, of course, the distinguished IAB members.

Mulroney chairs the IAB. He may be widely disliked in Canada, but he has an excellent reputation outside the country, having served as a diligent negotiator in many international disputes and having built friendships with many leaders of other countries. "[Chilean President Eduardo] Frei loves him," says Munk. "[Argentinean President Carlos] Menem loves him. When we appointed him, you wouldn't believe the hate mail we received. Yet, when we were walking down a street in Santiago once, a tour bus full of Canadians passed and they stopped the bus so they could get out and shake his hand and wish him well. When we walk on the streets of Toronto, taxi drivers stop and wave encouragement to him."

Barrick was the only board in Canada that Mulroney joined after he resigned as prime minister and he has worked very hard for Munk, traveling all over the world. He was the man who put the IAB together and his bonhomie is the glue that has got it going. Apart from Munk, Bob Smith, and Bush (who is not officially a member of the board), there are six other members,

319

who bring to the table an extraordinary reach and depth of international connections:

— Howard Baker, the former senator, who made his name in the Watergate hearings and went on to become Majority House Leader.

— Paul Desmarais, the chairman of Power Corp. of Montreal and probably among the top half-dozen businessmen in Canada's history. Desmarais has interests in the media, financial institutions, communications, power generation, and oil in Canada and Europe. He is half owner of the huge, sprawling conglomerate Pargesa Holdings S.A., based in Luxembourg, and through Pargesa, the equally enormous Groupe Bruxelles Lambert S.A. One of his sons is married to Prime Minister Jean Chrétien's daughter and several leading politicians have spent time learning the ropes in Power Corp. He is also the honorary chairman of the Canada–China Business Council, where he has built up extensive contacts in the upper echelons of the Chinese power structure.

— Vernon Jordan, a leading Atlanta lawyer who has been in public service in many capacities. He was chairman of Bill Clinton's transition team, and also president of the National Urban League, the Georgia point man for the NAACP (National Association for the Advancement of Colored People). He has served on numerous committees and councils for the federal government and holds directorships in 11 companies, 3 academic institutions, and 4 foundations (Ford, LBJ, National Academy, and Roy Wilkins).

— Andronico Luksic, the patriarch of Chile's wealthiest family and the founder of one of Chile's biggest and most diversified conglomerates. The assets he controls are estimated to be worth $9 billion. He dominates the Chilean market in brewing, banking, mining, pasta, copper manufacturing, and edible oils. He owns railways, telecommunications companies, Ford dealerships, iron-ore mines, coal mines, packaging companies, cattle ranches, and forest products in Chile, Argentina, Brazil, Peru, and Colombia. He is expanding his copper activities into China and exploring a partnership with the parent company of Southwestern Bell Corp.

— Karl Otto Pöhl, the man who headed Germany's Bundesbank from 1980 to 1991. The Bundesbank is probably Germany's most trusted institution and the rock on which all European monetary policy is founded. Pöhl has served at the highest levels in the Bank for International Settlements and the International Monetary Fund and now serves on several boards and university councils in Germany and the United States.

— José Rohm, managing director of Banco General de Negocios and one of the top Argentinean bankers. He is associated with Credit Suisse, Dresdner Bank, Rockefeller & Co., International Finance Corp., and the Chemical Bank.

321

The second meeting of the IAB was in London in the winter of 1996 and, like the first one, the people who attended gave rave reviews for the quality and intelligence of the briefings by this remarkable group of men.

That's all very interesting, some people have commented, both privately and publicly, but what purpose does the IAB serve? Some are not sure it can do something for Barrick that Barrick can't do for itself. This question may be partly a response to Bush's presence on the board, because that gives the appearance of shooting for prestige rather than commercial advantage, but that's not how Munk thinks. The idea of the IAB was born out of Barrick's needs, but its real value in the long term lies in the business and political associations it is building for both Barrick and Horsham.

The idea sprang from the shock Munk received when Barrick almost got sideswiped by Bruce Babbitt's lurch for royalties at Barrick's expense soon after Clinton took office. He realized that Barrick had no protection from sharp political swings. "I was very hurt," he said in 1995, shortly after his first IAB meeting. "I felt abused by Babbitt. I didn't think American contacts were that important. But when I had to go rushing down every week to Washington with Bob Smith last summer, seeing the ambassador, it just wasn't good. We needed access to [Vice President] Gore, and we needed Maurice Strong to take us to some key contacts to make sure our case was understood at the highest level. I just made up my mind, there's nothing like an ounce of prevention. So I lined up my defenses. Now I have people whom I can call. It's an important investment. I may not use it for five years, but now I can bring in the big guns. It's the best insurance policy in countries where we have an enormous investment."

Munk was motivated by more than a concern with the often unpredictable U-turns in American politics, however. "When I moved Barrick into international operations," he adds, "I was frightened I was very much behind the eight ball. Companies like Newmont and Placer Dome and Rio Tinto Zinc have been around the world for 50 years. We had to catch up in a hurry. We had never been international. We were a 10-year-old mining company that did business only in America. Those other companies were international when I was born. I had some international background, but I didn't know heads of state — and I can't cover every country anyway. I can't be in Brazil and Africa and Australia. I feel comfortable making one or two deals, but we suddenly had to have mining concessions everywhere. And I had to have entrée to the top."

As Barrick's mining interests expand in other parts of the world, Munk will add more members to his IAB. "We're going to expand it into the Far East," he says. "In the next two or three years, we are going to make some major strides in Southeast Asia — particularly Indonesia and the Philippines. That's the next move."

The defensive aspect of the IAB may be critical in a future crunch, but its more immediate, everyday purpose lies in its offensive role — the creation of a network of people with impeccable international connections, who can stitch together unparalleled business opportunities. "It's the Barrick advisory board and as such it's only for gold mining right now," Munk says. "But you know in countries like Peru or Chile and Argentina, the top families are into everything. So you know, for me to move into shopping centers in those areas, it won't be very difficult."

The first official acknowledgment of this aspect of the IAB

came when Greg Wilkins moved into the CEO spot in Trizec in the spring of 1996. Trizec's former CEO, Bill L'Heureux, stayed on to spearhead its international expansion, with specific responsibility to work with the IAB in generating real estate opportunities. A week after his appointment, L'Heureux left for the Philippines to chase an opportunity brought to Trizec by Hany Salaam, one of Munk's longtime associates. Salaam is not on the IAB, but he was on the Horsham board for a while and is in constant touch with Munk concerning opportunities all around the world. His main business is London-based Gulf Resources Corp., which has producing oil wells in Africa and the Middle East. At heart, however, he is a peripatetic trader, with ventures and partnerships all over the world. His partners include Occidental Petroleum, Kaiser Aluminum, the National Bank of Kuwait, Boeing, and ITT-Sheraton. He does business in 15 different countries on four continents. His ventures are in oil and gas, pipelines, petrochemicals, real estate, aluminum smelting, sales agencies, finance, construction, and engineering. Born in Jerusalem of a Lebanese father and a Palestinian mother, he has built a global empire, punctuated at regular intervals by his collection of plush apartments and houses in several countries around the world, including New York and Los Angeles.

One of Salaam's friends is the president of the Philippines, Fidel Ramos, who has facilitated introductions for Munk and several of his key executives to the appropriate decision makers in the Philippines. Another of Salaam's friends is Ray Irani, the chairman of Occidental Petroleum. Salaam arranged a meeting between Munk and Irani in Oxy's palatial Los Angeles offices (that used to belong to Howard Hughes). That meeting led to a major deal between Occidental and Clark Petroleum, negotiated with the help of Salaam. "We brought in Oxy as a partner,"

Munk said with some satisfaction the day after the announcement. "They got 20% odd of Clark in return for a contract to supply oil. They became a strategic partner. It's only a $200 million deal but it's better than a kick in the ass."

Munk is, in effect, gearing up his global network to start churning out business opportunities for all his companies. Luksic is smoothing the path in Chile. Pöhl has already helped in Germany with Horsham's development in Berlin. Rohm is introducing Munk to potential Argentinean partners, and Munk is establishing contact with Desmarais' gold-plated contacts in Europe and China. He doesn't limit himself to IAB, however. He has contacted Sir Jimmy Goldsmith and all the major business players he has met over the years.

"I'm calling all my buddies," he says. "We have to mobilize everybody, absolutely. We have to pull out all the stops." In the course of 1995, Munk mounted his campaign to blast Barrick and Horsham into the next phase of super-growth by placing about 20 key calls to all these people. "Everyone knows that people who were in business with me made money — so it's very easy. I tell them: 'We've got half a billion in cash, we want to invest it. We're not juniors. We don't want to promote our shares, we want to find mines. We don't mind spending $10 million for exploration. We need the concessions and we need them on a preferential basis.'

"In many of these countries, there's someone in the country who can do those things — the head of state maybe. So while our geologists go like everyone else, we can maybe find some other things or some other contacts. We take all the risks. A junior cannot lay out $10 million for drilling. We can. These countries need us because we can bring expertise and technology and resources. And I'm very happy to share.

"So, if you're sitting in the Philippines or in Hong Kong, and you are friendly with someone in Malaysia or in Venezuela, it's a hell of a nice phone call to get from Peter Munk to say, 'Hey, can you help me? If you do and if I find something, I'll make you a part owner.' It's not a difficult phone call for me to make. Brian [Mulroney] was very helpful, because he could make phone calls I couldn't make. He knew heads of state in Africa — and everybody takes a phone call from Brian. Doing business successfully in these countries is much easier once we've explained to the top people what development projects can do for their countries."

Munk's international network, centered around the IAB, but not limited to it, is working equally hard for both Horsham and Barrick. Its impact on Barrick, however, will be much more obvious. As the opportunities the network generates come flooding into his office, Munk's challenge will be to buy his expansion cheaply. The price he paid for Lac amounted to $133 per ounce of official reserves, but Smith was convinced he could convert half the resources into reserves, which lowered the cost to less than $90, and subsequent exploration results are driving the cost still lower. Goldstrike cost Barrick about $6 an ounce after the development drilling. Discoveries in grassroots exploration costs about $1 an ounce.

Barrick can still make a healthy profit on acquisitions such as Lac, but it cannot rely solely on them to grow. That's why Munk decided in 1995 to establish a network of joint ventures with prospectors and junior companies. The strategy had a false start before it even got underway, when Barrick miscued in its negotiations with Bre-X in early 1994.

Bre-X's Busang deposit was one of two discoveries that changed the mining world in 1995. The other mega-find was the nickel mine discovered in Voisey's Bay in Labrador by Bob Friedland's company, Diamond Fields Resources Inc. That mine was eventually bought by Inco for C$4.3 billion after Friedland played the Inco executives like a violin.

"Give him full marks. He played his cards like he won the grand slam," says Smith, with a tinge of admiration. "Now every prospector is trying to emulate him. And when investors see the monetary success of some of these juniors, there's a lot of money available for equity."

Between Bre-X and Diamond Fields, the market for juniors has been wrecked for companies like Barrick. The two prospectors, both of whom know what it was like to stare bankruptcy in the face, have injected stars into the eyes of every investor in Canadian stock markets and the market is flooded with capital ready to pour into exploration companies. Smith has seen it all before: "We're going to go through a period of a couple of years or more when there's going to be a lot of disappointments. A lot of big money is going into situations that won't come through. It's a cycle and eventually that source of funding will dry up."

At the same time, however, the next three or four years represent a window of extraordinary opportunity. The end of the Cold War persuaded developing countries to open up their economies to foreign investment. The major mining companies responded by signaling their intention to develop commercial deposits, which has triggered a tidal wave of prospectors from developed countries who are washing across every promising geological formation in parts of the world that have been ignored for years.

Barrick now finds itself in a race for time. Having arrived on the international scene many years after its major competitors, it has only just put its exploration strategy in place and must now conduct an effective exploration program for a three- or four-year period of heightened competition. In late 1993, Barrick hired a vice president of exploration, Alex Davidson. During his first two years at Barrick, Davidson established a comprehensive network over all the potential gold sites in the world. By the spring of 1996, he employed about 60 geologists based in ten offices — two in North America (the United States and Canada), five in South America (Chile, Peru, Argentina, Brazil, and Bolivia), one in Africa (Mali), and two in Asia (Indonesia and China, and the Philippines). The job of these geologists is to find mines big enough for Barrick — and that means a minimum of 3 million ounces of gold.

The geologists are chosen for their expertise in the particular type of geological formations in the area where they are based. "When a junior comes up with something," says Davidson, "we have a team in place that is familiar with the geology and probably familiar with the junior itself, ready to evaluate that property." If they decide to cut a deal with the prospector (which may be a junior gold company or a lone rock hound, equipped with a 4-wheel drive truck), Davidson prefers to do "earn-in options," whereby Barrick agrees to spend specified amounts on exploration drilling in order to earn anything from 50% to 90% ownership of any mines that may be developed. Usually, the options include payments of $100,000 to $300,000 to the prospectors to keep them alive while the drilling progresses. For example, Solitario Resources Corp. signed an option with Barrick in May 1995 to give Barrick a 60% interest in Solitario's land position in northern Peru in return for exploration spending of $6.25 million over four years plus $250,000 a year to Solitario. The earn-in in this case is a bit lower than usual because Solitario had already spent $1.5 million on the property.

In another option over four years, with Moneta Porcupine Mines Inc., Barrick has agreed to spend $7.5 million in exploration drilling on Moneta's northern Ontario land, as well as pay Moneta $1,125,000 a year in order to earn 80% to 90% of any mine that may be developed.

With an annual budget of more than $50 million, Davidson can afford to do a lot of these deals and, by the spring of 1996, he had already signed more than 50. He also does joint venture agreements with juniors, similar to the deal that was discussed with Bre-X. In these cases, Barrick buys shares in the junior and commits to spending specified amounts on exploration, but the junior usually manages the exploration program, in return for a fee (3% or 5% of the exploration funding). In January 1996, for example, Barrick agreed with Vancouver-based Yamana Resources to invest $14.7 million in the company, which gave Barrick the right to 75% of up to two discoveries that it may select for development. The prospective land is in the same area as Bre-X's Busang deposit in Indonesia, and Yamana is operating the exploration program itself, although Barrick's geologists are deeply involved.

The joint ventures with juniors are not as attractive as they were even a year ago, however. With so much money available on the stock market, many juniors can raise the funds to do more of the exploration themselves and thus drive harder bargains with the majors when it comes time to build the mine. Davidson says that 80% of his budget goes to options, where Barrick can put its own people in to run the exploration program.

Apart from these deals with prospectors and juniors, Barrick also does grassroots exploration on its own account. Most of its land position in Indonesia, for example, is a partnership with the Mutiyera group, controlled by an Indonesian timber and wheat baron named Piet Yap, who has 15% of the rights but no operating involvement at all. The biggest play in this partnership is on Irian Jaya, the huge, wild island at the eastern end of Indonesia, contiguous with Papua New Guinea.

"We're exploring thousands and thousands of square kilometers there," says Davidson. "Our target is another big deposit of 30 or 60 million ounces. The theory is that a 50-million-ounce orebody has a bigger signature, so we set our "filters" coarse. If we don't find anomalies that are really strikingly large, we'll walk away. You could never hope to mine a 2 million ounce mine profitably there — it's too remote."

By contrast, the filters are set very fine near existing mills. A 500,000-ounce discovery near Val d'Or, for example, might be highly profitable, because there is a mill nearby to process the ore. So Barrick still spends 50% of its $110 million-plus exploration budget on properties it already owns. In early 1996, it announced a new mine, Pasqua, near the El Indio mine in Chile. Lac had identified one million ounces at Pasqua, but Barrick has identified a whole new deposit nearby, which raised the reserves for the mine to 8.5 million ounces at a cost to Barrick of less than $1 per ounce.

In the two years since Davidson was hired, Barrick has put together one of the largest global exploration teams in the gold industry. Two years previously, its only exposure outside Canada and the United States was three projects in Peru and some flirting with the Chinese. In 1994, few Barrick employees traveled outside North America. In 1996, Barrick felt obliged to produce a medical book for its employees, detailing medical conditions and dangers in more than 20 countries where it has a presence.

In April 1996, Barrick had completed its transition into an

international powerhouse and Bob Smith started edging toward retirement. He gave up half of his responsibilities as chief operating officer, along with the title, which passed to John Carrington, whom Smith had hired away from Noranda in 1994. Carrington has responsibility for all the existing mines, while Smith concentrates on developing new prospects. He and Alan Hill sit on a new committee chaired by Munk and they will continue to exercise their rare ability to see gold where hundreds of other mining engineers have failed.

"I've seen so many companies get to this stage and become complacent, big, fat cats," says Smith. "The moment you sit back, you're history. How did we get where we are? By taking risks, by looking at things, and by saying, 'How do I make it work?' rather than 'Will it work?' So much of this business is being in the right place at the right time with the right amount of money. You have to be flexible and be prepared to strike various deals. We're looking for exposure."

Munk is elephant hunting again. Typically, the hunt is tightly focused, methodical, and comprehensive. He has set out to create his own luck again. He is no longer the man who, in the first half of 1993, pondered the dilemma of his success and concluded that perhaps Barrick had become a mature "commodity play" and that it was perhaps time to withdraw gracefully. When he apologized to his Horsham shareholders for failing to make their shares move, he told them that he had dramatically changed his mind about Barrick. "We are going to do some very exciting things. Barrick is poised to double."

11

THE MAN AND HIS MACHINE

I t's the annual staff lunch for Barrick and its sister companies, a week before Christmas and the day before he wings off to Klosters. Munk is giving his annual pep talk in the Harbour Castle Hotel. With Lake Ontario for a backdrop, sparkling in the clear December sunshine, he is introduced by three or four of the top executives who all thank him for the leadership he provides. It could be embarrassingly corny, but it is so sincere — and so expected by all the employees — that it works.

December is a hard time for Barrick, because Munk creates great waves of work in the flurry to complete all his tasks before he heads off for the Swiss slopes. The senior people have all endured a punishing round of meetings as they rushed to meet the deadlines set by their demanding boss. The load has filtered down to lower levels. By Christmas, they will be able to think about relaxing, but right now, they are tired.

Munk launches into his inspirational message. He talks about trust. Starting in a small voice, talking intimately with his 150 head office employees, he builds as he warms to his theme.

"We are a community of values . . . a company is people, not assets . . . we must share goals . . . we must learn to trust unknown people and take the responsibility . . . When we perform to our optimum potential, it does away with politics and paranoid suspicion . . . the work ethic . . . the highest order of human achievement is the commitment to decency . . . there are smarter people than I, who work harder — thousands of them. What makes it work for us is values — moral and spiritual commitment. Trust."

The employees leave the lunch with a sparkle in their eyes, their backs straight, ready to work right through Christmas.

His speeches are a legend in his companies, as much a celebration of the moral underpinnings of success in business as an outpouring of his own emotions and ideals. On another occasion, he stood up in a small group and extemporaneously launched into an impassioned discourse of the beauty of humility. Munk has perfected his inspiring speeches to the point where it has become an integral part of his leadership.

Consistent with his leadership by inspiration, Munk has built a structure that can house his entrepreneurial genius without exposing his lack of interest in detailed supervision. The bedrock foundation of this structure is his sense of ownership. As the owner of an enterprise, he is responsible for its ultimate survival, growth, and prosperity — and his rewards must come principally from ownership of the stock, rather than from bonuses and salary. While he doesn't expect his employees to feel the same way, the principal strategy of his leadership is to extend that sense of ownership throughout his organization. He sits at the core, surrounded by a series of concentric circles of managers and employees — the unquestioned leader who guides and draws strength from each of the circles, each of which has its defined role.

The core is composed of somewhere between two and four complementary co-owners who are his alter egos — the people to whom he confides his deepest secrets, whom he trusts unquestioningly, and each of whom has a special role to play in making the core completely effective. By the time he gained control of Travelodge, the core had already coalesced into Munk, Gilmour, and Birchall. Others came close, like Pat Samuel — always on the periphery but only occasionally an integral part of it. Only people whom Munk has known for a very long time can qualify.

The genesis of the core was Gilmour's and Munk's symbiotic relationship in Clairtone, when they discussed every issue together, thrashing it out until they reached agreement. The second step was Birchall's rite of passage — which demanded an extended period of total dedication to "the" business. "We had no other interests in life, except this," Birchall remembers of the days in the South Pacific and Egypt. "That was the way we had to operate. No outside interests — 80% of Peter's life was business, and 100% of my life, in those days, was business." They all paid a price, but the result is an extraordinary friendship, more like a marriage, really. Munk even calls them "darling" when they're in small groups.

"We live together here," says Munk. "We lived together with these people for decades. I spend much more of my time with these guys than with my wife, my children. Apart from

334

sleeping, this is my life. We've gone through great difficulties, great elations . . ." These men have shared so much, there are no secrets between them — and they all understand that their primary, overarching role is to help the business in whatever way their talents dictate.

Birchall is the policeman, the eagle eye who weeds out the second-rate proposals. He will find a flaw if there is one to be found. He will spot potential risks that everyone else ignores. "I can always be relied upon to give some negative thoughts on any particular proposal," he says with a big smile. "There's no point in everybody cheering in the room saying, 'Oh what a wonderful idea!' I've always been able to assess a particular proposition very quickly from a financial point of view."

Gilmour was always the door opener. He was the one who gained access to the wealthy and powerful people who could help the duo (or trio) advance their businesses. Once Munk got Barrick going, Gilmour's role faded — Munk had acquired his own access and became one of the best connected businesspeople in Canada. In recent years, Gilmour has not been in the core at Barrick, although he is reverting to his marketing roots in the real estate business, applying his instinctive understanding of what products or services will command a high enough price to make it a profitable business.

This core is all about ownership. They are investors, not managers. They know no limits or constraints to the opportunities they might consider. Everything is possible.

The members of the inner circle (around the core) are dedicated, hotshot managers who have been tested and found true. They are the Munk protégés — younger men (women are pretty scarce at this level) in charge of various businesses. They have all spent a great deal of time with him one-on-one or in small meetings. They have paid their dues and can be counted on to anticipate Munk's needs and responses to any situations they might encounter. Munk sees these people as critical resources to be deployed where they are needed most. They are totally trusted, very well remunerated, and disproportionately accountants.

Bob Smith is the exception in the conceptualization of Munk's structure. He almost has a circle all to himself, because he is trusted and relied upon to a degree beyond the members of the circle around the core, but he will never be in the core. He is a miner — the best in the world as far as Munk is concerned, but he belongs in the mining environment.

For Birchall, the Barrick culture was articulated best by David Newbigging, the taipan of Jardine Matheson and a director of SPP for five years. He took a fistful of six pencils in his hand and told them it was impossible to break them — but if he took them one by one, he could easily break them.

Munk's thirty-second golden rule:
You cannot build a team without mutual confidence, mutual trust, mutual reliability. And there's no team if you don't have the strength. You need the strength when you go into battle. Whatever you tackle — and in business you're always tackling things — the other party has to feel that there is total cohesiveness, there's total awareness of the objectives, and there's total support of each other.

"In order to get a group like that," Birchall explains, "you have to see that they're rewarded, you have to give them your trust, you have to give them your confidence, you have to be flexible in the way that you deal with them as human beings — which he's fully prepared to do because he expects these people to be around for the next 20 years. So he's prepared, very happily, to invest all his time and energy into the things that other people wouldn't do. Because, going back to the Newbigging concept, you've got to have a group, because as a group, you have strength. An individual has his frailties."

Talking of Greg Wilkins, one of the more senior members of the inner circle, Munk says, "He coped somehow or other with the complex deals and he was always smiling and he was always available and he always knew where to go and come back with the results. And he never lied. You develop respect. They are straight, they're honest, they're fun. Yet they are work-oriented. Their work ethic is there. How can you not have these people as partners? They create the wealth, they look after the shareholders."

Peter Sidebottom, a personal friend and a business partner, puts it succinctly: "He relies totally on you, which makes you really determined to deliver. His team is closely knit. We all live for Peter, really. He's certainly changed my life for the better."

"I'm so lucky," Munk says. "When we have a problem, these guys come up with what I would have thought of quicker than I can myself."

Beyond the inner circle is the outer circle, whom Munk sees as fundamentally technicians. Whereas the inner circle might be deployed in any situation where they might be needed, without necessarily worrying too much about their past work experience, the outer circle is bound by preconceived roles reserved for them. It means his perspective of these people is sometimes two-dimensional, heavily geared to their role in his business. Munk's intense focus does not allow time for leisurely explorations of people's lives outside his business. He expects the world from them, trusts their professionalism completely, inspires and motivates them, and rewards them generously.

In every business he has started or bought, Munk has gone first class. The product was always aimed at the upper niches in the market. The consultants were always the crème de la crème. The top performers are always paid extravagantly. The poor performers are shown the door.

His investment bankers have been the best in the business from the time he hired E. F. Hutton three years into his career as an entrepreneur. He hires the most innovative advertising agencies and the top mining consultants in the continent.

Munk's thirty-third golden rule:
If you have to worry about the consultants' pay,
you shouldn't retain any.

"I probably have a proclivity to go for the best names," he says. "It's better to deal with quality people — it gives you more credibility."

What really sets Munk apart is how he arrives at this philosophy. He doesn't earn the money and then decide to go first class. He decides to go first class, then figures out where he'll find the cash. It's quintessentially entrepreneurial and it applies to everything he does. True entrepreneurs never limit themselves just because they are short of cash. They set their goals, without regard to the resources they control.

A friend from Munk's schooldays in Switzerland, Steven Friedlich, offers a revealing story. When they lived in Zurich, penniless for the most part, Munk would drag him to the best hotel in the city, and order a sandwich and champagne. It was the cheapest champagne in the cellar, but it came, of course, with the trademark ice bucket and loud pop. He explained to Friedlich that it was essential to establish your standards for all to see. When Friedlich bought cotton shirts, Munk would reprimand him for not buying silk. If Munk didn't have the money to buy his champagne, even the cheap stuff, he would just go and make it. Often that meant being at the local car wash at 6 a.m. the next day, because that was when the owner selected who would work there for the day (the competition was fierce).

This ability to separate decisions on how to spend money from the act of securing money to pay for it means he never feels he has to cut corners to save money. He will strive mightily to cut costs if he feels the money is being spent inefficiently, but he will never settle for lower quality or quantity just because the ready cash is not available.

This attitude carries through to the people he hires (and fires). "I really pay very highly," he said in 1990. "The team running Goldstrike didn't exist three years ago. We offered the biggest challenges and we provide stock options, so we attract the top talent. But they also attract each other. The top man in metallurgy likes to talk with the top man in computerization and they both like to talk to the top geologist."

There is a real sense in Barrick that everyone feels they are working in a top-class operation. Bob Smith and many of his managers often say it's a privilege for them to have the opportunity to do things the way they really should be done. Whether it is the satellite system for tracking the trucks in the pit, or putting a Barrick page on the Internet, or perfecting the autoclave technology, there is a strong sense in the company of being at the cutting edge of technology. And he is not afraid of spending money to get there.

The ultimate objective, of course, is to maximize profits for the shareholders, but a lot of the money generated by Barrick dribbles into the pockets of employees — which is exactly the way Munk wants it to be. "I get a kick out of sharing wealth," Munk said in 1990. "Of the 16 employees and partners who came back to Canada with me in 1979, 14 are millionaires now." The count was a great deal higher in 1996. He is thrilled to reel off a list of current and former employees who have made $3 million to $10 million by working with him at Barrick. It is a source of lasting pride for him.

"I really believe that it's better to have a smaller portion of a bigger thing. I could be a billionaire if I had bought out my partners. I built more value than Ted Rogers did and I'm not a billionaire — I'm not even near it. I think it's the healthy way to go."

Munk's thirty-fourth golden rule:
Share the wealth.

He has done rather well himself, of course. By 1995, his personal wealth was rumored to be in the range of a quarter of a billion dollars, but he won't talk about it: "I created Barrick, I created Horsham. I work with major corporations, I'm heading up the planning committee at the Toronto Hospital. I'm providing input at my alma mater [the University of Toronto]. We have operations in Beijing and Chile. That turns me on a lot. Money just doesn't compare with that."

Munk has made most of his wealth through owning stock — unlike most of his employees, who have made their fortunes entirely through stock options.[1] He owned 22% of the company

---

[1] Stock options grant the recipient the right to purchase stock of the company at a fixed price (usually the price at which the stock is trading at the time the option is granted) at some time in the future. Usually, there is a waiting period of three years or so before the right vests fully and the options normally expire after a fixed term, usually seven years at Barrick. When the stock price rises quickly as in the case of Barrick, this enables options to be exercised at a significant profit.

that founded Barrick and later became Horsham (he now owns 8.4% of the Horsham shares). When he started Barrick, he granted stock options freely, but not to himself, because he felt that options were for employees who could not afford to buy shares — while owners bought stock on their own. In fact, he didn't even pay himself a salary until 1988 when Barrick started paying dividends.

He finally cottoned on to the power of Barrick's stock options through a curious incident in 1986. One of his key employees, Stephen Dattels, announced to his boss that he was quitting. Munk was devastated. He felt it was a personal betrayal. He sat Dattels down on his couch and turned the full force of his persuasive powers on him. "Nobody leaves me," he says with almost plaintive passion. Dattels didn't budge.

"We've worked our guts out together for four years," he told him, "and we're finally getting there and you want to leave. Are you insane?"

He told Dattels to bring in his wife and perhaps she could talk some sense into him. His wife, however, was getting tired of her husband's constant traveling and she rather liked the idea of his staying at home. Then Dattels delivered his punch line:

"I have so much money now that if I don't have the courage to be on my own, I'll be kicking myself when I'm 50."

"What do you mean — so much money," Munk replied. "You're too young, Stephen, you don't understand. You're confused. You think you've got a million bucks, but that's nothing. That's petty cash. We'll be doing big things here."

"Peter," Dattels shot back, "I don't have a million dollars, I have much more."

"So you've got two million dollars . . ."

"Peter, much more than that."

"Well how much can you have?" a by now exasperated Munk demanded. "I had to pay your mortgage three years ago, so you can't have that much."

"I'm worth seven million dollars."

That shook Munk. He hadn't realized just how powerful the stock options were. And it was a sobering thought that the very success of the company was encouraging his best employees to quit. He "allowed" Dattels to go (to Dattels's great subsequent regret) and went home and told his wife, as well as his closest friends. Soon afterward, he changed his mind about options and made himself available for awards by the Stock Options Committee. They obliged with one and a half million shares in 1987, which he exercised in 1988 and 1991 for a total profit of more than C$40 million.[2]

His remuneration has raised a lot of eyebrows in Canada, as it has for Frank Stronach, the mercurial founder and chief executive of Magna International. Both men have created enormous value for their shareholders and feel their rewards are totally justified. But many disagree. It's not made any easier for people like Munk and Stronach when stock options are awarded for services to the company over a long period, but they are cashed in all at once. Barrick's stock option plan awards options every four years and the options vest over a period of four years, so they represent compensation for four years' performance. So, in judging the fairness or otherwise of stock option awards, it is important to put it in the context of four years of rewards and performance.

---

[2] After adjusting for subsequent stock splits, he received six million options at an exercise price of C$3.50. He exercised the option for the first two million in 1988 at a price of C$5.65 and the second four million in 1991 at a price of C$12.65. The first transaction made a profit for him of C$4.4 million; the second made C$37 million.

On that score, Munk (like Stronach) can reasonably justify some big numbers. In the period from 1984 to 1986, he led the company as it increased its market capitalization from $28 million to $335 million — and the directors knew that it was about to go up a great deal more as a result of the purchase of the Goldstrike property. At the time of the award, those shares represented about 2.7% of the total outstanding shares of Barrick, which is generous by any standard, though perhaps reasonable considering he had not yet drawn any salary. Yet even this would not have excited a great deal of attention if the share price had not gone up so much subsequent to the award.

His subsequent stock option awards were for 2 million shares in 1991 and another 1 million at the end of 1994, prompted by the enormously successful takeover of Lac Minerals. At the end of 1995, these options (still to be exercised) were worth C$55 million[3] in unrealized profit.

"We don't get complaints from our shareholders," says Randall Oliphant, chief financial officer. "They think it's marvelous. It's much better to be paying what amounts to a kind of commission on tremendous gains than to be paying nothing on mediocre gains. If they make a billion dollars and Peter gets $30 million, they love that. They tell us, 'I want you to get it up another billion and give him another $30 million, we'd love that too.'"

Of course, Munk isn't the only one in the stock option plan. Barrick's plan reaches deeper into the organization than most companies in Canada. The current policy is to award stock options to all the 65 head office employees and to the managers in the operating companies down to the level of general foreman.

---

[3] The exercise prices for these (adjusted for stock splits) were C$11.87 and C$28.75 respectively, which, at the year-end stock price of C$36, meant he had an unrealized profit on his options of more than C$55 million.

In all, 10% of the employees (390) are in the plan. For people below general foreman, stock options are considered to be less effective than bonuses based on their productivity.

The number of options awarded to each individual is not always consistent, since there is an element of reward for performance, but the benchmarks are 2,000 to 5,000 for administrative staff, 12,000 to 18,000 for middle managers in the mines, and 50,000 for mine managers. Head office executives vary from 5,000 to 1,000,000. The power of these awards can be dramatic, even at the lower-paid levels. A receptionist, for example, whose options vested anywhere between 1987 and 1993 had a good chance of making a profit of C$20 on each share — and if the award was 5,000 shares, that meant a capital gain of C$100,000.

The Barrick stock option plan is almost certainly the most generous in Canadian business. It is based on a very clear premise, enunciated by Oliphant. "Peter is unequivocal about why a company is in existence, which is to create value for its shareholders. We're not in business to produce lots of gold, to set records in gold production, or to own more mines than anybody else — or to be big. Everything is evaluated from the perspective of how we maximize the value of the company's shares, whether it be Barrick or Horsham or any other entity. So he says, 'How do I get everybody motivated and focused on how to achieve this? I try to make them part of it. It will make a meaningful difference to them how the Barrick share performs and that's why I want a significant part of their well-being to be tied to that.' He has been able to attract people whom he considers to be the best in their respective fields in our industry. And people have the ability to really enhance their well-being by the stock performing well. This aligns their interest with those of the shareholders. It means that people who work at Barrick — or Horsham or anything else he's involved with — are focused on a common goal."

The 390 Barrick employees and directors in the plan had, between them, been granted options on 11% of the total shares outstanding at the end of 1995.[4] They had exercised slightly more than half of their available options to generate a profit totaling C$191 million — or 2.1% of the total increase in the company's market capitalization over the same period.

The distribution of the shares is weighted toward the executive suite. Of the total of almost 40 million stock options awarded, 23% (9 million) went to Munk himself, 6% (2.3 million) went to Bob Smith, and 5% (2 million) went to Greg Wilkins and Alan Hill. The remaining two-thirds of the options went to other corporate officers and employees (34%), the operating companies (20%), and the directors (12%).

Among the directors, the largest award — 800,000 options — went to the vice chairman, Angus MacNaughton of Genstar International. Brian Mulroney has received 500,000 options, as did Munk's long-time counsel, Howard Beck. David Gilmour and Bill Birchall received 400,000 and 700,000, respectively. The remaining six "outside" directors received among them 1.3 million options.

The decision to award options to directors has come in for some criticism, but Munk is almost certainly ahead of his time. Companies in the United States are turning increasingly toward forms of remuneration that put directors firmly in the shoes of

---

[4] Total shares outstanding were 357.2 million; total options granted were 39.2 million, of which 17.9 million were still outstanding.

the shareholders. A recent survey[5] of the 100 biggest firms in the United States found that more than a quarter are planning to change the way they pay their directors and the most common intention is to move toward stock ownership.

Of course, the stock option plan is only part of Barrick's munificent remuneration system for its executives and employees. Bonuses are also an integral part of the motivation system. "In the mines, every single person gets some form of bonus," says Oliphant. "Sometimes it's a number based on the overall performance of the mine. In other cases, it's based on individual performance — like the man drilling in the mine face underground."

The higher a person is in the organization, the more important the bonus becomes. At the senior corporate level, bonuses average about half of salary — and for the top half-dozen people, bonuses are often more than their salaries. Oliphant says Barrick sets its salary and bonus levels for its top people at about 75% of the rates paid by comparable companies. "We like to tie our compensation more to our shares than do our competitors," he says. That still means generous pay. In 1995, the top nine Barrick executives were paid cash (salary and bonus) totaling C$5.7 million — C$1,350,000 for Munk, C$1,100,000 for Bob Smith, and C$3.25 million for the other seven. In 1994, 15 Canadian executives made more cash than Munk (excluding stock options) although most of them had smaller companies and profits and a much slower growth rate. Munk, however, did have another string to his bow — he also received almost C$1.3 million in salary and bonus from Horsham, so his cash

---

[5] Conducted by Spencer Stuart, an executive search company.

compensation from the two companies comes to more than C$2.25 million, which puts him in sixth place among Canadian executives, ignoring stock options. However, Barrick was ranked the top company in Canada for creating shareholder value in *The Financial Post*'s survey of market value added.

Munk feels he has earned it — and he wants as many executives in Barrick as possible to earn lots of money, because they will have earned it too. It is not greed. It's almost like a mission. "The fundamental role of any company is to create wealth," he says. "Create wealth for its employees, create wealth for the communities in which it works, create wealth for the state. We are taxpayers at all levels, and we generate employment."

Peter Munk is a remarkably uncomplicated man. "I'm a very pragmatic guy. My first wife [Linda] always said I'm blessed because I have no doubts. I know black and I know white. Linda always said, 'You have a limited IQ, because people who are really well educated with a really high IQ know there are no blacks and whites.' I don't have this problem."

When he makes business decisions, he makes up his mind on purely strategic grounds, taking a long-term view in the context of where he wants his business to be in five years' time. He will watch his senior managers argue points back and forth until they have ironed out the wrinkles — but he is not really interested. That's their job. His job is to recognize when something makes strategic sense and then to see that it's done properly.

He also has a characteristic shared by many people who have to deal constantly with change — he has an immutable pattern of habits in his personal life. It gives a sense of permanence when nothing else does. "I'm a very stable, boring kind of guy," he admits cheerfully. "I really do a lot of routine. I go to my island like I've gone since the days when I was at Clairtone. My habits are frighteningly predictable. Linda — whom I divorced almost 30 years ago — knows when I brush my teeth. She knows exactly when I go to Switzerland — the 16th of December unless things are bad, then I go on the 18th of December.

"It's a great luxury that I don't have to think what I'm going to have for breakfast. I've had the same breakfast for 35 years. I dress the same way. I pretty well wear the same ties. I look at my photographs from I don't know how many years ago and I'm dressed the same way — I wore gray flannels, I wore blue shirts. I only wear three kinds of shirts."

Munk is the rock of Barrick. He may be mercurial, he may get emotional, but his commitment to his company is unwavering. When he's away from the office, everyone feels there's something missing. He's the same way. He loves to wander, but his base is Toronto and his home is the office in Royal Bank Plaza.

"It's my life. I like my life. I do exactly what I want to do and I wouldn't do it if I didn't like it. And I enjoy doing it with the Gilmours and the Birchalls and the Smiths and the Samuels — they stimulate me. I like them. I like to have dinner with them, lunch with them. They are in their own ways magnificent people. Ah! What a privilege to have people like that. To share my problems, with nothing to hide. Whether it's my sex problem, my marital problem, my financial problem. I mean there's nothing I haven't shared with those guys. Nothing. It gives you tremendous strength. You don't have to worry about bull. You can worry about what matters — how to get the company forward, how to formulate and execute strategic plans. It's good."

He never doubted, through all his ups and downs in Canada,

the South Pacific, and the United States, that he would become immensely successful. Failure was never an option. Yet he still has the occasional twinge of amazement at what he has achieved. "When you are the world's most profitable gold mining house, you've got to pinch yourself. It's the dream of your dreams. Few people achieve their objectives. Very few people achieve way more than their objectives. I don't have objectives — it's not that I'm a modest little guy. But there you are. The world's most profitable gold company."

But it's never enough. There is no end. "It's important that you can motivate yourself. The good thing about me, that I have in my personality, I respond really well to challenges. When I go into a confrontational meeting, I am not good, because I don't give up, I attack. It's awful. I think it comes from when I used to be beaten because I was a Jew."

As a young boy of 10 or 11, in 1938 or 1939, he was sent to a new school way outside Budapest for a year and a half. At that time, the Germans had occupied Austria but not Hungary — yet many Hungarians had allied themselves with the Nazis, especially those close to the Austrian border, where Munk's new school was. "I was the only Jew in the class and I was red-haired. Hungary was a very black-haired country and kids at that age hated red-haired kids. When the class disbanded, there were always half a dozen guys who felt that beating up a Jew was good fun. Especially because I came from Budapest and I was better dressed. I didn't have a single friend. I used to run. I remember the mountain road, I remember falling, I remember them jumping on top of me — stuff like that. But in the end, I didn't run, you know. You get beaten up anyway. In the end I looked into their eyes. In the end, I think, they got bored of beating me and some of them got hurt. But I wasn't beaten so often any more. It felt better to face the music. I often thought it made me less afraid of life."

Can he ever stop fighting? Can he ever stop pushing? More than half a century later, at 68, successful and powerful, he is starting to plan his legacy. He has his own foundation, to which he contributes 30% of his annual income. Now approaching eight figures, this fund has provided C$6 million to the Toronto Hospital for a new cardiac unit. The next goal is his gift to the University of Toronto, where he wants to encourage international study through the Faculty of Arts. "We have to create Canadians who are totally at ease internationally. Right now, we have very few. It will be a large center."

Beyond that, he will do one more project. "The balance of my money will go into my foundation which is going to be dedicated to promote the cause of free enterprise. That'll be its mandate. We're working on a mandate now. We have to do this, because it was free enterprise that created everything we have and now people are attacking it. We mustn't let it go. Free market states in general have been exceptionally successful, because they have created the enormous economic development globally from the industrial revolution onward. Conversely, all socialistic states, where you are trying to cap that potential, pull down everyone. Instead of creating wealth, they distribute wealth and eventually destroy wealth."

As for his legacy in the businesses he has created, Munk is struggling with the hardest of all dilemmas for entrepreneurs — succession. He has a devoted team, who have developed an impressive array of business skills. But there is only one boss. With a leader that strong, there is not a lot of room for the executives around him to swim on their own. Competence, professionalism, excellence, determination — all these things are there in abundance. But no one will know until Munk lets go if there is leadership there.

In the meantime, Peter Munk is not tired. He has not lost his enthusiasm.

"Armand Hammer was 93 when he was still providing that spark for Oxy. Roy Thomson was 87. I've got another 25 years to go. Please don't push me."

INDEX

Abdul-Aziz, Prince Nawaf Ben,
   158, 161
Abeles, Sir Peter, 103–04, 136
Adams, John, 57
Agnew, Rudolph, 232, 233, 260, 261
Allen, Peter, 276, 277, 281
American Barrick, 213
Anglo American group, 259, 260
Australia, foreign investment in,
   103, 116, 186
autoclaving, 245–47

Babbitt, Bruce, 264–65
Baker, Howard, 320

Barrick Explorations, 207
Barrick Gold Corp.
   Barrick-Cullaton Gold Trust,
      215–16
   ConsGold takeover attempt,
      231–33
   employee bonuses, 346
   equity financing, 252–57, 271
   exploration program, 8, 11, 13,
      26–28, 327–28, 329–31
   financing for diversification pro-
      gram, 20–23, 24
   Goldstrike mine, 8, 9, 236–39,
      240–43, 244, 245, 246–47, 271

Betze-Post development plan,
  248–49, 251, 263
Meikle Mine, 249
hedging program, 266–70, 271
International Advisory Board
  (IAB), 318–23
joint ventures with juniors, 329
Lac Minerals, 1, 9, 10, 18–19,
  259, 273–76, 279–80
takeover, 280–300
Mercur mine, 224–28, 244, 245,
  247
and Moneta Porcupine Mines,
  329
and Newmont Gold, 257–58, 263
  injunction, 263–64
Pasqua mine, 330
Renabie mine, 215
and Solitario Resources, 328
startup, 214–15
stock market performance, 1,
  5–6, 9, 25, 249–51, 255, 305
stock options, 340–46
Barrick Investments, 191, 211
Barrick Power Gold Corp. of
  China, 14–15, 17
Barrick Resources, 207–09
Beachcomber Hotel, 71
Beck, Howard, 75
Benson, Kevin, 310
Berlin, foreign investment in, 308
Biggar, Bill, 21
Bijur, Peter, 225
Birchall, Bill, 84–86, 120–21, 136,

139, 175, 334, 335
Bond International, 276
Boswell, J. G., 88
Boulevard Hotel, 111, 123, 182, 188
Bre-X, 27, 326
Brooks, Oliver, 122
Bush, George, 318–19

Camflo Mines, 216–17, 220,
  221–24, 249
Camp, Dalton, 50
Campbell, Helen, 39
Canadian Motor Industries (CMI),
  58, 61, 63
Carrington, John, 331
Caucubau, Ratu Edward, 69
Chile, foreign investment in, 272–73
China, foreign investment in, 14, 15
Chojnacki, Michael, 39
Clairtone Sound Corporation
  collapse of, 56–57, 64–66
  color TVs, 53–54
  expansion, 45–46, 48
  and Industrial Estates Ltd.,
    52–53, 54, 55, 56–57
  merchandising program, 49–51
  Project G, 50–51
  reunion, 30–32
  startup, 43–44
  stock market performance, 47, 52
Clark Refining and Marketing, 19,
  23–24, 306, 324–25
Commonwealth Trading Bank,
  152, 180

conglomerates, 316

Consolidated Goldfields PLC
(ConsGold), 231–33, 258,
259–61

copra plantation, 130

Crowther, Lord, 134

Cullaton Lake Gold Mines, 215

cyanidation, 243–44

Dattels, Stephen, 215, 341–42

Davidson, Alex, 328

Desmarais, Paul, 14, 320

Diamond Fields Resources, 327

Eacott, Graham, 277

Egypt, foreign investment in, 145,
150

Egyptian Tourist Development
Company (ETDC), 158

entrepreneurs, 302, 303, 338

Fasken, Bob, 217

Fell, Tony, 24

Fiji, 67–68, 75–76

Forte, Sir Charles, 112, 134, 189–90

Fouad, Dr. Nemat, 149

Friedland, Bob, 327

Friedlich, Steven, 338

George, Sir Arthur, 135, 136, 138,
139, 141

Gilmour, David
contacts, 42, 142
early career, 35–36

education, 33

family background, 33

management style, 35

partnership with Peter Munk,
40–43, 335

and Pyramids Oasis project,
142–44, 147, 149, 150, 151,
158

Gilmour, Doris, 33

Gilmour, Harrison, 33

Gold Company of America, 223

gold mining industry, 7, 211, 213,
289–90

Goldsmith, Sir Jimmy, 262–63

Goldstrike mine, 236–38

Gould, Irving, 46

Greenway, Alan, 104, 105–11
feud with Peter Munk, 117–120,
124–29
managerial style, 124
and takeover of Travelodge
Hotels, 111–20, 124, 132,
133–41

Gregson, Brian, 221, 222

Hahn, Ziggy, 31, 46

Haines, George, 132, 168, 175

Hancock, Mac, 79, 80

Hanson PLC, 261–62

Hill, Alan, 26, 226

Hoare, David, 113, 131–32, 184

Hogarth, Mac, 75

Holt, Dit, 226

Horsham Corp., 3, 19, 20, 305

Berlin development plan, 307–09
diversification, 306
stock market performance, 25,
    304–05, 316

Iacocca, Lee, 156–58
Inchcape, Lord, 162
Industrial Estates Ltd.(IEL), 52
International Advisory Board
    (IAB). *See* Barrick Gold Corp.
Irani, Ray, 324

Jardine Matheson, 87–88, 111
Johnson, Mark, 128
Jones, Norman, 135, 139
Jordan, Vernon, 320

Keswick, Henry, 87
Khashoggi, Adnan, 133, 152–65,
    209–10
King Fung Development Co., 100,
    101
King, Scott, 108
Kirby, Roger, 120, 128, 131, 168,
    174, 175, 177, 196
Klein, Hanno, 309

Lac Minerals, 1, 9, 10, 18–19, 259,
    273–77, 279–80
    takeover by Barrick, 280–300
Lakshman, 76–77
land development, 81–84, 96
Latin America, foreign investment
    in, 272

Leys, Arthur, 69, 71, 76
L'Heureux, Bill, 310, 311
Luksic, Andronico, 321

MacMahon, Frank, 59, 60, 61
Marwan, Ashraf, 142, 143
McGovern, Peter, 132
McLaughlin, Earl, 60
Meikle, Brian, 226, 238
Melnuk, Paul, 20
Mercur mine, 224–28
Minami, Koji, 93, 94
Minorco, 259–61
Mitsubishi Trading Co., 108–09,
    123, 125
Mitsui, 63
Moneta Porcupine Mines, 329
Monex, 191
Muldoon, Robert, 130
Mulroney, Brian, 13–14, 17,
    265–66, 318, 319, 326
Munk, Melanie, 10
Munk, Peter
    business philosophy, 3, 338
    business strategies, 13, 19, 23,
        58, 80, 96–97, 166, 176, 205,
        207, 214, 252, 296, 312, 314,
        326
    early career, 37–40
    education, 12, 37
    family background, 36–37
    foundation, 350
    golden rules, 23, 24, 40, 47, 52,
        70, 78, 98, 103, 115, 133,

138, 147, 159, 170, 179, 190, 192, 205, 209, 210, 212, 223, 230, 255, 257, 269, 280, 295, 303, 314, 336, 338, 340
inner circle, 333–37, 348
management style, 2, 4, 15–16, 113, 169, 171, 172–74, 176, 195, 294, 334, 347
partnerships with:
  Adnan Khashoggi, 162, 191, 209–10
  Alan Greenway, 117–20, 124–29
  Bill Birchall, 84, 85
  Bob Smith, 217, 219, 229
  David Gilmour, 40–43
  Pat Samuel, 74
personal wealth, 340–41, 342, 347, 350
and senior executives, choice of, 174–75, 339
speeches, 178–79, 333
views on:
  business cycles and timing, 313
  business deals, 315–16
  business partnerships with government, 65
  Latin America, 17–18
  secondary manufacturing industry, 51–52
  stock market, 12
Mutiyera group, 329–30

Narita Airport hotel, 123, 182, 188
Nelson, D. O. "Swede," 207, 208

Newbigging, David, 88
Newmont Gold, 236, 238, 257–59, 260–61, 262, 263
New Zealand, foreign investment in, 130
Novelly, Tony, 19

Occidental Petroleum, 324–25
O'Connor, Jerry, 311, 317
oil and gas industry, 205–06
Ord-BT, 113
Osman, Osman Ahmed, 143–144
O'Toole, Marty, 200

Pacific Harbour
  development plans, 90
  and Jardine Matheson, 87–88
  marketing program, 90–91
  and 1974 recession, 91–92, 120–21
  sale of, 95
  and Slater Walker, 87
  startup, 74–81, 84, 86–89
  and Taisei Corp., 92–95
Pacific Hotels and Developments, 75. *See also* Pacific Harbour
Page-Williams mine, 276
PanCana, 236, 238
Parker, Gordon, 260
Pendock, Simon, 87, 88–89
Peninsular & Oriental Steam Navigation Company (P&O), 88, 111, 122, 162
Peter Munk Associates, 38–40
Pickens, T. Boone, 258, 259

Pitblado, Jim, 281, 282

Placer Dome, 5, 6, 8

Pöhl, Karl Otto, 308, 321

Power Corp., 107

Project Planners Ltd., 79–81

Pyramids Oasis project
    and Adnan Khashoggi, 158, 159
    and Anwar Sadat, 144–46, 148
    cancellation of, 148–51
    development plans, 146

Ramos, Fidel, 324

real estate industry, 309–10, 312

reverse takeover, 98–99

Roberts Real Estate, 78–79

Rohm, José, 321

Rothchild, Evelyn, 94

Rotman, Joe, 205, 207, 211,
    233–36, 313

Royal Oak Mines, 278, 279
    Lac Minerals takeover attempt,
    273–77, 279–80, 284–86,
    288, 290, 291, 292, 296–99

Sabri family, 149–50

Sadat, Anwar, 144–46, 147–48

Salaam, Hany, 324

Samuel, Pat
    and Berlin development project,
    308
    career, 58–60, 62, 63, 72–74
    and negotiations in Fiji, 70–71
    and negotiations with Japanese,
    93–95

partnership with Peter Munk, 74

Sarlos, Andy, 306–07

Short, Norman, 205, 207

Sidebottom, Peter, 307, 337

S. J. Groves, 236, 237

Slater, Jim, 87, 88, 98

Slater Walker, 87, 88, 99, 100, 102,
    111, 121–22

Smith, Bob, 15, 214, 216–17,
    218–21, 225, 228, 331, 336

Smith, Ike, 55

Sobey, Frank, 53

Solitario Resources Corp., 328

South Africa, foreign investment
    in, 211–12

Southern Pacific Hotel Corp., 200,
    202. *See also* Travelodge
    Hotels

Southern Pacific Properties (SPP),
    88, 89
    and Adnan Khashoggi, 161–65,
    191
    and Commonwealth Trading
    Bank, 152
    and 1974 recession, 121
    privatization of, 190–94
    and Slater Walker, 88, 99, 100,
    102
    stock market performance, 98,
    102, 115, 129, 160, 190

SPP (Middle East), 158, 159, 161

Stanfield, Robert, 55, 61

Steen, Peter, 287–88

stock options, 340

Strong, Maurice, 107
Studebaker Corp., 61–62
Sultan of Brunei, 203

Tahiti Beachcomber, 123–24, 182,
    183, 188–89
Taisei Corp., 92–95
Tan Sri Khoo, Teck Puat, 203
Texaco, 225, 227, 228
Thompson, Bill, 135, 138
Toyota, 62–63
Travelodge Hotels, 97–98, 107,
    108–11. *See also* Southern
    Pacific Hotel Corp.
    acquisition of remaining shares,
        180–87
    art collection, 127
    Boulevard Hotel, 111, 123, 182,
        188
    and Mitsubishi, 108–09, 123,
        125, 188
    Narita Airport hotel, 123, 182, 188
    and 1974 recession, 122–24
    Parkroyal chain, 110
    sale of, 202–03
    Slingshot campaign, 132–41
    stock market performance, 111,
        112, 129, 181
    Tahiti Beachcomber, 123–24,
        182, 183, 188–89
    takeover, 98–102, 103–04, 109,

111–17
    tariffs, 196–99, 200
    turnaround strategy, 166–71,
        179–80, 188, 200–01
    upgrading of, 194–95, 200
Treuhandanstalt, 308, 309
Triad Holding Corp., 153–54, 156,
    158
Trizec, 16, 25, 309–10, 311
    stock market performance, 305,
        311
    turnaround strategy, 311–12
Trust Houses Forte, 112, 134, 189

van Eendenburg, Dam Carel
    Frederik, 55
Vansittart, Shelagh, 35–36
Viking Petroleum, 207, 208
Viti Levu chalet, 11
Volvo Canada, 58–59

Western States Minerals Corp.,
    236–37
Wicks, Frank, 228
Wilkins, Greg, 16, 20, 206, 311, 337
Witte, Peggy, 273–74, 277–79, 284
Wolfensohn, James, 109, 110
Wynne-Morgan, David, 14–15

Yamana Resources, 329
Yap, Piet, 330